GLORIANA'S FACE

Frontispiece Darnley portrait, *Elizabeth I*, unknown artist, *c.* 1575

GLORIANA'S FACE

Women, Public and Private, in the English Renaissance

Edited by

S.P. Cerasano and
Marion Wynne-Davies

WAYNE STATE UNIVERSITY PRESS   DETROIT

U.S. Edition published by
Wayne State University Press
Detroit, Michigan 48202

Printed and bound in Great Britain

Library of Congress Catalog
Card Number 92–080266

ISBN 0–8143–2426–6

1 2 3 4 5   96 95 94 93 92

For our parents,
especially for Arthur P. Cerasano (1924–91)

Contents

CONTENTS

List of Figures

Acknowledgements

S.P. Cerasano wishes to acknowledge the generous support of the Public Record Office, the National Endowment for the Humanities, and the Colgate University Research Council (as well as the University's administrative officers), each of whom contributed to this project in significant ways. She also wishes to thank the Warden, Sandra Lello, and the Accommodation Secretary, Helen Burrows, of William Goodenough House, for pleasant accommodation during the preparation of this manuscript. Not least of all, she is grateful for having worked through this book with Marion, a co-editor and friend of the best sort. Marion Wynne-Davies would like to thank the Newberry Library for enabling her research into Lady Mary Wroth's *Urania* by awarding her a fellowship, and Liverpool University's Renaissance Seminar Group for their valuable suggestions when her essay was at an early stage. She would also like to thank Geoff Ward, who acted as mediator over the stickiest editorial problems and unfailingly advocated a generous decision; and finally, her co-editor Susan, whose meticulous scholarship and enthusiasm over her work have made this project not only easy, but fun.

Barbara J. Bono would like to thank the Society for the Humanities at Cornell University (1982–3), the Mellon Foundation Fellowship at Harvard University (1983–4), and the Research Foundation of the State University of New York at Buffalo (summer 1985) for their support during the years when she began her intensive work on Sidney, and the Institute for Advanced Study at Princeton, New Jersey, which offered her its hospitality during the year when she completed this article. In the interval Heather Dubrow and her many patient and intelligent graduate students have helped immeasurably in the crafting of its particulars. Akiko Kusunoki wishes to thank the British Council in Tokyo for a research fellowship which enabled her to engage in the research for this essay at the British Library in spring 1989. Helen Wilcox wishes to acknowledge the support of the University of Liverpool. Georgianna Ziegler would like to thank the members of the Delaware Valley Women's Seminar at the University of Pennsylvania, and colleagues from the session on Women in the Renaissance at the Renaissance

Society of America Conference (1988) for their interest in reading and commenting on her paper.

Also, the editors acknowledge their gratitude to Jackie Jones of Harvester Wheatsheaf for her sustained support of this project.

Notes on Contributors

S.P. CERASANO is Associate Professor of English at Colgate University, New York, where she teaches courses on Shakespeare and theatre history. She is the author of articles on theatre architecture, Renaissance theatrical entrepreneurship, and the socio-political aspects of the Elizabethan theatre. She is currently writing a biography of Edward Alleyn, the actor who memorialised Doctor Faustus and an influential theatre magnate of Shakespeare's day.

MARION WYNNE-DAVIES is Lecturer in the English Department at the University of Keele. She is the editor of *The Bloomsbury Guide to English Literature* (London: Bloomsbury, 1989), published in the United States as *The Prentice Hall Guide to English Literature*. She has also published on Yeats and Arthurianism, the Renaissance romance epic, Chaucer's treatment of women in *The Wife of Bath's Tale* and *The Clerk's Tale*, and Shakespeare's *Titus Andronicus*.

BARBARA J. BONO is Associate Professor of English Literature at the State University of New York at Buffalo, where she teaches courses on the range of English Renaissance literature. She is the author of *Literary Transvaluation: From Vergilian epic to Shakespearean tragicomedy* (Berkeley and Los Angeles: University of California Press, 1984) and articles on English Renaissance literature which seek to extend the concept of the 'sources' of writing from literary antecedent to gendered and material conditions of production. She is currently working on two extended projects articulating a feminist theory of literary influence to account for the revisions and influence of Sidney's *Arcadia* and the intertextual relationships among Shakespeare's plays.

HILARY HINDS teaches literature at Fircroft College of Adult Education in Birmingham, and is a Fellow of the Institute for Advanced Research in the Humanities at the University of Birmingham. The chapter in this collection is drawn from her doctoral research on radical sectarian women writers. She is co-editor, with Elspeth Graham, Elaine Hobby and Helen Wilcox, of *Her Own Life: Autobiographical writings by seventeenth-century Englishwomen* (London: Routledge, 1989) and is currently working with Elaine Hobby on another anthology of seventeenth-century women's writing.

AKIKO KUSUNOKI is Associate Professor of English at Tokyo Woman's Christian University, and has published articles on women in English Renaissance drama and society. She is currently writing a book on rebellious women in drama and society in seventeenth-century England.

LAURIE MAGUIRE is Assistant Professor of English at the University of Ottawa. She has contributed articles on aspects of Elizabethan staging and textual studies to *Cahiers Elisabéthains, Medieval and Renaissance-Drama in England* and *Theatre Notebook*, and is currently completing a book on memorial reconstruction.

FRANCES TEAGUE is Professor of English at the University of Georgia. She has published *The Curious History of 'Bartholomew Fair'* (Lewisburg, PA: Bucknell, 1985) and *Shakespeare's Speaking Properties* (Lewisburg, PA: Bucknell, 1991). With John Velz, she edited *One Touch of Shakespeare: The letters of Joseph Crosby* (Cranbury, NJ: Folger, 1986). Her publications on early women writers include articles on Frances Brooke, Christine of Pizan, Bathsua Makin and Elizabeth I, as well as entries for *The Encyclopedia of British Women Writers* (New York: Garland, 1988).

HELEN WILCOX is Professor of Post-medieval English Literature at the University of Groningen in the Netherlands. She is the author of essays on seventeenth-century poetry, music and autobiography; editor of Longman's Annotated edition of George Herbert's poetry; and co-editor of *Her Own Life: Autobiographical writings by seventeenth-century Englishwomen* (London: Routledge, 1989), *Teaching Women: Feminism and English studies* (Manchester: Manchester University Press, 1989), and *The Body and the Text: Hélène Cixous, reading and teaching* (Hemel Hempstead: Harvester Wheatsheaf, 1990).

GEORGIANNA ZIEGLER is Curator of the Horace Howard Furness Shakespeare Library at the University of Pennsylvania and teaches Shakespeare in the College of General Studies. She has edited the anthology *Shakespeare Study Today* (New York: AMS Press, 1986), and has published articles in *Shakespeare Quarterly, Shakespeare Studies, Theatre Survey, Textual Practice*, and other journals.

'From Myself, My Other Self I Turned': An Introduction

S.P. Cerasano and Marion Wynne-Davies

The representations of Elizabeth I have become at once eternal symbols of glorious majesty and individual portraits which appear, through intricate interpretations, to offer a glimpse into the private life of the Queen herself.[1] More intriguingly, the intellectual delights inspired by her image had their origin during her own lifetime. For example, in February 1602 Sir John Manningham recorded an event in his diary which focused specifically upon the way a representation of the Queen's face could be perceived contiguously as a metaphor for truth as a moral virtue:

> Sir Christopher Hatton and another knight made challenge whoe should present the truest picture of hir Majestie to the Queene. One caused a flattering picture to be drawne; the other presented a glas, wherein the Queene sawe hir selfe, the truest picture that might be.[2]

At one level the Queen becomes simply the means by which truth can be seen to triumph over flattery in a political context. Indeed, we cannot but be influenced by Manningham's admiration for the cleverness of the knight who presented the mirror, and persuaded by the neat rhetoric of his final words. However, the account also carries us briefly to a position not identical with the Queen's, but perhaps gazing over her shoulder; we perceive Elizabeth seeing herself in the mirror. In this position we almost become voyeurs, intercepting a personal exchange between the individual and her reflection, intruding upon a brief moment of private contemplation.[3] In Renaissance illustrations, mirrors are commonly used as emblems of vanity; they closet the subject in an inner world of the individual, which neither needs nor allows anyone else to sustain and satisfy itself.[4] Of course, Elizabeth's reaction to her reflection is not recorded, and she might have looked at herself with dissatisfaction or self-irony. What is important is the difference between mirror and portrait: the former is meant for private contemplation, the latter for public consumption.

Manningham's tacit criticism of court flattery also presents us with an interesting subtext, for the purpose of the Queen's public representations was purely propagandist. From the Coronation portrait with its surfeit of gold, to the Rainbow portrait with its overt idealisation of an aged Queen, flattery was the essential element.[5] These were images of a monarch to be reproduced, copied and transmitted across her realm; they encoded a political identity which could not allow for self-obsession or self-doubt.[6] The portraits of Elizabeth I were for the adulation of her subjects and, inasmuch as they represented her royal identity, were as 'true' as the mirror which reflected her private self. Manningham's delight in discovering this private woman, reduced to an intimate and feminine form – vanity was often represented as a woman – reveals a discomfort felt by many of the Queen's male courtiers.[7] In a society whose hierarchy offered absolute privilege to men, the ideological shift required to accept a female ruler was considerable, if not impossible.[8] Thus the conventional view of women which focused upon their containment within a private world had somehow to coexist with the reality of the public show necessary for a monarch.[9]

Elizabeth I was, without doubt, a female ruler accepted by her contemporaries because of her own exceptional qualities; they condoned the individual, not the concept of female majesty.[10] But the same biplay between private and public selves does occur repeatedly in the representations and writings of other Renaissance women. The essays in this collection deal specifically with the continual interaction of such internal/externalisation, from sixteenth-century conduct books to the sermons of Puritan women. Since in titling this volume we chose to use Elizabeth's face as a metaphor for the (self)presentation of women, this introduction, like Manningham's diary, participates in a continuing intellectual debate about her portraits. We focus specifically on the way in which the Queen's pictures change, seeing this as parallel to the manner in which the female identities considered in the following essays appear to metamorphose. In so doing, we incorporate previous conventions, the more recent demands of materialist and feminist criticism, the multiple interpretations made possible by our chosen trope and, not least, the limits of aesthetic and historical credibility.[11]

As an analysis of the representations of Renaissance women, the essays presented here construct themselves as poised between historicity and art, offering a picture which is both an object for popular consumption and an interrogation of individual subjectivity. As such, the critical prose offered by our contributors is faithful to the interpretative structures of the image on the jacket.[12] In this self-conscious historical positioning and in our concentration upon the roles of women we have broadly followed materialist feminist criticism – for example, the approach taken by Judith Newton and Deborah Rosenfelt in their pathbreaking text *Feminist Criticism and Social Change* (1985). They write:

> This kind of dialectical, as opposed to static and linear, mode of analysis distinguishes feminist-materialist criticism from many other feminist criticisms. It is a way of seeing that prompts us to locate in the same situation the forces of oppression and the seeds of resistance; to construct women in a given moment in history simultaneously as victims and as agents.[13]

The essays which follow discuss the oppression and resistance of women in the English Renaissance; they are therefore grounded in materialist feminism. But rather than structuring their arguments about dialecticism, the writers here often seem to be breaking down the divisions earlier criticism set up. Repeatedly, definitions dependent upon difference – such as subject and object, the work of art and its social environment, the inner and outer selves – are shown to be inadequate when we try to understand just how Renaissance women fitted into the cultural, domestic and political worlds they inhabited. The temptation to determine where women should be placed in the ledger-like summation initiated by Joan Kelly-Gadol's now famous question – 'Did women have a Renaissance?' – has been avoided.[14] This diversion from conventional feminist criticisms of the Renaissance occurred not because there was no conclusive sum at the end of our accounting, but simply because a credit for the resistance of women always encoded, simultaneously, a debit to the benefit of the suppression of women.[15] What became apparent from the texts and portraits was a dialogue in which dynamic interaction rather than confrontational dialecticism took place. The works of Bakhtin proved useful in theorising this area of communication, especially his definition of the dialogic principle:

> The word in living conversation is directly, blatantly, oriented toward a future answer-word: it provokes an answer, anticipates it and structures itself in the answer's direction.[16]

Obvious examples of these double-voiced texts are the pamphlets produced in the *querelle des femmes,* which debated the vices and virtues of women from the medieval to the late Renaissance periods – each text carrying within it the hidden polemic of its adversary.[17]

The deprivileging of sole authorship implied by the dialogic principle allows female voices to be anticipated within any work, whether written by a man or a woman.[18] Moreover, it opens the interpretative process in a parallel democratisation, where the roles of subject and object, personal and public, art and society, are no longer trapped in an authoritarian polarisation.

The representations of Elizabeth I do not have to be seen as a site of confrontation between the Queen's different identities, provoking us into either allowing one element to dominate, or invoking an uneasy compromise between, say, all-powerful monarch and conventionally chaste maiden. Instead we can allow them, and ourselves, greater manoeuvrability through accepting an interlocution between the Queen's public and private faces, and between the simultaneous invitation and re-creation of the viewer in response to the work of art.[19] The Darnley portrait, which we chose for the jacket of our book, and which may be seen as the frontispiece, is a case in point.[20] It is one of the more sensitive and sympathetic portrayals of Elizabeth I: her clothes and hair are simple, allowing the focus of our gaze to rest upon her face. The eyes are almost black, and their intensity compels and returns our stare.

Not surprisingly, because she actually sat for it, this portrait has been interpreted as evidence for both her private and public identity: for the Queen's personal life and her affection for Essex, and for the overwhelming iconicity of all her pictures. Roy Strong, in *Gloriana* (1987), suggests that the artist was the Italian Federigo Zuccaro, who also drew two companionate sketches of Elizabeth and Essex during his stay in England.[21] Thus the less formal costume and soft Titian-like style suggest, for Strong, the private emotions of a woman in love. Alternatively, Andrew and Catherine Belsey, in 'Icons of Divinity: Portraits of Elizabeth I' (1990), call our attention to the crown and sceptre on the table, the inflated shoulders recalling the portraits of Henry VIII, and the shape and decoration of the bodice, which suggest an ornamental breastplate.[22] Here Elizabeth is a warrior queen or martial maid, in whom the 'iconic character is [already] in the process of construction'.[23] Without denying that Elizabeth I was indeed constrained by the iconography which sur-rounded her all her life, and without ignoring the fact that Strong has an almost Manningham-like desire to present the Queen in the more conventional female role of a woman in love, the Darnley portrait seemed to us to encode an interaction with the viewer that neither of the interpretations mentioned above acknowledges. Strong comes close when he notes that the Darnley portrait was the face pattern used throughout the 1580s and 1590s, and that 'no other face pattern of the Queen was to be so widely disseminated'.[24] Both private emotion and public show may be encompassed by the image, but the pivot of the painting's production and consumption – the latter on a massive scale – is the Queen's power over her own representation. The licensing of multiple copies enabled this contemporary 'self-fashioning' to flourish.[25] Still, one suspects that the material evidence of the artistry ensured the portrait's immediate success, as well as its continued power.

The resolutely black background and reduced veil and ruff endow the Queen's face with total domination over the picture's other elements. But it is the eyes, those inner orbs of the same infinite blackness, which suggest the full power of her gaze, for it is ultimately the viewer who is constructed by the Queen's obdurate stare. There are other personal paintings, such as Hilliard's well-known miniatures of the Queen, and

Figure 1.1 Coronation portrait, *Elizabeth I*, unknown artist, *c.* 1605

many more iconographic engravings and portraits, but there is no other likeness of Elizabeth I with eyes so powerful and commanding.[26] The Darnley portrait may be interpreted as personal, iconographic and majestic, but any prolonged contemplation of the work ensures that these qualities are perpetually opening themselves for debate along the subject/object axis between the beholder and the Queen.

The extant paintings of Elizabeth I were produced over a period of almost fifty years, and the Darnley portrait is simply one of many, looking Janus-like back to the Coronation portrait of 1559 and forward to the death mask of 1603.[27] So too, the essays in *Gloriana's Face* encompass a chronological field covering the sixteenth and seventeenth centuries, encoding a series of divergent representations of Renaissance women. We accept wholeheartedly Betty Travitsky's statement that '*all* women had come to be considered inferior to men by virtue of their sex; regardless of class', and correspondingly we perceive a constant and determined effort by men to construct women within highly constraining predetermined roles.[28]. The small expressionless face surrounded by the pomp of formal rulership in Elizabeth's Coronation portrait is evidence of this. It was first commissioned by the Lord Chamberlain and then copied under the auspices of a male ruler, James I.[29] The young Queen was treated as a blank and impersonal page upon which the statesmen of her reign and afterwards could inscribe their own version of female majesty.[30] Correspondingly, in literary terms, the conduct books required the good wife to:

> Stay indoors, guarding her chastity as she guards the other property of her husband. As her body is locked within the walls of the house, her tongue is locked in her mouth.[31]

Yet these same conduct books and their progeny, while attacking women, simultaneously presented a hidden polemic for their defence. It has been claimed that two such texts – *The Schoolhouse of Women* (1541), which attacked women, and its opposer *Mulierum Paean* (1542), which praised them – were both written by the same man, Edward Gosynhill.[32] The author of the earlier text was clearly aware of an existing argument to the contrary, which he answered. The later text then formally voiced the supposed original statement, perhaps implying that it, in turn, would be refuted by yet another work in the future. The books appear to be part of an ongoing debate, this dialogism being combined in *The Schoolhouse* with an attitude resembling Manningham's interest in truth at the expense of woman's good name:

> Wherefore as now in this treatise,
> Whatso be said in rude sentence,
> Virtue to increase and to lay vice
> Is chief occasion of my pretense,
> And where that truth is, is none offense.

Whoso, therefore, that blameth me,
I say he deemeth wrongfully.[33]

Here, 'truth' becomes an excuse for an attack upon women that Gosynhill erects against a blame which is already present within the *querelle*'s discourse, but has not yet been actively voiced by 'Whoso' may be. Georgianna Ziegler, in her essay on representations of Penelope in the Renaissance, identifies the same issues: the male voice of restraint and the female confutation of that control:

> While her [Penelope's] chastity and busyness are praised by Renaissance men in their various representations of her for the benefit of women, it is also true that as a woman she asserts power over her own body with her conscious decision to remain chaste by repulsing the advances made to her by men.[34]

The overt discourse of the Coronation portrait, the conduct books and Penelope is that of acquiescent containment; yet even in these absolute examples of authoritarian male power, whispers of an ongoing and irrepressible debate may be heard.[35]

An essential aspect of any criticism which highlights the relationship between women and cultural artefacts is the space given to works produced by those women themselves. By ignoring female productivity in an artistic arena, we collude with the myth of female muteness which polices women's utterance and ultimately attempts to suppress female power in the public domain.[36] From Manningham and Gosynhill to Strong, women's proper domain is seen to be in silent and private contemplation. Yet even within this domestic or emotional realm, women were capable of expressing views and giving voice to an emotive rejection of such a monochrome existence. The diaries discussed by Helen Wilcox cannot be neatly categorised as 'private texts'. She writes:

> Autobiographical writing appears to be introverted, and these texts the most inward-looking of the genre; however, the act of inscribing a self involves the creation of a new self, a publicly accessible one, available in the shared language in spite of an absent or limited audience.[37]

Women's diaries are, at one and the same time, for introspective study and an external, general readership. No choice between these purposes is required, and both do – and, indeed, must – coexist in the female self-representation considered. In the Renaissance men may have attempted to construct women as 'chaste, silent and obedient', but what they were presented with instead was not bold opposition – the archetypal shrew – but the invitation to a dialogue which guaranteed both private and public images of women.[38] It was this latter argument, complex and subtle, that was ultimately harder to refute than any angry diatribe.

7

A similar double voice may be found in the writings of Elizabeth I. Her poem 'On Monsieur's Departure' has been explained as commemorating the leaving in 1582 of Francis Duke of Alençon, whose wooing of the Queen represented a political alliance.[39] The poem has also been accounted for as a description of Elizabeth's prohibited love for the Earl of Essex, in which case the interpretation would be essentially intimate.[40] The words of the poem add to the impression of shifting identity:

> I am and not; I freeze and yet am burn'd;
> Since from myself, my other self I turn'd.[41]

Whatever regret or poignancy may have been involved, the authorial voice carries the same painful paradox, that acute awareness of a double self, which penetrates the writing of Renaissance women. Frances Teague, in her analysis of Elizabeth I's speeches, discusses the Queen's manifest rhetorical ability to alter her language according to political demands:

> . . . one must be conscious of Elizabeth I's own manipulation of her image, her politically knowing alteration of her own texts. To borrow Stephen Greenblatt's phrase, Elizabeth has fashioned herself: she invented a persona, the proud Virgin Queen of England adored by her servants . . .[42]

The portraits of Elizabeth I retain a certain objectification perpetrated by the iconicity of her public role – as, for example, in the Armada portrait – and they barely escape tonal rigidity.[43] But her speeches shift and change; she rewrote several of them, including the one addressed to her troops at Tilbury on the eve of their battle against the Spanish Armada, and her position is never stated forthrightly.[44] The dialogic representation of herself moves so subtly about the contemporary ideas of women and majesty (private, chaste, silent, weak, strong, public and vocal) that divisions can no longer be sustained, or even distinguished. Our own clear definitions, marked above in parentheses, cannot do justice to the sinuous fluidity of Elizabeth's linguistic technique. We are fixed by the need to decode, to clarify, to explain, whereas her political and personal power came from precisely the opposite effects – to obfuscate, to conflate, to entrance and to mystify.

There was, of course, always something artificial about the court world, which Elizabeth chose to manipulate. The court's own self-reflexiveness and pervasive intrigue necessitated the production of a double-edged discourse in which veiling and masking were commonly accepted. In such an arena, where nothing could be certain, educated women had more freedom to create for themselves an identity that could be simultaneously private and public. Ironically, it was not until the reign of James I that the full impact of Elizabeth's unconscious example as an independent intellectual woman was felt. The young women influenced by the memory of the Queen, no less than the male subscribers to Elizabethan nostalgia, sometimes gathered about the less compelling, but still defiant, figure of Queen Anne;[45] or enacted a Sidneian retreat from the corrupted world at the Jacobean court to the havens of pastoralism.[46] Marion Wynne-Davies, in her essay on the court masque, reveals the radical, but somewhat crude, challenge to patriarchal authority attempted by Anne and her ladies in 'The Masque of Blackness' (1605), when they shocked the court by literally painting themselves black.[47] She goes on to discuss how one of the lady masquers, Mary Wroth, wrote her own entertainments, thereby liberating women politically and linguistically. Still, as Wynne-Davies concedes,

> the masque is transient, like the female voice it empowers, and indeed when Pamphilia [Wroth's heroine] recognises its limitations she sadly accepts the renewed conformity of her gendered role and the twilight nature of a feminised masque discourse.[48]

Wroth's emphasis on 'twilight' and the Queen's desire to obscure her face with black make-up coincide with the veiled meaning of Elizabeth's speeches, and indeed with the prevalence of allegory in her last portraits, such as the Ditchley and Rainbow paintings.[49] In each case signification floats between two elements which are inseparable: twilight is an expression of a moment which is neither night nor day; make-up both is and is not the face which it coats and which has absorbed it; a veil is meant to reveal partially, rather than to obscure totally; and allegory provokes decoding rather than any denial of meaning.[50] Renaissance female power lay precisely at this point of interaction. Consequently, Elizabeth's image became increasingly absorbed into the realm of public property.

The territory between the mirror, showing Elizabeth's intimate self, and the portrait, revealing her public likeness, needed to be negotiated through a sense of 'licensed individuality'. The nature of this metamorphosis can be traced in the progression from the Sieve portraits (1579–83) to the Armada and Ditchley portraits (1588 and c. 1592).[51] In order to sift the mixture of public and private, Elizabeth was represented in the first Sieve portrait (1579) as a combination of imperial aspirations and Petrarchan motifs of chastity. In the second series the political symbols were elaborated to assert the Queen's power and ambition: a globe showing England and an arcade filled with the Queen's gentlemen pensioners were added. Yet in each of the Sieve portraits the face was derived from the life-model shown in the Darnley picture. This mixture of the personal and the iconographic may be found, with a similar sense of balance, in Edmund Spenser's definition of the Queen:

> She beareth two persons, the one of a most royall Queene or Empresse, the other of a most vertuous and beautifull Lady.[52]

9

Figure 1.2 Armada portrait, *Elizabeth I*, George Gower, c. 1588

That the Queen's person could emerge from her public function only if she controlled the movement between the two is emphasised even more in the Armada portrait. Here, the globe (again showing England) is brought forward so that the Queen's right hand may rest firmly upon it, while in her left hand she carries a fan of feathers, denoting her personal feminine side, as in the Darnley portrait. By the time the Ditchley portrait was painted, the imperial theme had become fully invested alongside the Queen's face. In it she stands on the globe, her feet planted staunchly in Oxfordshire, in the vicinity of Ditchley, home of her loyal supporter, Sir Henry Lee. She wears earrings made of smaller, celestial globes, further evidence of her political and military superiority. Here the woman and the kingdom become interchangeable. Nevertheless, even though she has been abstracted into an emblem of rulership and virtue, she holds in her hands a fan and a pair of gloves, the personal accoutrements of any fashionable lady.

Bringing the traditional prescription of feminine virtue into the political arena, literally and metaphorically, was particularly problematic for the female ruler. Virtue for women was often advocated through that popular Renaissance trope, the mirror. In the case of virtue the glass was intended to provoke women to concentrate upon their moral advancement, rather than to embellish their physical adornment. As Thomas Salter argued in *The Mirrhor of Modestie* (*c.* 1579), women were too conscious of their outer appearance:

> Maidens now adaies, dooe onely take delight daiely to tricke and trim their tresses, standyng tootyng twoo howers by the Clocke, lookyng now on this side, now on that, least any thyng should bee lackyng needefull to further Pride.

Instead he advised young women to learn how

> a vertuous demeanour & honest behaviour, would be a more sightlier ornament.[53]

The 'mirrhor of modestie' – that is, the textual didactic mirror – was of greater value than any 'crystall glass'. Women must cultivate and present a spiritual face, and relinquish fine embroidered fabrics, wigs, powder, rouges, tints, lotions, perfumes, corsets, precious stones (each of which we associate with Elizabeth) because they signify arrogance, pride, vanity and indecency. In the light of these stringent moral discourses, Elizabeth's self-presentation as the 'ornament of her age' required a delicate balance designed both to dazzle her populace with the pomp considered essential to a Renaissance monarch, and to reassure them of her feminine virtue and wisdom. In *Hymnes to Astraea* (1599) John Davies characterised Gloriana's rule as captivating her subjects with an authority based on honour and 'straight rule':

B y this straight Rule she rectifies
E ach thought that in her hart doth rise;
T his is her cleare true mirror,
H er *looking glasse*, wherein she spies
A ll forms of Truth and Error.[54]

But at the same time we cannot deny the centrality of ornament in the Queen's calculated sense of 'licensed individuality'. Her privy chamber was stocked with cosmetics and lotions intended to preserve the whiteness of her skin. She had a penchant for silk stockings, and rooms overflowing with jewels, gowns and outer robes. Nor was she the least bit shy about requesting dresses off the backs and racks of her noblewomen if she saw a gown that caught her fancy. In her later years Elizabeth wore more and more make-up in order to hide the natural signs of ageing – a trend that biographers and historians make much of in assessing her personality. However, they frequently overlook the fact that this 'vanity' seems to have been grounded in a sense of insecurity that Elizabeth had felt from her youth. To her brother's request for a portrait in 1547 she replied: 'For the face, I graunt, I might well blushe to offer, but the mynde I shall never be ashamed to present'.[55]

From the mid 1580s onwards her face ceased to be painted from life. What followed were a series of orders that every portrait had to be approved by her Master Serjeant Painter. A group of government-licensed face patterns were issued periodically to be copied by painters, each producing her official 'likeness'. While a few of Elizabeth's courtiers might have glimpsed the woman behind the mask, during her last decade her subjects saw only the 'Mask of Youth' invented by Nicholas Hilliard. It was an image which conveyed eternal beauty and freshness, far distant from the reality of the sixty-year-old Queen.[56] Indeed, the official order in favour of youth given to Hilliard might well have been motivated by the notorious failure of his predecessor, Isaac Oliver, to please the royal sitter. Around 1592, Oliver was granted a private sitting, which was an oddity at that time, and from this he produced an *ad vivum*, the only one of its kind to survive. From the evidence of the one miniature which makes use of the pattern (and which distinctly softens the original image) it is thought to have been judged unacceptable because it was too truthful a depiction. If this was not enough to stir up bad feelings, the *ad vivum*, having found its way to an engraver named Crispin van de Passe, eventually developed into a full-length engraving of the Queen by William Rogers in which she is placed next to a window, shedding light on her face and thus showing her advanced age and physical decay. Not surprisingly, government censors suppressed this unflattering image.[57]

Another aspect of this seemingly paranoid vanity, which is often sidestepped by biographers and historians, was the political necessity of maintaining a stable and vigorous image of the Queen. It could not be acknowledged that a monarch, particularly one without an heir, was subject to the usual tides of mortality, if she or he wished to sustain their full authority. Moreover, Elizabeth's male advisers quickly realised that if they emphasised her chastity and youth, England would be able to wield considerable influence in marriage negotiations with foreign princes. The

Figure 1.3 Ditchley portrait, *Elizabeth I*, M Gheeraerts the Younger, *c.* 1532

promise of an heir – preferably male – in direct descent from the previous monarch was unquestionably the most valuable commodity a woman had to offer in return for an advantageous dynastic union. After all, Elizabeth I's mother, Anne Boleyn, had been married and beheaded because she had fed and then disappointed Henry VIII's desire for a son. However, through the lure of her virginity, which implied a restrained and dutiful sexuality, and the common expectation of fertility, which reassuringly proffered male heirs, an independent woman could begin to bargain for herself. Indeed, it was during that brief period of maidenly promise before a marriage contract was arranged that pledges could be made without any expectation of consummation; it was an interlude when women were neither daughter nor wife, when they could entice, inveigle, tantalise and cajole without the threat of repercussion. For Elizabeth I, however, the time of 'courtship' extended from her accession, when marriage was first talked of by her advisers, until her death forty-five years later. During this time she had fully mastered the art of manipulating her image as the 'Virgin Queen', so that she appeared perpetually youthful, even perpetually desirable, in the marriage stakes of Europe.

One of the ways in which she encouraged this identification with youth and chastity was through symbolism. For example, in the Sieve portrait she is seen carrying the eponymous object in her left hand; to a twentieth-century person viewing the painting, this might appear as an anomaly against the background of rich garments and opulent jewellery which otherwise characterise the Queen's accoutrements. As an emblem the sieve is somewhat graphic in its analogy; the ability to carry a sieve containing water without spilling any was meant to confirm to onlookers a woman's own physical impenetrability. The inclusion of this symbol of chastity in the Sieve portrait of 1580 allowed the forty-seven-year-old Queen to project a still youthful face in the 1579–83 marriage negotiations with Anjou.

Thus Hilliard's myth of the Queen's eternal youth was intended to maintain the fiction of her generative power. Though this was physiologically a complete fiction after the mid 1580s (indeed, there was some doubt that she could procreate in the years of the Anjou negotiations) the proliferation of youthful portraits/faces into the last years of her reign functions as an ironic comment upon the absence of children. The portraits can be seen as her offspring, nurtured by Elizabeth's 'maternal subtext'. The imaginative power of these images could not be erased, and if there were to be no flesh-and-blood assurances of monarchic continuity, at least the portraits preserved the semblance of a dynastic perpetuation that could not be seen as 'nothing'. We have taken the phrase 'maternal subtext' from Barbara Bono's essay, in which she reminds us that patriarchal discourse is, in part, a response to women's ability to reproduce, and that motherhood cannot be easily dismissed since it rivals masculine systems of power and meaning. It cannot be, as Lear would have it, reduced to 'nothingness'. In the absence of Cordelia's mother, the maternal subtext emerges to haunt Lear, and in the last scene, as Bono explains:

the great father has now become the mother, cradling a prefiguration of love's redemptive power.[58]

14

Ironically, it was the Virgin Queen's decision not to marry that enabled her to exert authoritative monarchic control and to act as a redemptive force for the Protestant cause. Like Lear, she came to embody both male and female, both father and mother; paradoxically, her childless 'nothingness' contributed to her victories and enhanced her ascendancy.

The Queen's persistent urge to fashion her public identity – in a combination of monarchic stagecraft and the ever-so-slight disclosure of a personal self – relates closely to the steady stream of epithets with which her subjects sought to capture her essence. These terms, which were as mutable as the faces in her portraits, not only acted as a verbal mapping-out of her authority but also, intriguingly, invoke specific paintings where visual image and name appear to unite. Epithets such as 'Virgin Queen', 'Gloriana' and 'Eliza Triumphans' orientated viewers to the symbols which they could expect to 'read' in the artistic representations. For example, 'Virgin Queen' recalls the allegorical signification of the Sieve portraits, while 'Gloriana' and 'Eliza Triumphans' might remind us of the sumptuous Coronation and celebratory Armada portraits respectively. However, few of these portraits seem to have been given names at the time they were painted; when they did, shortly after their exhibition, acquire titles, they were associated either with the icons that dominated the image, or with the patrons who commissioned them. As a result, the Ditchley portrait was named after the location at which it resided, while the Ermine portrait came to be identified by the creature displayed prominently on the Queen's left sleeve.[59]

In her essay on 'Household Kates', Laurie Maguire explores the significance of this propensity for 'naming', suggesting that it was only through such linguistic determinism that a subject was either defined as, or could itself lay claims to, an independent identity. Maguire finds that in Shakespeare's plays, unlike Elizabeth's self-construction, the male characters use 'naming' as a device whereby they may 'frame' and 'tame' the women they pursue. Concentrating on Hotspur's wife, Henry V's wife-to-be, and Petruchio's beloved, she explains that to be *called* something is, in fact, to *be* something. Nomenclature, whether used benevolently or malignantly, is crucial to the transformation of identity. In the plays Maguire analyses, these names are used to create a sense of 'doubling' – not as this is usually meant (two roles played by one actor) but between the private and public facets of the female character. The 'naming of a shrew' (Petruchio insists that his wife will be called 'Kate', not 'Katherine') demonstrates the degree to which men can determine a woman's public image. However, the necessity of negotiating a compromise between personal and political identities was not exclusive to women; Maguire points out that:

> Like Katherine Minola, Henry V is performing a public role in defiance of the on-stage audience's prejudgements, and, like Katherine, Henry realises that public order requires the adoption of a public persona.[60]

The emergence of the private woman into the public domain, therefore, depended upon persons and circumstances not wholly within her own control. As the Queen realised, the steady issue of portraits and epithets carried with it the important purpose of renewing her image in the eyes of her subjects. But because she was constantly forced to balance their expectations of traditional femininity with the power of rulership, this image was only tenuously held in place. During times of faith and pride in the monarchy, personal and intimate touches such as jewels, gowns, miniatures and affectionate glances were a potent way of manipulating the Elizabethan courtiers. In less auspicious times, however, the same characteristics observed in an unmarried woman could easily fuel charges of 'looseness' and other slanderous comments. As S.P. Cerasano illustrates in her essay on *Much Ado About Nothing*, the degree to which legal language creates a dramatic fiction of identity – in the courts and on stage – is central to locating women as plaintiffs and characters. The fragility of a woman's public image, the ways in which her reputation could be penetrated and destroyed, and the ways in which legal language so clearly privileged those who created it, all bring to light the intricacy of those fictions mediating public life. It was the mechanism of drama which provided a unique opportunity to explore how identity could be balanced between public and private, and how it is language that both fashions identities and continually threatens to undermine and reshape them. Considering, then, the tenuous nature of feminine repute and regal fame, it is significant that the Queen's image took such a strong hold in the popular consciousness. In a posthumous portrait, 'The Queen in a Petrarchan Triumph of Eternity' (1620), Elizabeth is recrowned in heaven, and in an engraving, 'Truth Presents the Queen with a Lance' (1625), the Armada, glimpsed in the background, continues to be vanquished long after the original event took place.[61]

The death of Queen Elizabeth is thought, by some historians, to have prompted a recession for women. The presence of two male sovereigns in the first half of the seventeenth century contributed to the growing prejudice against female education. Since women were not expected to assume positions of power, it was thought difficult to justify the education of girls. 'Learned women' were once again open to depiction as defeminised freaks threatening the social order; and the wives and daughters of the Stuart monarchs were, perhaps in consequence, not on the whole as well educated in classical subjects as Elizabeth had been. Yet despite these trends at court, numerous schools for girls were started in the seventeenth century. The Quakers, in particular, were committed to educating young men and women equally.[62] While the progress of women might have seemed to be impeded by royal precedent, Elizabeth's Protestant example seems to have persisted in the lives of young Puritan women who realised that the path to change – and, ultimately, to social revolution – lay through godly self-fashioning. Akiko Kusunoki describes how, while male preachers such as Thomas Adams asserted that as women were formed from Adam's rib they were somehow less substantial than men, female Puritans such as Rachel Speght argued that the rib attested to the equal integrity of women. Having been allowed to discuss alternative ways of interpreting the Scriptures, Puritan women were able to find spiritual justification for non-traditional marriages, for teaching men, for a basic independence of thought, and for feedom of speech. They realised that if this image of women as self-possessed and self-assertive was to be maintained, the private world must necessarily become public. As Kusunoki writes:

> In spite of her apologetic tone, Speght's pamphlet consistently demon-strates her firm belief in the necessity for women to speak out against injustice and to use their capacities for rational thinking.[63]

In certain plays of the Stuart period – for instance Thomas Drue's *The Duchess of Suffolk* (1624) – levelling attitudes were endorsed in overt parallels with the political circumstances of Queen Elizabeth of Bohemia (James I's daughter).[64] As staunch Protestants, she and her husband were forced to wander the European continent in order to escape religious persecution. Not surprisingly, the younger Elizabeth was frequently as-sociated with Elizabeth I who was seen, with the political opportunism of hindsight, to have defeated the Catholic Antichrist in the guise of the Spanish Armada. In addition, the speech of the female characters in plays like Drue's was itself an embodiment of the outspoken woman, whose rhetorical skill was meant to question conformist assumptions and to open out the possibility of female equality. As Elizabeth I used her speeches to create an independent identity, so the voices of Puritan women laid a new foundation for female activism – one which was shared, moreover, by non-Puritans.

While the urgent proliferation of courtesy books written by men at-tempted to hold women in their place, sectarian women rejected formal constructions of feminine virtue by taking up the pen themselves and creating their own portraits. At this time spiritual autobiography, which we in the twentieth century often consider to be for personal contem-plation, was recognised primarily as a political genre. Amidst charges that they were 'disorderly women', these writers could gain a certain protec-tion when they declared themselves to be the vehicles of divine inspira-tion. Hilary Hinds concludes that the very existence of writing by women offended men, since it broke what they considered to be the bounds of silence and restraint. As she notes:

> even the most 'private' of texts had overtly 'public' and didactic ends.[65]

Women were thought to be completely out of place in the political arena. Nevertheless, 'who may binde where God hath loosed?' What man had the right to stand in the way of women articulating their faith? Women became engaged in prophesying, in tract-writing, and in producing spiritual autobiography. A new spiritual equality carved out a space for female expression that could not be possessed or supervised by men, be they fathers, husbands or clerics. The best way of serving one's family and Church was by serving God, even if doing so required that women preach in the market square.

Like their Elizabethan predecessors, those women who had become adept at negotiating the boundary between public and private worlds, the sectarian women frequently suffered recrimination for not adhering to the 'bounds of silence'. Consequently, women were silenced forcibly through the use of iron bridles. Verbal abuse and physical assaults were common. Charges of witchcraft, vagabondage, whoredom and sedition were equally familiar. When, in 1605, the Court of the Star Chamber complained that women were 'hiding behind their sex', the judges misconstrued the level of individual consciousness that sectarian women were venturing for the purposes of political action.[66] As Hinds perceives:

> The decisive factor is internal, an individual apprehension of the 'spirit of God'. . . . Consequently, it was difficult, if not impossible, to define boundaries beyond which [female] writers should not go; for if God called, a writer could not refuse to follow.[67]

No area of a woman's life was out of bounds for commentary; the possibilities for female independence had become, if only theoretically, limitless. As Elizabeth had once brandished her divinely sanctioned monarchy for political gain, so finally, moving towards the Restoration, spiritual authority was wielded in order to grant a more widespread female autonomy.

The essays gathered here uncover a model of female life that may be represented by the trope of 'Gloriana's Face': they reveal the crucial possibilities for the women of Elizabeth's time and beyond to enact both their real and their fictive selves. For a woman the most potent and lasting creation of an independent and self-determining identity resided, as Elizabeth knew full well, in the public image. She fabricated and protected the way in which she was perceived, in art, in language, and in life. Indeed, she hid any signs of her mortality from even her closest confidantes. A well-known example links this defiance of age to the shattered vanity of an old woman: the Earl of Essex is said to have sealed his fate at the moment when he burst into the Queen's chamber and saw her:

> in a state of undress, her red wig still on its stand, her face bare of the elaborate make-up behind which it was now habitually concealed, and her grey hair in wisps about her temples.[68]

There is another apocryphal story of the Queen's idiosyncratic behaviour as she grew old; it is said that she refused to examine her reflection in a mirror during the last twenty years of her life. This rejection of what Elizabeth would have known to be an accurate image reveals a fear of mortality bred from such self-awareness, and a contiguous, almost desperate, desire to sustain the fiction of youth and beauty. What she saw in Manningham's glass, then, the year before her death can only be left to conjecture: did she see the ravaged complexion and teeth blackened with eating too many sweetmeats?[69] Or did she collude with the allegorical

Figure 1.4 Elizabeth I's tomb effigy, Maximillian Colt, 1603

game invented by her courtiers and perceive the glimmering mirage of a timeless self, the immortal Queen of her portraits?

At the Queen's death in 1603 John Colt made a wax effigy of Elizabeth I which was carried at her funeral.[70] This impression was later transformed under the command of James I, the direction of Robert Cecil and the execution by Maximillian Colt into the splendid tomb which we can see today in Westminster Abbey. Replicas of the tomb were erected in many churches, and descriptions of it began to occur in contemporary histories and guides by writers such as William Camden, John Stowe and Henry Holland.[71] Through an increasingly iconographic process, the

19

Queen's death mask became public property; an assurance of the Stuart succession and a monumentalised body used to fix in national memory the glory of the Elizabethan age.[72] Yet that same image reminds us of the human life which, first in wax and then later in stone, was transfixed at the very moment of its mortality. The face is old, the cheeks are sunken and the neck muscles are sagging with age. The bones protrude, recalling the skull which lies beneath, and the eyes are quite blank.

It is the same subject as the Ditchley portrait, but the death mask is more personal, more intimate than any two-dimensional oil representation could be. Here we have the Queen, defenceless against death, lacking control over the artist who formed her visage, over the King and statesmen who commissioned her tomb, and over the male writers who later chose to inscribe her final image in their texts. At this intensely private moment she seems to be completely vulnerable. Although Elizabeth's tomb presents the possibility of majesty on earth, it also reminds us of our own mortality. The threshold of death allows, tragically and fleetingly, the ultimate meeting of public and private selves; it offers, perhaps, 'the truest picture that might be'.

NOTES

1. Interpretations of Elizabeth I's portraits may be found in Roy Strong, *Portraits of Queen Elizabeth I* (Oxford: Clarendon Press, 1963) and *Gloriana* (London: Thames & Hudson, 1987); Frances Yates, *Astraea* (London: Routledge & Kegan Paul, 1975); Lucy Gent, *Picture and Poetry 1560–1622* (Leamington Spa: James Hall, 1981); Philippa Berry, *Of Chastity and Power: Elizabethan literature and the unmarried queen* (London: Routledge, 1989); and Andrew and Catherine Belsey, 'Icons of divinity: Portraits of Elizabeth I', in Lucy Gent and Nigel Llewellyn, eds, *Renaissance Bodies* (London: Reaktion Books, 1990), pp. 11–35.
2. Manningham, *The Diary of John Manningham*, ed. J. Bruce (London: J.B. Nichols & Sons, 1868), pp. 130–31.
3. For a discussion of the relationship between representations and mirrors, see Michel Foucault, *The Order of Things* (London: Tavistock, 1974), pp. 3–16.
4. For example, see the description of Lucifera in Edmund Spenser, *The Faerie Queene*, 1590, ed. A.C. Hamilton (London: Longman, 1977), I. iv. 10. For a more general discussion, see Guy de Tervarent, *Attributs et Symboles dans l'art profane 1450–1600* (Geneva: Librairie E. Droz, 1958), p. 274.
5. Coronation portrait: *Elizabeth I*, unknown artist; the original work, painted in 1559, was destroyed, but we have a replica made in the first decade of the seventeenth century (National Portrait Gallery, London). See also Strong, *Gloriana*, p. 163. Rainbow portrait: *Rainbow Portrait of Elizabeth I* by Isaac Oliver, 1600–3 (Hatfield House, England).
6. Strong, *Gloriana*, pp. 14–16; Gordon Kipling, *The Triumph of Honour* (Leiden: Leiden University Press, 1977), pp. 3, 11–13, 94–5.
7. For a discussion of the political problems endemic upon Elizabeth's gender we are indebted to Fran Teague's essay; see below, pp. 67–9.

8. Louis A. Montrose, '*A Midsummer Night's Dream* and the shaping of fantasies of Elizabethan culture: Gender, power, form', in Margaret Ferguson, Maureen Quilligan and Nancy Vickers, ed, *Rewriting the Renaissance* (Chicago: University of Chicago Press, 1986), pp. 65–87.

9. The ideal Renaissance court lady is described in Book III of *The Courtier* by Baldassare Castiglione, translated by Sir Thomas Hoby as *The Courtyer of Count Baldessar Castilio* (London: Wyllyam Seus, 1561), pp. Aaiii v.–Mmii r. For a feminist reading of women's domesticity, see Roberta Hamilton, *The Liberation of Women* (London: George Allen & Unwin, 1978), pp. 15–46.

10. A similar phenomenon may be seen in the British Conservative Party's loyalty to Margaret Thatcher during the 1980s; see Marina Warner, *Monuments and Maidens* (London: Weidenfeld & Nicolson, 1987), pp. 38–60.

11. Cultural materialism and new historicism have, by now, influenced the majority of critical writings about Renaissance texts; for an outline of the American new historicism, see Jean E. Howard, 'The new historicism in Renaissance Studies', *English Literary Renaissance*, **16** (1986), pp. 13–43; and for British cultural materialism, see Jonathan Dollimore, *Radical Tragedy* (1984) and Dollimore and Alan Sinfield, *Political Shakespeare* (1985). Two critics who link these approaches with feminism are Lynda Boose, 'The family in Shakespeare Studies', *Renaissance Quarterly*, **40** (1987), pp. 707–42, and Catherine Belsey, *The Subject of Tragedy* (London: Methuen, 1985) and 'Disrupting sexual difference: Meaning and gender in the comedies', in John Drakakis, ed., *Alternative Shakespeares* (London: Methuen, 1985). Feminist writing on Renaissance literature has proliferated radically over the past decade; it is possible to name only a selection of those texts which have shaped our thinking: Lisa Jardine, *Still Harping on Daughters* (Rutherford, NJ: Barnes & Noble, 1983); Retha M. Warnicke, *Women of the English Renaissance and Reformation* (Westport, CT: Greenwood, 1983); Linda Woodbridge, *Women and the English Renaissance* (Urbana: University of Illinois Press, 1984); Margaret P. Hannay, *Silent But for the Word* (Kent, OH: Kent State University Press, 1985); Ferguson, Quilligan and Vickers, *Rewriting the Renaissance*; Mary Beth Rose, *Women in the Middle Ages and the Renaissance* (Detroit: Wayne State University Press, 1986); and Anne M. Haselkorn and Betty S. Travitsky, *The Renaissance Englishwoman in Print* (Amherst: University of Massachusetts Press, 1990).

12. The Darnley portrait, *Elizabeth I*, unknown artist, *c.* 1575 (National Portrait Gallery, London).

13. Newton and Rosenfelt, *Feminist Criticism and Social Change* (London: Methuen, 1985), p. xxii.

14. Joan Kelly-Gadol, 'Did women have a Renaissance?', in R. Bridenthal and C. Koonz, *Becoming Visible: Women in European history* (Boston, MA: Houghton Mifflin, 1977), pp. 137–64.

15. Since Kelly-Gadol proposed the seductive question 'Did women have a Renaissance?', feminist critics have felt impelled to answer it, either positively or negatively. We suggest that the question of whether women experienced greater freedom or renewed repression in the sixteenth and seventeenth centuries should perhaps adopt the terminology of that period itself and concentrate upon a *querelle*. The move away from reductive absolutes has already occurred in the field of art history; see, for example, Griselda Pollock, *Vision and Difference* (London: Routledge, 1988), pp. 1–17.

16. M.M. Bakhtin, *The Dialogic Imagination*, ed. M. Holoquist; transl. C. Emerson and M. Holoquist (Austin: University of Texas Press, 1981), p. 280.

17. For a discussion of the *querelle des femmes* in the Renaissance period, see Linda Woodbridge, *Women and the English Renaissance* (Sussex: Harvester Press, 1984).
18. For a discussion of authorship, see Peggy Kamuf, *Signature Pieces. On the Institution of Authorship* (Ithaca, NY: Cornell University Press, 1988), pp. 59–67. For a more specific analysis of Bakhtin's relevance to feminism, see Anne Herrmann, *The Dialogic and Difference* (New York: Columbia University Press, 1989), pp. 3–31.
19. For this idea we are indebted to Georgianna Ziegler; see below, pp. 25–31.
20. Darnley portrait: see Note 12 above.
21. Strong, *Gloriana*, pp. 84–9.
22. A. and C. Belsey, 'Icons of divinity', pp. 18–20.
23. Ibid., p. 20.
24. Strong, *Gloriana*, p. 89.
25. The term 'self-fashioning' has gained precedence in Renaissance criticism since the publication of Stephen Greenblatt's influential new historicist work *Renaissance Self-Fashioning* (Chicago: Chicago University Press, 1980).
26. For a full catalogue of Elizabeth's portraits, see Strong, *Portraits;* for example, *Queen Elizabeth I* by Nicholas Hilliard, 1572 (National Portrait Gallery, London).
27. The death-mask image may be seen in two forms: either as part of the stone monument in Westminster Abbey itself, or as the effigy in the Abbey's museum. This face is, however, only a copy of the original.
28. Haselkorn and Travitsky, *The Renaissance Englishwoman in Print*, p. 12.
29. Strong, *Gloriana*, p. 163.
30. Susan Gubar, ' "The blank page" and issues of female creativity', in Elaine Showalter, ed., *The New Feminist Criticism* (London: Virago, 1986), pp. 292–313.
31. Ann Rosalind Jones, 'Nets and bridles: Early modern conduct books and sixteenth century women's lyrics' in Nancy Armstrong and Leonard Tennenhouse, eds, *The Ideology of Conduct* (London: Methuen, 1987), pp. 39–72; the quotation may be found on p. 52.
32. Gosynhill, *op. cit.*, in Katherine Usher Henderson and Barbara F. McManus, eds, *Half Humankind* (Chicago: University of Illinois Press, 1985), pp. 136–70.
33. Ibid., pp. 137–8.
34. See below, p. 40.
35. Suzanne W. Hull, *Chaste, Silent and Obedient: English books for women* (San Marino, CA: Huntington Library, 1982), pp. 1–30.
36. On the idea of female mutedness, see Shirley Ardener, *Defining Females, The Nature of Women in Society* (London: Croom Helm, 1978), p. 21.
37. See below, p. 60.
38. See above, Note 35.
39. Frances Teague, 'Elizabeth I: Queen of England', in Katharina M. Wilson, ed., *Women Writers of the Renaissance and Reformation* (Athens, GA: University of Georgia Press, 1987), pp. 522–47.
40. Ibid., p. 526.
41. Ibid., p. 536.
42. See below, p. 75.
43. Armada portrait: *Elizabeth I* by or after George Gower, c. 1588 (Woburn Abbey, England).
44. Teague, 'Elizabeth I', pp. 542–3.
45. These women include, for example, Lucy, Countess of Bedford, Elizabeth Cary, Lady Anne Clifford, Margaret Hoby, and Lady Mary Wroth; see Pearl

Hogrefe, *Tudor Women: Commoners and queens* (Ames: Iowa State University Press, 1975); Katharina M. Wilson, ed., *Women Writers*, pp. 449–608; and Haselkorn and Travitsky, *The Renaissance English woman in Print*, pp. 347–60. For James I's treatment of women, see Juliet Dusinberre, *Shakespeare and the Nature of Women* (London: Macmillan, 1975), p. 81, 303.

46. Roy Strong, *The Cult of Elizabeth* (Wallop, Hampshire: Thames & Hudson, 1977), pp. 186–8, and Anne Barton, 'Harking back to Elizabeth: Ben Jonson and Caroline Nostalgia', *English Literary History*, **48** (1981), pp. 706–32. The pastoral ideal world was associated with Penshurst, the home of the Sidney family, as may be seen in Ben Jonson's poem 'To Penshurst' in George Parfitt, ed., *Ben Jonson, The Complete Poems* (Harmondsworth: Penguin Books, 1975), pp. 95–8.

47. Ben Jonson, *Ben Jonson*, eds. C.H. Herford, Percy and Evelyn Simpson (Oxford: Clarendon Press, 1925–52), vol. VII, pp. 169–80.

48. See below, pp. 98–9.

49. Ditchley portrait: *Elizabeth I*, M. Gheeraerts the Younger, c. 1532 (National Portrait Gallery, London); Rainbow portrait: see Note 5 above.

50. The popularity of the veil image in Renaissance writing may be seen in Spenser's *The Faerie Queene*, that which covers but simultaneously reveals Acrasia's body: II. xii. 77; and in Sir Philip Sidney's *An Apology for Poetry*, ed. Geoffrey Shepherd (Manchester: Manchester University Press, 1973), pp. 99–103. For a more detailed discussion of veiling devices in relation to allegory, see Michael Murrin, *The Veil of Allegory* (Chicago: University of Chicago Press, 1969).

51. Sieve portrait: *Queen Elizabeth of England* by Federigo Zuccaro, c. 1580 (Pinacoteca Nazionale di Siena, Siena); Ditchley: See Note 49 above.

52. Spenser, from 'A Letter of the Authors', p. 737. See also Strong, *Gloriana*, pp. 95–107.

53. Thomas Salter, *A Critical Edition of Thomas Salter's The Mirrhor of Modestie*, ed. Janis Butler Holm (New York: Garland, 1987), pp. 61, 101–17. We are indebted to Holm for the above argument.

54. John Davies, 'Of her Wisedom', Hymne 22 from *Hymnes to Astaea*, in Robert Krueger, ed., *The Poems of Sir John Davies* (Oxford: Clarendon Press, 1975), pp. 83–4. The first letters of the sixteen-line poem spell out 'ELISABETHA REGINA'.

55. Strong, *Gloriana*, p. 9; Christopher Hibbert, *The Virgin Queen* (London: Viking, 1990), pp. 100–22, 247.

56. Strong, *Gloriana*, pp. 147–8.

57. Ibid., pp. 143–5. *Ad vivum, Elizabeth I*, Isaac Oliver, c.1590–92 (Victoria and Albert Museum, London). First engraving, head and shoulders, *Elizabeth I*, Crispin van de Passe, 1592 (see Strong, *Portraits*, Plate E21). Full-length engraving by window, *Elizabeth I*, William Rogers, 1595–1600 (British Museum, London).

58. See below, p. 123.

59. Strong, *Gloriana*, pp. 135, 115. Ermine portrait: *Elizabeth I*, William Segar, 1585 (Hatfield House, England).

60. See below, p. 157.

61. Strong, *Gloriana*, p. 165.

62. Margaret J.M. Ezell, *The Patriarch's Wife* (Chapel Hill, NC and London: University of North Carolina Press, 1987), pp. 1–12.

63. See below, p. 199.

64. Thomas Drue, *The Duchess of Suffolk* (London, 1631). The play was first performed in 1624.

65. See below, p. 207.
66. Natalie Zemon Davis, *Society and Culture in Early Modern France* (London: Duckworth, 1975), p. 146.
67. See below, pp. 219–20.
68. June Osborne, *Entertaining Elizabeth I* (London: Bishopsgate Press, 1989), p. 93.
69. Hibbert, *The Virgin Queen*, p. 247; Osborne, *Entertaining Elizabeth I*, p. 97.
70. Charles Wall, *The Tombs of the Kings of England* (London: Sampson, Law, Marston & Co., 1891), pp. 409–17; H.M. Colvin, *The History of the Kings' Works* (London: Her Majesty's Stationery Office, 1975), vol. III, p. 120; Strong, *Gloriana*, pp. 43, 163; Margaret Whinney, *Sculpture in Britain 1530–1830*, 2nd edn, ed. John Physick (Harmondsworth: Penguin, 1988), pp. 60, 433; and Nigel Llewellyn, 'The royal body: Monuments to the dead, for the living', in Gent and Llewellyn, ed, *Renaissance Bodies*, pp. 218–40.
71. William Camden, *Reges, Reginæ, Nobiles, Et alij in Ecclesia Collegiata B Petri Westmonasterij sepulti* (London: Melch. Bradwoodus, 1603), pp. D3 r–v; John Stowe, *Annales or A General Chronicle of England* (London: Richardi Meighen, 1631), pp. 812–15; Henry Holland, *Herwologia Anglica* (Arrhemiensis: Jansonij Bibliopola, 1620), pp. 35–44; and for a later description, Thomas Fuller, *The Church History of Britain* (London: John Williams, 1655), Book 10, pp. 4–5.
72. Llewellyn, 'The royal body', pp. 228–30.

2

Penelope and the Politics of Woman's Place in the Renaissance

Georgianna Ziegler

On 15 May 1540, just about a year after their marriage, Duke Cosimo de' Medici and Eleonora of Toledo took up residence at the Palazzo Vecchio in Florence. At the age of twenty, the Duke had already weathered the intrigues of a scramble for power following the murder of Alessandro de' Medici, and had chosen his own bride, in spite of several politically motivated offers. His decision to remake the ancient fortification of the Palazzo Vecchio into a gracious home for his dynasty reflected artistically his own consolidation of power in Tuscany. The responsibility for organising and carrying out this grand plan was given in 1555 to the artist/writer Giorgio Vasari. Part of the rebuilding involved the addition of a chapel, study, and suite of four rooms for Eleonora, which unfortunately were not quite completed at the time of her death in 1562. Nevertheless, the programme for Eleonora's rooms, like the design for the rest of the building, is an attempt to read myth and history within the context of Medician power. While the stories of Penelope, the Sabine women, Queen Esther, and the virtuous Gualdrada painted on the ceilings and walls of these rooms all depict the politics of female virtue, it is the designs for the Sala di Penelope which will form the focus of this discussion.[1]

Twenty-five years later, in 1587, Robert Greene, one of the University Wits and a prolific generator of Elizabethan prose, had just published a small tract entitled *Penelope's Web*, offering his image of 'a Christall Myrror of Faeminine perfection'. It was dedicated to the noble sisters Margaret, Countess of Cumberland and Anne, Countess of Warwick. Both women were cultured patronesses, supporting such writers as Spenser and Samuel Daniel, and Lady Margaret appears to have tried her own hand at verse. In addition, Anne was influential at Elizabeth's court, serving as maid of honour, then Lady of the Privy Chamber; she was with the Queen at her death.[2]

These two creative endeavours – a decorated room and a piece of prose – have the same focus on Penelope and were both designed for noblewomen. Nevertheless, they are generally considered to be worlds apart in what we term 'artistic value'. While the room is privileged in our cultural ideology, the prose piece has been all but lost. What interests me about them is not at all a question of influence but one of inscription. Each of these works is based on a discourse which involves certain shared assumptions held about women during the Renaissance.[3] I am interested in the ways in which these assumptions are both inscribed in and subverted by the artistic endeavours which embody them.

Both works partake of that 'self-conscious stylization' which John Shearman has called 'the common denominator of all Mannerist works of art'.[4] Both achieve their effect through a union of disparate discourses, and here I broaden the term 'discourse' to include not only 'a particular way of talking (and writing and thinking)'[5] but, by extension, particular modes of visual representation as well. The iconography of the room is meant to be read like a text; for as Foucault reminds us, in the sixteenth century knowledge was acquired by constant (re)interpretation of all signs, both visual and verbal:

> The face of the world is covered with blazons, with characters, with ciphers and obscure words. . . . And the space inhabited by immediate resemblances becomes like a vast open book. . . . All that remains is to decipher them . . .[6]

The programme for the Sala di Penelope combines the discursive modes of impresa, heraldry and allegory with that of history painting to create a unified programme which invites reading(s) and both defines and breaks its architectural space. The eye moves from the friezes around the top of the walls which tell of Ulysses' travels, punctuated by representations of the four Cardinal Virtues, upwards to the ceiling, where personifications of four Italian rivers alternate with the Medici impresa and Medici/ Toledo coats of arms. The whole frames the central tondo in the ceiling, showing Penelope at her loom, surrounded by her women engaged in spinning and other wool-making activities. Although the ceiling is flat, this central scene is painted within a *trompe d'œil* circular frame, creating a dome-like effect. The eye moves through the dome and out to sky beyond, for Penelope sits in an open loggia topped by a balcony from which spectators look in on her and down on us.[7]

In a recent article on the Camera degli Sposi, painted in the Ducal Palace at Mantua a hundred years earlier, Randolph Starn notes that Alberti advised artists to include 'at least one figure that seems to address the viewer . . .', with the result that 'by positing a contingent response, the painting acknowledges the need for a beholder'. He goes on: 'In responding, the viewer becomes in turn patron, impresario, producer, *and* production of a command performance.'[8] Foucault situates such interaction in what he calls 'this precise but neutral place' – that is, the space

Figure 2.1 Penelope at the Spinning Wheel, Giovanni Stradano, 1555–62

between viewer and painting where 'the observer and the observed take part in a ceaseless exchange'. In this dynamic space, the viewer is seized and forced to enter the picture by those who gaze out from the painting, and s/he is assigned 'a place at once privileged and inescapable'.[9]

We know from a recently discovered cartoon that Giovanni Stradano, the artist who designed the central tondo of Penelope, changed the woman holding a spindle at lower left so that on the ceiling she is facing out and looking down towards the viewer, rather than inwards at the spinning wheel.[10] Furthermore, we have a clear profile of the woman at the spinning wheel, rather than a three-quarter back view as in the drawing. Both these figures, then, as well as the spectators on the balcony, elicit a response from the viewer by inviting him/her into the painting. The viewer, whether male or female, both reads the painting and is in turn validated by it. A man will feel contented by the orderliness of the noble household of Ulysses, which provides a busy domestic retreat from the vicissitudes of the masculine world of action, depicted around the lower wall in Ulysses' adventures. A noblewoman, like Eleonora, will see inscribed her place as organiser of this domesticity, and will by implication understand what is expected of her as keeper of both home and self for her husband. And finally, the setting of this painting in its emblematic Medician framework, within the larger structure of the Medici dynastic palace, produces and validates the court positions of these viewers.

The simultaneous invitation/re-creation of viewer in response to the painting has its counterpart in Greene's work, where the handmaids and old nurse who listen to Penelope's tales suggest the largely female readership of the work itself. In addition, just as the painted and 'real' spectators provide more than one point of view through which the painting can be seen, so Greene's multiple dedications to two noblewomen, to gentlemen readers, and to 'the Courteous and Courtly Ladies of England' set up various groups of readers with different expectations of the text.[11] Again, the assumption is of a primarily courtly rather than a general audience, from which the men are invited to participate as voyeurs of the text, while the women are to read it for instruction.

The text itself is composed of a variety of discourses, with their own framing devices.[12] Besides the author's letters of dedication and introduction, there is the omniscient narrator's placement of his material within the Homeric subtext. This placement in turn frames Penelope's discourse, which consists of three stories, punctuated during the intervals by the conversational discourse of herself and her ladies. Furthermore, the three tales which she tells them include narration, conversation, a letter, a poem, a song, and oration. While this piling up of discursive modes, one within the other, might seem as web-like as Penelope's cloth, the text, like the Palazzo ceiling, offers a glimpse beyond. It stands as a kind of time-warp within the *Odyssey*, as though Greene had stopped Homer's poem, inserted his own text, and then left the outcome open-ended. At the conclusion of Penelope's third night of tale-telling, the omniscient narrator takes over and reports that Ulysses has arrived at the port of Ithaca. Penelope sends her son to verify the report, and the narrator says:

> . . . what newes he heard of his father I knowe not. But thus abruptly this night was the discourse broken of [*sic*]: but for that fell out after his home comming, I referre you to the Paraphrase, which shortly shalbe set out vppon *Homers Odissea*: till when let vs leaue *Penelope* attending the returne either of her husband, her sonne, or of both.[13]

As far as we know, Greene never produced such a paraphrase, and the outcome of Penelope's predicament is thus left open. But just as the ceiling of Eleonora's room only *seems* to dissolve through the *trompe d'œil* effect of the painted sky, so Penelope's story only *seems* receptive of infinite endings, because the outcome mandated by the Homeric text would have been familiar to most readers of Greene's work. The constant possibility of re-creation is thus simultaneously offered and withdrawn, remaining ever in suspension.

Such appropriation of time and history is inherent in both the painting and the text, and represents what the critic Thomas Greene defines as the heuristic imitative strategy, one of several adopted by Renaissance writers as a way of coming to terms with texts of the classical past: 'Heuristic imitations come to us advertising their derivation from the subtexts they carry with them but having done that, they proceed to *distance themselves* from the subtexts and force us to recognize the poetic distance traversed.' He continues: 'a living culture is one which assumes historical responsibilities, one which remembers, preserves, resuscitates and recreates.'[14] In his total plan for the interior decoration of the Palazzo, Vasari consulted the historians and humanists surrounding the Duke: Cosimo Bartoli, Vincenzo Borghini, author of the *Discoursi*, and Giovambatista Adriani, who wrote the official history of Cosimo's dukedom. Vasari then orchestrated a vast plan paralleling past and present Medici history, integrated with terrestrial and celestial deities, classical antiquity, and Medici emblems and signs: 'Each room is arranged according to a system that the eye can easily grasp and these systems usually relate to each other room by room.'[15] In the Sala di Penelope, the Homeric past is given new life in a Cinquecento setting of Medici arms and Italian rivers. Penelope and her ladies sit within a landscape reminiscent of Florence itself, a hub of textile production.[16] The effect is both to suggest a past stretching back to heroic Greece and to display a present proud of its own achievements and eminently worthy of such a comparison. Eleonora de' Medici, it is implied, is a Renaissance Penelope.

A similar intent is stated by Greene in his Dedicatorie Epistle to the Countesses:

> For if trueth be the daughter of tyme, and tyme the Heralt that best embla-zeth affections: the report that the Gretians made of the Princesse of Ithaca, may seeme but a fiction compared with the fame of your Ladiships ver-tuous resolutions . . . (p. 142)

Greene's Penelope stands within time and outside it, for as she waits for Ulysses to return, she tells stories about other women who will live after her and whose fortunes she cannot yet know. Greene's work

> becomes a kind of *rite de passage* between a specified past and an emergent present. . . . The passage of history will never be as simple as the *rite de passage* suggests. But by the reductive simplifications of its historical con-struct, [Greene's prose fiction] confronts the threat of history and asserts its own limited freedom from it.[17]

Its open-endedness and fluid sense of time invite the reader to enter the ruptured space between past and present where the creative process occurs.

The stories Greene retells through Penelope's voice he chose and em-broidered from a variety of sources, including La Primaudaye's *French Academie*[18] where, in the author's address 'Av Lectevr', La Primaudaye asks rhetorically:

> Was it in vaine and fruitles, that an infinite number of famous personages, whom Historie, the mother of antiquitie set before our eies, imploied so great travell, passed infinite watchings, forsooke and contemned riches, pleasures, honors, and worldly commodities, to get and treasure up vertue only?[19]

The implication, of course, is that they did not suffer so much in vain, but that later generations might learn from them. La Primaudaye's book is set forth as an Academy to teach moral behaviour in all aspects of society. The book is dedicated to Henry III of France (son of Catherine de' Medici, Cosimo's cousin), for whom La Primaudaye served as Gentleman of the Chamber; thus, like the Palazzo Vecchio, the book politicises history and morality.

In Greene's adaptation, history also serves a moral function to a courtly and to a more general audience. In Elizabeth's England, history was often understood as a mirror for the present, and the full title of Greene's work is: *Penelopes Web: Wherein a Christall Myrror of faeminine perfection represents to the viewe of euery one those vertues and graces, which more curiously beautifies the mynd of women, then eyther sumptuous Apparell, or Iewels of inestimable valew: the one buying fame with honour, the other breeding a kynd of delight, but with repentance. In three seuerall discourses also are three especiall vertues, necessary to be incident in euery vertuous woman, pithely discussed: namely Obedience, Chastitie, and*

Sylence: Interlaced with three seuerall and Comicall Histories. The mixed metaphor is curious for the mirror is *in* the web, which is woven in part by the interlacing of the three comical histories; comical in the sense of a story which ends happily. But also embedded in the title are the 'sumptuous Apparell' and 'Iewels of inestimable valew', the obverse of the web and mirror, which constantly threaten to subvert their positive influence. A woman looking into a mirror can see only the pleasing decoration of her body, or she can look deeper and see the state of her mind and soul. In like manner, the reader of this 'Web' can merely enjoy the 'Comicall Histories' for pleasure, or she can take instruction from them. Paraphrasing the popular Horatian dictum, the motto which rounds off the title page declares: 'He carries every point who mixes the useful and the pleasant' [*Omne tulit punctum qui miscuit vtile dulci*], a sentiment repeated by Sidney when he writes of poetry that it is 'a speaking picture – with this end, to delight and teach'.[20]

During the Renaissance, the figure of Penelope was abstracted from Homer's account and used to represent the ideal chaste and faithful wife. Her attribute became the loom on which she wove and unwove the web that enabled her to maintain this chastity against the importunities of many suitors.[21] Various works of art represent this theme, and Penelope likewise appears in numerous literary works besides Greene's, including Boccaccio's *De Claris Mulieribus*, Brathwait's *The English Gentlewoman*, Breton's *The Praise of Women*, Elyot's *Defence of Good Women*, Gosynhill's *Mulierum Paean*, and Vives's *Instruction of a Christen Woman*. In all these works, created by men for the edification of women, Penelope is one of a set of images which inscribe what Peter Stallybrass calls 'the production of a normative "Woman" within the discursive practices of the ruling elite'.[22] This 'normative "woman" ' is chaste, silent and obedient, and busies herself with needle or spindle at home among her maids rather than going abroad. Such an ideology, however, as Dollimore, Sinfield and others have reminded us, is in itself a construct, hiding rather than revealing 'the prevailing social order'.[23] Both the Palazzo room and Greene's prose piece are forceful examples of the simultaneous construction and subversion of this ideology.

Painting and text are presented as courtesy pieces, as morally uplifting exempla for their female audiences. Stradano includes the four Cardinal Virtues – Prudence, Fortitude, Charity and Temperance – in his programme, and Greene designs his stories to illustrate 'three especiall vertues, necessary to be incident in euery vertuous woman . . . namely Obedience, Chastitie, and Sylence'. The central figure in each piece is Penelope at her loom, the faithful wife steadfast at home, drawing back to her Ulysses' wandering bark. The painting emphasises the creative act: all the women engaged in wool-processing and Penelope in weaving, as though she were weaving out the tales of her husband's adventures which encircle the walls below. In Greene's work, Penelope is both maker and unmaker. Each evening when we see her, she picks apart the web of cloth she has woven during the day to delay for a little longer the advances of the suitors, while she weaves with words the figure of a chaste woman through the story she tells. These verbal tapestries of Obedience, Chastity and Silence, when taken together, represent the perfect wife as embodied in herself. Penelope constructs herself through words as she deconstructs the fabric or ploy which enables her to maintain that chastity which is the core of her identity.

The artist/writer creators of these pieces assume, with their times, that it is the male prerogative to offer moral instruction to women. Once she married Cosimo, Eleonora, like all Italian women of the age, belonged to her husband's family and was responsible for maintaining the male line.[24] This duty was made quite clear to her in the elaborate entertainment celebrating her wedding which, like the Palazzo itself, contained allegorical figures with pointed significance for the Medicis. In particular, as she entered the city of Florence, Eleonora passed under a triumphal arch at the top of which sat the figure of Fecundity, while singers greeted her thus:

> Come in, come in, under the most favorable auspices, Eleonora, to your city. And, fruitful in excellent offspring, may you produce descendants similar in quality to your father and forebears abroad, so that you may guarantee eternal security for the Medici name and its most devoted citizenry.[25]

Following through with this emphasis, Eleonora continued to be associated with Juno as Fecundity in various artistic representations throughout her lifetime.[26] Her portrait was painted around 1545 by Bronzino with her eldest son Francesco (then about four), the heir apparent, marking 'the first appearance of this combination in the history of the state portrait'. In it 'Bronzino presents her as the ideal princess praised by Vasari as *serena* and *fecunda*, the ideal consort of the stoic prince'.[27]

With the habit of reading such imagery, Eleonora would have understood very well the message of the decor in the suite of rooms, including the Sala di Penelope, designed for her. Vasari's earlier idea for these rooms, as indicated in a letter to Cosimo dated 28 January 1560/61, was to show the stories of royal women of long ago whose virtuous deeds compared with those of men, but eventually the programme specified itself into the stories of virtuous Roman, Hebrew, Greek and Tuscan women.[28] The Sabine women, Esther, Penelope and Gualdrada all showed loyalty to their husbands and/or the state, and they were all strategically placed politically.[29] The iconography in each of the four rooms containing their stories includes Medici impresa and heraldry, emphasising again that connection between past and present which, as we have seen, pervades the design of the entire Palazzo.

The patriarchal intent of the whole project is underscored by Vasari at the beginning of his *Ragionamenti,* a staged dialogue with Cosimo's son, Francesco, in which Vasari compares the revival of the building with the revival of the republic itself under Duke Cosimo:

> Now, the head of this republic has preserved the laws, justice, and the dominion for his citizens. He has, in fact, gloriously enlarged and improved them all. And the very same thing is indicated by these strong walls: in their ugliness, without harmony or unity, they reflected the disorder of the changing past governments; but our duke now demonstrates precisely in this building his beautiful method for correcting the architecture, just as he has done in the government – which is to subject it no longer to the will of many, but to one alone, *his* will.[30]

These four rooms, then, with their stories of faithful wives, create perpetual moral settings in which the line of Medici wives will be expected to live out their own lives in dutiful emulation. In these rooms of their own, they will never entirely escape the obligations of their patriarchal society.

Greene's work is specifically directed towards women, but with the expected modesty of dedicatory epistles, he downplays its importance. It is revealing, however, to see how his attitude towards his work changes between the two epistles he writes to women readers and the one to men. In his dedication to the Countesses of Cumberland and Warwick, Greene disclaims his own 'harsh style and methode' in comparison to Homer's 'sugred eloquence'. *Penelope's Web*, he says, is valuable 'for the vertue of the woman that first wrought it, though the Cloath workers arte [i.e. his own writing] haue given it so bad a glosse' (pp. 142, 143). In his letter to the 'Ladies of England' he suggests that his work is an unfinished piece and apologises for having 'intermedled' in women's matters, but it was, he says, 'in discouering the vertues of your sex, not in censuring seuerely of your actions' (p. 146). In these instances, he seems to lay blame on his own writing skill while simultaneously lauding the value of his subject matter. In the letter to 'Gentlemen Readers', however, he reverses his claim and denigrates his subject matter, calling it 'womens prattle' and saying that at first he was not even going to appeal to male readers. He decides to address them, nevertheless, in a manner which makes them voyeurs of the text: 'considering', he says, 'that *Mars* wil sometimes bee prying into *Venus* papers, and gentlemen desirous to heare the parlie of Ladies' (p. 145). A touch of prurience is thus thrown over this work which advertises itself in the title as a virtuous discourse.[31]

It is a little more difficult to specify an audience for Greene's work than for the Sala di Penelope, in part because the printed book had the opportunity for a much wider circulation than the painting; however, the immediate audience for both works was the aristocracy. Furthermore, Greene's book was published in only one edition, and its classical subject matter and multitude of literary references did not have the more popular appeal of his 'coney-catching' pamphlets. Nevertheless, the dedications allow us to postulate a gendered reader-response; both men and women would have enjoyed the work for its stories, which sweeten the moral instruction for the female audience. This audience would also have found appealing the female-centred community of the work, where women tell stories about love problems to other women. For male readers, a window on to such a private female world provided the appeal of voyeurism, while giving perhaps a false sense of security that the women are 'in their place'.

Both the book and the room inscribe a mixture of sexual enjoyment with sexual restraint, the former acting to subvert the latter. In Greene's work, this mixture is presented largely through Penelope's conversations with her Nurse and maids while they discuss such topics as passion and lust versus true love; the several kinds of marriage; virginity and wantonness; and the popularity accorded the sensual in contrast to the relative obscurity conferred upon the chaste. As the old Nurse says:

> . . . for long haue I mused why only in al the whole world *Dyana* hath a Temple in *Ephesus*, and *Venus* is as commonly honored as the household God *Lar*, that had a corner in euery mans kitchen . . . (p. 196)

Each sex likes to imagine the conversations of the other, and Greene depicts here a little community of women whose talk ranges from the moral to the risqué. He presents their conversation ostensibly as an incitement to female virtue, but implicit in the discourse of virtue is the discourse of passion which the first never quite succeeds in suppressing, and which would have been enjoyed, not only by his Gentlemen Readers but by his Ladies as well.

The paintings of the Sala di Penelope provide an obvious sensual delight through the appeal of their colour and form. The four rivers painted in the corners of the ceiling surrounding the tondo are depicted as muscular and sensual male and female nudes, while the carefully modelled female forms of the four Cardinal Virtues display the very sexuality which they also keep in check. On the walls beneath, the inclusion of scenes showing Calypso's release of Ulysses and Ulysses' release of his own men from Circe's bestial imprisonment not only celebrates the triumph of restraint over sensuality but in so doing invokes that sensuality itself. Perhaps the painting exceeds the text in its power to portray the sensuous through the use of form and colour that appeal directly to our sight. Certainly this was one argument used in the early debates on *ut pictura poesis* concerning the relative effectiveness of the visual versus the verbal. Even Ismena and the Nurse in *Penelope's Web* discuss the danger of sight as a sense especially conducive to passion, 'for in deede that is not loue which pearceth the eye, but which pleaseth the mind, not that is founded vpo[n] the superficial sight of beautie, but vpo[n] the touchstone of delight, which is vertue.'[32]

In addition to sexual enjoyment versus virtuous restraint, there are other forms of subversion operating in Greene's work. The need for women to be instructed in the first place is both asserted and denied by the text. Penelope relates her tales as a way of instructing her opinionated maids:

> because my mayds are young, and may in tyme trye the fortune of mariage, we will this night discourse of this poynt . . . that both we may beguyle the night with prattle, and profite our mynds by some good and vertuous precepts. (p. 162)

On the other hand, Penelope herself, the maids and Nurse, and some of the women in the stories have their own supply of wisdom. Some of this comes from the popular proverbial lore generally associated with women, such as 'the greatest prodigalitie is the expence of the eye'; 'better one house troubled than two'; or 'no man is happy before his end'. Other wisdom grows out of experience, as in the cases of Penelope herself and the old Nurse, as well as the injured wives in the first two stories, Barmenissa and Cratyna. A third kind of wisdom, largely masculine and authorial, is that derived from mythology and literature. There are numerous references to characters from legend and history: Paris, Venus, Diana, Cleopatra, Octavia, Antony, Lucrece, Juno, Theseus, Medea – the list could go on – and to famous authors: Plato, Aristotle, Dionysius, Anacreon, Menander, Ovid, Ariosto, and others. It is ultimately, of course, Greene – the male author – who is supplying these references, but the fact that he places them in the mouths of women both reinforces and subverts the very assumption that women should receive their instruction from a man.

The exhortations to obedience, chastity and silence are similarly questioned in the very process of representation. Penelope's first tale, the longest of the three, recounts the efforts made by the faithful Barmenissa to win back her husband, the Sultan of Egypt, from the grasp of the concubine Olynda. Barmenissa meets the concubine's monetary demands secretly out of her own purse, she goes into exile complacently, and she even admonishes her son to remain faithful to his father in spite of everything. Denied her own home and relegated to poverty, Barmenissa takes up that icon of the chaste housewife, the needle, for the Sultan has decreed that she and her ladies must earn their own maintenance by the work of their own hands. Rather than staying passively indoors and waiting for something to happen, however, she goes out and seeks action as a way of resolving her fortunes: 'taking her work in her hand (for the vse of her needle was her yerely reuenues)' (p. 177). On her way to court to discover what is happening to her son, Barmenissa tries to reason herself out of her melancholy over the state into which she has fallen. When reason fails, she picks up her needlework again to combat the melancholy, and while sewing she composes a madrigal, in which she comes to terms with her lowly state, deciding that one can achieve greater contentment in a 'Cottage seated in the hollowe dale' than in a palace with 'The Sceptre and the glittering pompe of mace' (pp. 179–80). Song and sewing are thus stitched together as the same creative act, producing a kind of moral sampler in Barmenissa's story, which itself forms part of the larger web of words woven by Penelope.[33] Her song is a little soliloquy which she sings while hidden in a thicket, but a moment later this privacy is intruded upon by 'a great noyse, which at the first amazed her, but at the last she perceiued it to be the voyce of men: desirous therefore to bee a partner of their secrecie, she kept her self silent within the thicket' (p. 180). The cacophony of the male world breaks the ordered music of the female lament, but this cacophony in turn soon produces its own order in the form of an 'Oration' by one of the Egyptian lords, revealing a plot to poison Olynda, who has ingratiated herself into the Sultan's favours and marriage bed.

After some soul-searching, Barmenissa decides to warn Olynda about the plot. When she confronts Olynda and the Sultan out walking, the concubine asks her where and how she lives. Barmenissa replies, 'I dwell Madame . . . in a little Cottage adioyning to the Subburbs of the Cittie, where accompanyed with three friendly companyons, I passe the day in labour with quiet, and the night in securitie with sweete slumbers.' The Sultan then asks if she works for a living, and Barmenissa reminds him that although her own background is royal, her father 'the great *Chan* of *Tartaria*', knowing that high position is no safeguard against ill-fortune, 'learned me to vse the Needle and the Wheele, that both I might eschue ydlenesse in my youth, and (if the Destinies had so decreed) the better brooke pouerty in my age' (p. 185). No longer a privileged member of the court, Barmenissa is now marginalised, dwelling in the suburbs and using her sewing skills not for recreation, but for profit. In a recent study, Ann Rosalind Jones points to 'a set of connections made throughout early modern Europe between women's handiwork and the virtues of simpler and purer days – connections made by men intending to maintain their ownership of language and their control over women's behavior'.[34] Barmenissa's seemingly contented life in the country, where she spins her threads like some pastoral shepherdess, is a myth which cloaks the actual hardships she endures. Playing the game, she actually perpetuates this myth as part of a scheme to ingratiate herself with Olynda and eventually to win back her own position. As her needlework is a weapon against poverty, so her verbal assaults are weapons against the injustice of her condition. When she tells the Sultan about the poisoning plot, he has a change of heart and plans to depose Olynda for his rightful wife. Once again, Barmenissa sends Olynda a warning, this time in verse, to change her ways, but it has no effect on the concubine. Barmenissa thus remains chaste, obedient, loyal to her family, in spite of her husband's infidelity, and appears to take her downfall with good grace. Her virtue is rewarded by his reformation. At the same time as we see her representing these wifely virtues, however, Barmenissa also uses her wits, speaks out and takes bold action.

In a sense, Olynda the concubine is Barmenissa's alternate self, and the true wife appeals to her husband indirectly through this alternate identity. Olynda is everything Barmenissa is not; she is selfish, seductive and vindictive, and her ultimate punishment is one she designed for Barmenissa: to be banished from the Sultan's lands. Through her position as courtesan and her final banishment, Olynda is permanently marginalised, while Barmenissa is removed from her cottage in the suburbs to her rightful place at court. Olynda is what the Sultan calls her, 'a very mirror of vicious affections', standing against the example of Barmenissa, who reflects the example of the ideal obedient wife (p. 190). Both positions are fragile, but one is not possible without the other. Each mirror has its obverse image:

> *Socrates* was wont to say, that when a maried wife holdeth her looking glasse in her hand, she should speake thus to her self, if she be foule: what then should become of me if I were also wicked? and if she bee faire: how shall my beautie be accounted of if I continue wise and honest: for a hard fauoured woman that is renowned for her chastitie, is more honorable then she which is famous for her beautie. (p. 201)

The heroine of the second tale, Cratyna, also uses policy and subtlety to get out of an unfortunate situation, much as Penelope herself does, using her web to fool the suitors. In this story, a nobleman named Calamus lusts after Cratyna, the chaste wife of a poor farmer. When Calamus comes to their home, Cratyna treats him first with hospitality; then, when she ascertains his real purpose, she sees what persuasive rhetoric can do. Neither kindness nor morality moves Calamus, however, and he abducts Cratyna and would also kill her husband, Lestio, but he manages to flee to safety in the service of a collier. Cratyna escapes from the palace and travels alone and at night until she finds her husband. She then cuts her hair, puts on boy's dress, so that not even her husband recognises her, and works with him in the colliery. Cratyna's disguise enables her to speak out even more bluntly to Calamus when he comes searching for her. He is dressed in more humble garb than usual, but she recognises him and says, 'If I could [tell you where she has gone] thinke not so little courtesie in me as to bewray her: for by thy straight inquirie I perceiue thou art seruant to that dishonorable *Calamus*, that spareth neither wife nor widdowe to satisfie his vnbridled lust' (p. 215). When Calamus eventually learns of Cratyna's disguise and hardships, he has a change of heart and confesses the story to his overlord, Prince Menon. The Prince invites the

Collier, Cratyna, and her husband to court, but when he offers to keep the 'boy' as his page, Lestio becomes so upset that Cratyna once more tries her rhetorical skills:

> [She] fell down vpo[n] her knees, and unfoulded to the King what she was, and from point to point discoursed what had happened betweene her and *Calamus*, intermedling her speeches with such a fountaine of teares, as the King pittying her playnts, willed her to be of good cheere: for none in all his Kingdome should offer her any vyolence. (p. 218)

The use of disguise and impassioned rhetoric in this story brings it close to the world of the stage, and the theatrical metaphor is fore-grounded when 'the King praysing *Calamus* for his good mynd, willing to be an actor in this Comedie, commaunded his steward to furnish them with apparell, and afterward to conuay them to *Calamus* Pallace, where they liued long after in prosperous and happie estate' (p. 219).[35] As in so many of Shakespeare's comedies, the heroine's chastity is preserved, but in the process she has acted very much as an independent woman, travelling by herself, speaking in her own defence, dressing as a man, and doing men's work. In other words, she engages in those very activities to *save* her chastity which would have been forbidden her as means to *losing* it.

It may not have been Greene's intended point, but what both these tales show is that women are capable of resolving difficult situations with their own ingenuity and resourcefulness. In addition, both women work within and against the politics of the state as each outwits a ruler. As wife of the Sultan, Barmenissa is a woman of some political power. She loses that power, then regains it by appearing to behave as the 'normative "Woman" ' (taking her punishment, plying her needle, remaining humble), while in reality using the secret intrigues of the male political world to regain her position. Cratyna, a poor woman with no power, defends herself against the patriarchal power of the duke who lusts for her by 'becoming' a member of the patriarchy through disguise.

By a strange twist of fate, the life of Margaret, Countess of Cumberland, one of the dedicatees of Greene's book, provides a real-life parallel, especially to the story of Barmenissa. Margaret was caught in the political web woven by that astute politician Queen Elizabeth, and victimised by a system that, while headed by a female ruler, still gave preference to patrilineal inheritance. She was betrothed at a very early age to George Clifford, Earl of Cumberland, whom she married in 1577 when she was seventeen and he was nineteen. This alliance, graced by the presence of Queen Elizabeth herself, had been a political arrangement from the time when the child George, with the Queen's permission, was made a ward of Margaret's father, the Earl of Bedford. The marriage fell apart in 1591, when Margaret left her husband and took her small daughter Anne to live for a time with her sister. The Earl was quite a favourite of the Queen's, but this disintegration of the marriage shows the darker effects on families of the glittering court life Elizabeth offered her followers. The separation seems to have occurred because of the Earl's dalliance with another lady at court, but the situation must have been exacerbated by his gambling, his wasting of the family's estate, by his long absences on voyages, by the death of their only two sons at the age of five, and by what appears to have been some incompatibility of personality.[36]

Margaret was an intelligent and resourceful woman. Determined that her daughter Anne would be well educated, she hired Samuel Daniel as her tutor. Allowing for natural bias, there is a perceptive account of Margaret by Anne:

> She was naturally of a high spirit, though she tempered it by grace. . . . She had a discerning spirit, both in the dispositions of human creatures and natural causes, and into the affairs of the world. She had a great, sharp, natural wit, so as there was few things worthy of knowledge but that she had some insight into them. . . . [And she was] endowed with a large share of those four moral virtues, prudence, justice, fortitude, and temperance.[37]

In spite of his waywardness, the Earl evidently recognised the virtues of his wife, for he sent her a conciliatory letter just before his death which ends: 'Thus out of the bitter and greedy desire of a repentant heart, begging thy pardon for any wrong that ever in my life I did thee, I commend these my requests to thy wonted and undeserved kind wifely and lovely consideration.'[38]

Mother and daughter were present at his death in 1605. This being a real-life situation, not a romance, the man is not completely redeemed and rewarded by living happily ever after with his wife, as in the story of Barmenissa. Instead, just before his death, the Earl changed his will, cutting his daughter Anne out of her inheritance and placing it instead in his brother's male line. In the same letter in which he asks his wife's forgiveness, the Earl requests that she not bring a suit against his brother but accept his disposition of the estate. Margaret, however, spent most of the rest of her life fighting for her daughter's rights in court, and the case was not settled until after her own death.[39]

In 1587, when Greene's book appeared with its dedication to her, Margaret could not have known all the vicissitudes of life in store for her, though perhaps she already realised the incompatibility of her marriage. What she would have found in this text was not only another courtesy book for women but stories that insist on the independent thinking and action of women who, like Barmenissa and Cratyna, are asked to test their values and family loyalty under duress from the political hierarchy.

The third tale in *Penelope's Web*, which discusses silence, is by nature of that virtue the shortest text.[40] It is an interesting variation on the King Lear story, in which a king tries to decide which of his three equally worthy sons should succeed him by discovering which of their wives is most virtuous. The original plan is for each son to prove his wife's virtue, but the first son is interrupted by his wife, who says that the only recommendation *she* needs is her own fame:

> I referre my self to those whom fame hath made to glorie in my weldoings . . . referring my cause to the generall report of the world, both for obedience and chastitie, the two speciall ornaments that gardeth and preserueth a womans honour: I will not inueigh against the vertuous dispositions of my sisters, sith enuie in a woman is like a pibble stone set in the purest gold. (p. 228)

She, in turn, is interrupted by the second sister-in-law, who accuses her of self-love and warns: 'Take heede, Sister, fame hath two faces, and in that resembleth tyme, readie as well to backbyte as to flatter' (p. 229). The Janus-faced image of fame recalls the double mirror in Barmenissa's story and the larger mirror in *Penelope's Web* itself, wherein women can see/read what they are and what they ought to be.

If this wife had stopped there, her chances would have been better, but she is even more loquacious than her sister-in-law, and after saying with some venom, 'I set not my good name at so small a price, as to hazard it vpon the chaunce of the tongue . . . although I am sure my bordring neighbours so esteeme of my doings, as they take my vertues for a president [*sic*] of their actions', she argues her own case by referring to her virtuous ancestry (pp. 229–30).

Like Goneril and Regan, the wives of the two eldest sons protest too much. The third wife says only, 'He that gaineth a Crowne getteth care: is it not follie then to hunt after losse.' When the king questions her further she adds, 'This . . . that whe[n] others talke, yet being a woman I can hold my peace' (p. 232). Needless to say, she and her husband are the ones rewarded. Ironically, *male* worth is here determined by a *female* virtue which is privileged by the patriarchy. While this story supports the virtue of silence in women, the work as a whole again presents contrary evidence, through the ingenuity of Barmenissa who speaks through action, word, and poem, through the rhetorical skills of Cratyna, and through Penelope herself, the teller of these tales.[41]

It is to Homer's story of Penelope that we must finally return and ask it to reveal its own alternative reading. While her chastity and busyness are praised by Renaissance men in their various representations of her for the benefit of women, it is also true that as a woman she asserts power over her own body with her conscious decision to remain chaste by repulsing the advances made to her by men. When the game is up, and the suitors discover her deception of undoing the shroud she is weaving, Homer says, 'So against her will and by force, she had to finish it.' This shroud, which those in the masculine power world force her to finish, ironically becomes their own, for the suitors are killed by Ulysses at the end. But though she relinquishes her web, she does not relinquish her self. Antinous, spokesman for the suitors, praises Penelope's wisdom, 'beautiful work', 'good character' and 'cleverness', but he says, 'in this single matter she did not think rightly;/ . . . She is winning a great name/ for herself, but for you [Telemachus] she is causing much loss of substance.'[42] In the end, at Ulysses' return, the loss of substance is rectified, but it is her name – 'circumspect Penelope', as Homer calls her – which remains a signifier of that 'self' which she has so closely guarded, even testing Ulysses to make sure it is really he before she shares her bed and her tale with him. The creative process here becomes one with the sexual act, reminding us of the prevalent use of birth imagery by female *and* male authors to describe both the process and the result of writing.[43]

Of the three historic women to whom our Penelope pieces were dedicated, two worked successfully within the political systems in which they were born and wed. Married to a man who valued highly the female duty of maternity to support a dynastic line, while discouraging female meddling in affairs of state, Eleonora evidently complied gracefully with Cosimo's wishes. At the same time, she maintained her identity by choosing to speak her native Spanish and by acts of generosity, such as founding the Jesuit College in Florence. On her early death, most of her possessions were left to Cosimo, but in her will she also remembered the single women of her court and the slaves, who were freed.[44] Anne, Countess of Warwick, wife of Ambrose Dudley (brother of Robert Dudley, Elizabeth's favourite), must have been a woman of great sensitivity and discretion to have survived her whole life in favour at Elizabeth's court, serving the Queen for many years as a lady-in-waiting. Like many women in power who may feel insecure in a patriarchal role, Elizabeth did not make life easy for the women who served her. Nevertheless, Anne's niece wrote that the Countess of Warwick was 'more beloved and in greater favour with the Queen than any other woman in the kingdom. . . . She was a great friend to virtue, and a helper to many petitioners and others in distress.'[45]

Only Anne's sister, Margaret Clifford, openly opposed a system which had led her into an unhappy marriage and a forfeiture of her daughter's patrimony. The stories of Barmenissa and of Penelope herself suggest, however, that it can take just as much skill for a woman to work successfully within the power structure as to break completely from it. Each woman creates a 'self', a life of her own, within the 'frame' she is given. She may break out of this frame, or she may choose to weave her life within its bounds, adding colours and twisting the threads to create an individual pattern or identity.

In a recent article, Nancy K. Miller rereads the story of another ancient weaver, Arachne, and coins the term 'arachnology', by which she means:

a critical positioning which reads *against* the weave of indifferentiation to discover the embodiment in writing of a gendered subjectivity. . . . Arachnologies, thus, involve more broadly the interpretation and reappropriation of a story, like many in the history of Western literature that deploys the interwoven structures of power, gender, and identity inherent in the production of mimetic art.[46]

We have read the Medician painting and the Elizabethan text from this critical stance, drawing on the 'localisation' of each within its social/ historic context and then reading against that context to discover that 'other' private female self behind the 'normative' public woman. This kind of reading has been defined by Hans-Georg Gadamer as consisting 'in a dialogue between past and present'. In his discussion of Gadamer's theory, Terry Eagleton writes:

> All understanding is *productive*: it is always 'understanding otherwise', realizing new potential in the text, making a difference to it. The present is only ever understandable through the past, with which it forms a living continuity; and the past is always grasped from our own partial viewpoint within the present. The event of understanding comes about when our own 'horizon' of historical meanings and assumptions 'fuses' with the 'horizon' within which the work itself is placed. At such a moment we enter the alien world of the artefact, but at the same time gather it into our own realm, reaching a more complete understanding of ourselves.[47]

The web of Penelope, which Greene calls 'the only trophee of her chastitie', is structurally and metaphorically the unifying principle of both text and painting, making each in some sense a work *about* the creative act as well as an example of it. This artistic self-consciousness invites us as reader/viewers to participate in the creative act ourselves, alert to the ideologies of the writer and painter which are inscribed in the works, as well as the implied structures of power to which these works respond, to find new richnesses at the juncture of woof and warp.

NOTES

1. My main sources for information concerning the Medici and the Palazzo Vecchio are Ettore Allegri and Alessandro Cecchi, *Palazzo Vecchio E I Medici* (Firenze: Studio Per Edizioni Scelte, 1980) and Jerry Lee Draper, 'Vasari's decoration in the Palazzo Vecchio: The *Ragionamenti* translated with an Introduction and Notes' (PhD dissertation, Chapel Hill: University of North Carolina, 1973). For a recent discussion of the design for the central tondo by Giovanni Stradano (Johannes Stradanus) see R.A. Scorza, 'A "modello" by Stradanus for the "Sala di Penelope" in the Palazzo Vecchio', *Burlington Magazine*, **126** (July 1984), pp. 433–7.
2. For biographical information on the two countesses, see Kathy Lynn Emerson, *Wives and Daughters: The women of sixteenth century England* (Troy, NY: Whitston, 1984), pp. 185–6, 188. For Margaret Clifford, see also *Dictionary of*

National Biography (New York: Macmillan, 1908), vol. IV, p. 524; and George C. Williamson, *Lady Anne Clifford, Countess of Dorset, Pembroke & Montgomery. 1590–1676 . . .* 2nd edn. (Wakefield, Yorkshire: S.R. Publishers, 1967; rpt of 1922 edn.).

3. On ideology and discourse, see Catherine Belsey, *Critical Practice* (London: Methuen, 1980), p. 5.
4. John Shearman, *Mannerism* (Harmondsworth: Penguin, 1967), p. 35.
5. Belsey, *Critical Practice*, p. 5.
6. Michel Foucault, *The Order of Things* (New York: Vintage, 1973), pp. 40, 27.
7. On the viewer-subject in Renaissance painting, see Svetlana Alpers, 'Interpretation without representation, or, the viewing of *Las Meninas*' *Representations*, 1 (1983), pp. 30–42.
8. Randolph Starn, 'Seeing culture in a room for a Renaissance prince', in Lynn Hunt, ed., *The New Cultural History* (Berkeley: University of California Press, 1989), pp. 211, 217.
9. Foucault, *The Order of Things*, p. 5.
10. Scorza, 'A "modello" '. p. 434.
11. In his study of narrative, Ross Chambers calls it 'a transactional phenomenon', partly because there is 'an initial *contract*, an understanding between the participants in the exchange as to the purposes served by the narrative function' which 'assigns meaningfulness to the discourse'. Because Chambers is dealing with the modern novel, he has something less obvious in mind than dedicatory epistles, but these may certainly set up a contract. See his *Story and Situation: Narrative seduction and the power of fiction* (Minneapolis: University of Minnesota Press, 1984), p. 8.
12. Patricia Waugh writes: 'The novel assimilates a variety of discourses (representations of speech, forms of narrative) – discourses that *always* to some extent question and relativize each other's authority', in her *Metafiction: The theory and practice of self-conscious fiction* (London: Methuen, 1984), p. 6. Exactly how this works in Greene's work, an early experimental attempt at English prose fiction, deserves further investigation.
13. Robert Greene, *Penelope's Web*, in *The Life and Complete Works . . .*, ed. Alexander B. Grosart, 'Huth Library' ([London]: For private circulation, 1881–3), vol. V, pp. 233–4. All references are to this edition.
14. Thomas M. Greene, *The Light in Troy: Imitation and discovery in Renaissance poetry* (New Haven, CT: Yale University Press, 1982), pp. 40, 41.
15. Draper, 'Vasari's decoration', p. 28.
16. Allegri and Cecchi, *Palazzo Vecchio*, p. 204.
17. Thomas Greene, *The Light in Troy*, p. 41.
18. Ernest A. Baker, in what now seems an old-fashioned demand for historical rectitude, castigates Greene for playing 'ducks and drakes with chronology' in *Penelope's Web*. See his *The History of the English Novel* (London: Witherby, 1929), vol. II, p. 98. For discussions of Greene's sources, see H.C. Hart, 'Robert Greene's prose works', on Greene and Primaudaye, in *Notes & Queries*, series X, vol. V, pp. 204, 343, 444–5, 463–4; and René Pruvost, *Robert Greene et ses romans . . .*, 'Publications de la Faculté des Lettres D'Alger', (Paris: Société d'Edition 'Les Belles Lettres', 1938), IIᵉ série, tome XI, pp. 234–9.
19. Pierre de la Primaudaye, *The French Academie . . .* (London, 1589; STC 15234), sig.[Biiiᵛ]. The work was first published in English in 1586 but had appeared earlier in French. See Pierre de la Primaudaye, *Académie Françoise . . .*, 3 vols (Paris: Guillaume Chaudiere, 1581; rpt Slatkine, 1972).

20. Sir Philip Sidney, *An Apology for Poetry*, ed. Forrest G. Robinson (New York: Bobbs-Merrill, 'Library of Liberal Arts', 1970), p. 18. The mirror is, among other things, closely related to the idea of mimesis in the period, of literature as 'holding a mirror up to nature'. For a recent discussion, see Wendy Steiner, *The Colors of Rhetoric* (Chicago: University of Chicago Press, 1982), pp. 7 ff.

21. As Scorza writes, 'Spinning and weaving were almost emblematic of female virtue.' Boccaccio makes this association, and 'the theme had also been celebrated in art'. A fresco at the Palazzo Schifanoia in Ferrara, for example, shows weavers to illustrate '*virtu femminile*' (p. 434). Pintoricchio's 'Return of Telemachus and Ulysses' of 1509, originally a fresco for a palazzo in Siena (now in the National Gallery, London) has the men come in upon Penelope sitting at her loom, with one of her maids spinning at her side. Finally, Giovanni Stradano himself designed tapestries 'for the upper chambers where the Princess has her habitation, which are four, dedicated to the virtues of women . . .' (Vasari, *Lives of the Most Eminent Painters . . .*, transl. Gaston De Vere [London: The Medici Society, 1915], vol. 10, p. 18).

22. Peter Stallybrass, 'Patriarchal territories: The body enclosed' in Margaret W. Ferguson *et al.*, eds, *Rewriting the Renaissance . . .* (Chicago: University of Chicago Press, 1986), p. 127.

23. See, for example, Jonathan Dollimore and Alan Sinfield, 'History and ideology: The instance of Henry V', in John Drakakis, ed., *Alternative Shakespeares* (London: Methuen, 1985), pp. 206–15.

24. Lauro Martines writes, 'At Florence . . . a family name and the bulk of the family possessions and fortunes moved along a patrilineal route.' See 'A way of looking at women in Renaissance Florence', *Journal of Medieval and Renaissance Studies*, 4 (1974), p. 19.

25. *A Renaissance Entertainment: Festivities for the marriage of Cosimo I, Duke of Florence, in 1539*, ed. Andrew C. Minor and Bonner Mitchell (Columbia, MO: University of Missouri Press, 1968), p. 103.

26. See Janet Cox-Rearick, *Dynasty and Destiny in Medici Art* (Princeton, NJ: Princeton University Press, 1984), p. 290. From the evidence, it appears that Eleonora's marriage with Cosimo was one of mutual love, which surely made 'doing her duty' more pleasant. In the event, she produced eleven children in fifteen years of marriage. See Arnaldo D'Addario, 'Eleonora di Toledo, Duchessa di Firenze e di Siena', in *Donne di Casa Medici* (Firenze: Edizioni Arnaud, 1968), pp. 33, 42–3.

27. Karla Langedijk, *The Portraits of the Medici: 15th–18th centuries* (Firenze: Studio Per Edizioni Scelte, 1981), vol. I, p. 99. Cosimo was apparently interested in creating a gallery of family portraits, adding to those of the fifteenth century, and forming a dynastic collection. See Langedijk, p. 100.

28. Letter, G. Vasari to Cosimo de Medici, 28 January 1561, in *Der Literarische Nachlass Giorgio Vasaris*, ed. Karl Frey (Munich: Georg Muller, 1923), vol. I, p. 601. The later account reads thus: 'E per le stanze disopra, dove abita la principessa, che sono quattro dedicate alla virtu delle donne, con istorie di Romane, Ebree, Greche e Toscane, cioe le Sabine, Ester, Penelope e Gualdrada . . .' in Giorgio Vasari, *Le Vite* (Novara: Istituto Geografico de Agostini, 1967), vol. VIII, p. 39.

29. The Sabines, known for their virtue and religious fervour, were one of the ancient tribes in Italy. During the time of Romulus, the Romans carried off many Sabine women in a notorious mass rape, causing the Sabine men to rise up against the Romans. The biblical story of Esther, wife of King Ahasuerus, tells how she successfully pleaded for her life and the lives of all the Jewish

people in Persia, against the insidious plots of Haman. Gualdrada is mentioned in Canto XVI of Dante's *Inferno* as the grandmother of Guido Guerra. She was known for her virtue because, in spite of her father's encouragement, she refused to kiss the Emperor Otto IV when he was struck by her beauty one day in church, saying 'that no man might kiss her unless he were her husband. Otto was so impressed by the modesty and propriety of this remark that he married her to one of his noblemen and settled a large estate upon the couple. It was from this marriage that the counts Guidi de Modigliano . . . were said to descend'. See Dante Alighieri, *The Inferno*, transl. John Ciardi (New York: New American Library, 1954), p. 147, Note 38.

30. Draper, 'Vasari's decoration', p. 92; emphasis added.

31. In a recent article, Wendy Wall discusses the ambiguity many English Renaissance writers felt towards seeing their private verse and prose come into the public eye in print. Often, the prefaces to these works 'cast the reader in the role of voyeur, one who partakes of forbidden and private discourse and is complicitous in stealing a glance at clandestine words'. 'Disclosures in print: The "violent enlargement" of the Renaissance voyeuristic text', *Studies in English Literature*, 29 (1989), p. 38.

32. *Penelope's Web*, p. 158. Greene's comments on the appeal of the senses are a much-diluted version of a full-blown philosophical discussion of the matter, such as that found in Castiglione's *Courtier*. See especially the remarks of Pietro Bembo in Book IV. Baldessare Castiglione, *The Courtier*, transl. George Bull (Baltimore, MD: Penguin, 1967), pp. 325 ff.

33. The popularity of emblematic embroidery in sixteenth-century England and the growth of moralistic samplers in the seventeenth century are described by Rozsika Parker in *The Subversive Stitch* (London: The Women's Press, 1984), chapters 4 and 5.

34. Ann Rosalind Jones, 'Distaff and spindle in the gender debate, 1400–1660', p. 1, presented to the Workshop on 'Contested Domestic Spaces and the Fashioning of a Renaissance Woman' at the conference 'Attending to Women in Early Modern England', University of Maryland, 8–10 November 1990. Jones points out the difference between needlework done to pass the time by wealthy women and that produced out of necessity by the poor. 'But men writing conduct books were imagining female behavior in ethical and symbolic terms rather than addressing the economic need for textile work in private households' (p. 4). I am grateful to Ann Jones for permission to quote from this unpublished paper.

35. The theatrical motif is further suggested in Cratyna's story by an exchange between the King and Lestio when the group have been brought to court in their colliery garments. Trying to discern the real identity of the 'boy', the King asks Lestio, 'Is not this boy your man: No my Lord (quoth he) only my bedfellowe, and that is all the service I crave at his hands. At this answere the King and *Calamus* smyled, and *Cratyna* fearing she was discovered began to blush' (pp. 217–18). The innuendos concerning the sexuality of the disguised 'boy' are similar to those used on the stage by Shakespeare and his fellow dramatists for their boy actors in disguise. On this topic see Phyllis Rackin, 'Androgyny, mimesis, and the marriage of the boy heroine on the English Renaissance stage', in Elaine Showalter, ed., *Speaking of Gender* (New York: Routledge, 1989), pp. 113–33.

36. For details on the life of Margaret, Countess of Cumberland, see George C. Williamson, *Lady Anne Clifford* . . .

37. Ibid., p. 38.

38. Ibid., p. 33.

39. The *Dictionary of National Biography* tells us that the lawsuit was settled after Margaret Clifford's death by a compromise in 1617. Lady Anne eventually came into her father's estates after the death in 1644, without male heirs, of her cousin, Henry, last Earl of Cumberland. See Williamson, *op. cit.*, p. 186.

40. On women and silence, see Christine Brooke-Rose, 'Woman as a semiotic object', in Susan Rubin Suleiman, ed., *The Female Body in Western Culture* (Cambridge, MA: Harvard University Press, 1986), pp. 308–12; and among Renaissance women in particular, Catherine Belsey, *The Subject of Tragedy: Identity and difference in Renaissance drama* (London: Methuen, 1985), Chapter 6.

41. In Shakespeare's play, Cordelia's brief response angers Lear, though Kent understands the real value of her restraint. Here, the King is at first puzzled by the youngest wife's 'short and sweete' response, and he questions her further, as Lear does Cordelia, but when her reply is again brief, the King and nobles debate the matter and honour her 'that contrary to her naturall disposition [she] could so well bridle her affections': *Penelope's Web*, p. 232.

42. References are to Richmond Lattimore's translation of *The Odyssey* (New York: Harper & Rowe, 1967): Bk II, 110, 117–27.

43. Wendy Wall discusses the common Renaissance metaphor that 'equates textual production with reproduction. Writing is represented as childbirth, and the site of writing is the female genitalia, the veiled, enclosed space within the female body', 'Disclosures in print', p. 40.

44. See D'Addario, 'Eleonora di Toledo', pp. 41, 42, 56, 58.

45. Williamson, *Lady Anne Clifford . . .*, p. 37.

46. Nancy K. Miller, 'Arachnologies: The woman, the text, and the critic', in Miller, ed., *The Poetics of Gender* (New York: Columbia University Press, 1986), p. 272.

47. Terry Eagleton, *Literary Theory* (Minneapolis: University of Minnesota Press, 1983), pp. 71–2.

3

Private Writing and Public Function: Autobiographical Texts by Renaissance Englishwomen

Helen Wilcox

I

In the mean time she beg'd we might write to one another every day.
I did not faile to do that, and she had show'd me a place in the mated galary just by my chamber dore where she hid her letter's. I constantly went thether every day with great joy to loke for her's, which (according to her order's) I carefully kept in my bosome till I found a good opertunity of burning it.[1]

Lady Elizabeth Delaval's account of a youthful exchange of letters, expressed in a language of secrecy, introduces precisely the kind of auto-biographical texts with which this essay is concerned. The writing is private ('we might write to one another'), intimate ('kept in my bosome'), obscure ('a place . . . where she hid her letter's) and threatened with transience ('till I found a good opertunity of burning it'). It is a most private instance of what is generally considered to be itself the most private mode of writing. The focus of this essay will be on eight such autobiographical texts written by women between 1570 and 1676. The forms taken vary widely – from letters and diaries to journals and memoirs – and they differ significantly in their relationship to spirituality, materiality and history. However, what they share is a discourse of privacy and the absence of an intention to publish. The earliest of the eight texts is the matter-of-fact daily diary of Lady Margaret Hoby (1571–1633), kept at Hackness in Yorkshire between 1599 and 1605. This is followed, in chronological terms, by the early seventeenth-century journal of a Northamptonshire gentlewoman, Grace Mildmay (1552–1620), the diaries of the indomitable Lady Anne Clifford (1590–1676) and the pious, melancholic journals of Mistress Alice Thornton (1626–1707). The animated letters of Dorothy Osborne (1627–95) date from the mid seventeenth century, as do the memoirs of the romantic yet practical Lady

Anne Halkett (1622–99). Last come the youthful autobiographical meditations of Lady Elizabeth Delaval (1649–1717) and the family memoirs of the much-travelled Royalist Lady Ann Fanshawe (1625–80). Clearly the social background of these literate and self-aware women was aristocratic or, at the very least, genteel. By contrast, the middle-class or radical women who wrote in autobiographical forms as the seventeenth century progressed tended to commit their lives to print as part of an exemplary or prophesying literary tradition.[2] However, for those women who eschewed print during the earlier period, and chose instead to explore their lives and their language in the obscurity of a manuscript notebook, the function of autobiography was very different.

In many cases, the initial impetus to write was devotional and the framework for repeated self-analysis took the form of prayer or confession. Lady Margaret Hoby's diary entry for Monday 13 August 1599 begins: 'In the Morninge after privat praiers and order taken for diner, I wrett some notes in my testament tell: 10: a clock.' She ends: 'then I walked tell supper time, and, after Catichisinge, medetated awhill of that I had h[e]ard, with mourninge to god for pardon both of my omition and Commition wherin I found myselfe guiltie, I went to bed.'[3] Though less overtly hemmed in by daily self-examination than this diary of Margaret Hoby, Alice Thornton's 'Book of Remembrances' none the less announces itself as an account of God's providential dealings with her, shown in 'all the remarkable deliverences of my self, husband and children', an optimistic title which is startlingly at odds with the gloom of her autobiographical record.[4] A more secular desire to keep some kind of record of her own achievements and relationships would seem to be the chief motivation of Lady Anne Clifford, who kept diaries intermittently from 1603, when she noted how she was not allowed to be a mourner at Queen Elizabeth's funeral because 'I was not high enough',[5] until her death in 1676. Lady Ann Fanshawe wrote her memoirs in this same tradition of inscribing a personal history; she wanted specifically to pass on an account of the 'most remarkable actions & accidents'[6] of the Fanshawe family to her only son.

While the constraints of religion and the anxiety of anonymity were important motivators for these 'private' autobiographers – encouraging, paradoxically, a self-effacing form of self-expression – more practical considerations also spurred them to write. Grace Mildmay's journal, written around 1617, contains a narrative of her upbringing and adult responsibilities alongside the family accounts and recipes for herbal remedies.[7] Dorothy Osborne's spirited love letters also arose from the practical need to communicate with William Temple and maintain her hopes for their relationship against the opposition of their families.[8] However, Osborne's letters, like so many of these autobiographical texts, display most vividly a delight in the process of writing itself, and this would also seem to be a powerful force in the imaginative, almost novelistic, memoirs of Lady Anne Halkett, despite their ostensible commitment to a religious self-justification.[9] Lastly, a devotional framework may also disguise – or enable – a desire simply to analyse one's own being; this would seem to be the case with the 'Meditations' of Lady Elizabeth Delaval, the burden of which was 'sad yet true' but led to the writer's being 'strangely amaized' (as well as remorseful) at the events of her own life (pp. 27, 173).

Despite the range of forms and apparent purposes, these texts have in common an inwardness of focus and an unpolished mode of writing. In many ways this textuality reflects the reality of the women's lives: constrained, confined to a socially specified role[10] (even when not physically in the 'confinement' of childbed) and often hidden away from the public world and the subsequent attentions of history. The closeness of writing and experience is exemplified in an incident of Anne Halkett's youth, when she was forbidden by her mother to 'see' her beloved 'Mr. H.':

> In the midst of this dispute with my selfe what I should doe, my hand being still upon my eyes, itt presently came in my mind that if I blindfolded my eyes that would secure mee from seeing him, and soe I did not transgrese against my mother. And hee might that way satisfy himselfe by speaking with me. (p. 18)

The limited possibilities for this young woman are suggested by the pressure not to 'transgrese' and the necessity to 'blindfold' herself, an unconsciously apt metaphor for her restricted world-view and her partial visibility to others. Her devious and witty solution to the dilemma, built on the pun of 'see' as meaning 'encounter' as well as to 'view' her lover, draws attention to Halkett's linguistic sensitivity, and parallels the writing of her private memoirs by which she remains obedient in her apparent silence, yet simultaneously expresses herself.

II

These autobiographies reveal, not surprisingly, the private, domestic basis of Renaissance Englishwomen's lives. For several of the women, this frequently meant loneliness: in 1616 Anne Clifford describes herself as 'like an owl in the desert' in her house at Knole, in significant contrast to her husband, the Earl of Dorset:

> All this time my Lord was in London where he had all and infinite great resort coming to him. He went much abroad to Cocking, to Bowling Alleys, to Plays and Horse Races, & [was] commended by all the World. I stayed in the Countrey having many times a sorrowful & heavy Heart. (p. 33)

Grace Mildmay also recorded how her husband was 'much away' and she consequently 'spent the best part of my youth in solitarinesse'. However, the constraint here seems to have included her own refusal of company, since she had absorbed the ideology of the domestic holy wife:

> Myne answer was that God had placed me in the world in this house; and, if I found no comfort here, I would never seeke it out of this house; and this was my certaine resolution. (p. 125)

Figure 3.1 Lady Anne Clifford, Countess of Dorset, after Van Somer, 1620

Despite their separateness of function, the husband in the 'world' and the wife in the 'house', these women often found their lives, and hence their texts, structured around their husbands. Grace Mildmay's journal comes to an end with the death of her husband, as though her life, written or lived, could not continue independently. Anne Halkett's memoirs show her dependence on a masculine shaping force by the fact that they fall into three sections, one for each of the men with whom she had romantic attachments. The second of these, the Royalist spy Colonel Bampfield, dominates Halkett's text; by contrast, Anne Halkett is utterly absent from Bampfield's autobiography, which took its pattern instead from his public 'affairs'.[11] Similarly, while Ann Fanshawe's memoirs gain much of

their colour and energy from Ann's participation in her husband Richard
Fanshawe's escapades and travels, there is nothing reciprocal about this;
when Ann Fanshawe urges her husband to take her into his confidence
over affairs of state, he replies: 'my honour is my own' (p. 116). A
woman's 'honour', her chastity, belongs to her husband, but a man's
public reputation remains his own property.[12]

It would be wrong, however, to suggest that these autobiographical
writings reveal only the privateness of the lives of Renaissance Englishwomen. The paradox which this essay seeks to explore is that out of these
most hidden texts – often produced in secret and serving a primarily
private function for their authors – comes an impression of considerable
public activity by the women who wrote them. The dichotomy was a
familiar one to the women themselves, beginning with the contrast regularly made by Margaret Hoby between 'private prayer' (intimate, largely
silent dialogue between her soul and her Maker) and 'public prayer'
(communal, formal, liturgical worship). Dorothy Osborne draws a teasing contrast between the public world of London society and the life of
obscurity she is forced to lead:

> I rise in the morning reasonably Early, and before I am ready I goe rounde
> the house til I am weary of that, and then into the garden till it grows to hott
> for mee. About ten a clock I think of makeing mee redy, and when that's
> don I goe into my fathers Chamber, from thence to dinner. (p. 89)

There is a knowing, satiric edge to this account, indicating a consciousness of the limitations of a retired life. Elizabeth Delaval, on the other
hand, asserted that she would

> chuse rather to pass all my day's away unknown (even) in a private cottage
> then live publickly amongst all the pleasures of the court. (p. 134)

The contrast between 'private' and 'public' was, then, a polarity used by
these writers to delineate modes of living. However, it is clear that
Delaval perceives them not as spheres associated rigidly with women or
men but as possible choices, with moral implications, for any individual
to make.[13]

III

In what ways were these women's lives public? Anne Clifford's later
diaries reveal that even that most private domestic setting, the house,
which Grace Mildmay regarded as the sphere in which God had set her,
was also potentially emblematic of a woman's public function.[14] In her
maturity Anne Clifford inherited, after a long legal struggle, her father's
lands in Westmoreland, and her diaries record the energetic rebuilding of

'her father's house' in the fullest sense of the phrase: the family's many castles, her genealogy and inheritance, even the founding of a church, the house of her heavenly father. In 1651 she notes:

> And in this yeare the one and twentieth of Aprill I helped to lay the foundacion stone of the mill wall in the great tower of Apleby Castle in Westmerland called Caesar's Tower to the end it may be repaired againe and made habitable (if it please God) after it had stood without a roof or covering or one Chamber habitable in it ever since about one thousand five hundred sixtie nyne, a little before the death of my Grandfather of Cumberland. (p. 110)

There is evident pride here in reconstructing a public monument identified with her male ancestors, in the making rather than the unmaking of history. That same year, Anne Clifford also laid the foundation stone of an almshouse for women in Appleby, reminding us of the public extension of the traditionally private, maternal, caring role often exercised (sometimes with dubious results) by women of the gentry. Elizabeth Delavel records, for example, how a woman in her neighbourhood lives 'upon my aunt's charity'. However, the public duty of charity was not confined to women of status; Delavel's autobiographical meditation goes on to admire the 'true charity' of this poor widow who herself dispensed food and assistance to an impoverished charcoal-burner in the village (p. 95).

Closely related to the relief of the local poor was the public, recognised function of medical care by women in their community. Margaret Hoby notes how on 15 August 1599 she 'went to awiffe in trauill of child, about whom I was busey tell: I a Cloke, about which time, She being deliuered and I haueing praised god, returned home' (p. 63). Women assisting other women in childbirth is perhaps to be expected; but for Hoby it was clearly part of a significant public role. Later in her diary she notes men and boys coming to her for the dressing of wounds, and on 5 February 1600 she refers to them as 'my patientes' (p. 101). Grace Mildmay, further, gave advice to those 'who minister Phisick' (p. 130) – a ministration often taught, as well as enacted, by women. Anne Halkett's memoirs contain the dramatic account of her care of 'many poore wounded soldiers' during the Civil War:

> A youth about 16 . . . had beene run through the body with a tuke. Itt wentt in under his right shoulder and came outt under his left breast, and yett he had little inconvenience by itt, butt his greatest prejudice was from so infinitt a swarme of creatures that itt is incredible for any that were nott eye wittneses of itt. (p. 55)

Halkett's memoir fulfils the function of just such an 'eye wittnes', rendering 'credible' and permanent not only the youth's foul condition but also her own role in curing it. The memoir goes on to note how another contemporary witness 'had given the King and Councell an account of what hee had seene and heard I had done to the poore soldiers', and she was thanked by the King 'for my charity' (p. 56). The consequence of visible function in the world of men (a definition, perhaps, of the 'public') was reputation, the morally charged meeting point of private self and public name.

The King may have thanked Halkett, but generally Renaissance women risked a distinctly unwanted reputation by entering the public sphere, particularly in areas less well sanctioned for feminine activity than charity and nursing. It was quite common for a woman to manage the financial and even legal affairs of a household, as in the example of Margaret Hoby, who not only 'took order for things about the house' but also discussed with a tenant 'the purchasinge his owne farme' (p. 74). However, to challenge one's husband's decision in matters of money, as Anne Clifford did, signified a dangerous entry into the public arena of the law, represented for Clifford by the full panoply of king, bishops, legal advisers, husband, uncles – all of whom she defied in the King's own chamber in 1617 by refusing to give up her claim to her family estates in Westmoreland.[15] However, the diary entry not only records how the King 'grew in a great Chaffe' at her defiance, but is significantly charged with her husband's fear that 'the King would do me some Publick Disgrace' (p. 47). After this memorable audience at court, the diary records details of Clifford's subsequent reputation. On 30 January 1617, for example, a visitor tells her that 'they began to think at London that I had done well in not referring this Business to the King, & that everybody said God had a hand in it' (p. 48). A woman brought into public affairs, through acting independently from the patriarchal will, would, it seems, be acceptable only if she could claim divine sanction.

It is clear from these autobiographical texts that women were by no means immune from financial anxieties, despite the fact that for most of them the main burden was borne by male relatives. Elizabeth Delaval comments in 1671 that 'God has blest me with the kindnesse of a husband and the unspeakeable comfort of haveing pay'd my creditors' (p. 209), with the contrast between mere 'kindnesse' and heartfelt 'unspeakeable comfort' suggesting which blessing she valued the more. Ann Fanshawe relates to her son how she sought financial assistance on behalf of her husband who, in 1649, was in exile in France:

> My husband thought it convenient to send me into England again there to try what sums I could raise both for his subsistance abroad and mine at home; and though nothing was so grievous to us both as parting, yet the necessity both of the publick and your father's private affaires obliged us often to yeld to the trouble of absence, as at this time. (p. 122)

As Fanshawe herself notes, the inseparability of 'publick' and 'private affaires' led to her own involvement in financial transactions. She set off for Dover as part of an all-female party – 'with Mrs Waller, and my sister Margarett Harrison, and my little girle Nan' – and soon managed to raise 'near 4000 lb which at that time I thought a vast sum' (p. 122).

Fanshawe's activities, though extreme, serve to remind us how significant travel was in the public aspects of these women's lives. To be seen, to be known beyond the confines of their own homes, was to begin to breach the boundary between private and public worlds. In her later years Anne Clifford travelled between her castles in Westmoreland like a queen on a royal progress:

> The 27th day of Januarie in this year [1664] about 10 a clock in the forenoone did I goe out of Pendraggon Castle in Westmoreland in my Coach drawn by 6 Horses, and most of my familie with me on Horsback into Applebie Castle . . . (p. 169)

Some sixty years earlier, Margaret Hoby regularly recorded in her diary: 'I took my Cotch and went abroad' (p. 85), no doubt in a smaller scale but just as public outing around the local Yorkshire villages. It is Ann Fanshawe's memoirs, however, which contain the most detailed accounts of travel and its particular difficulties for a woman. In 1646 she set sail from Land's End for Jersey:

> The next day, after having been pillaged and extreamly sick and bigg with child, I was sett a shore almost dead in the Iland of Silley. When we had got to our quarters near the castle where the Prince lay, I went immediatly to bed. . . . But when I awaked in the morning, I was so cold I knew not what to doe, but the daylight discovered that our bed was near swimming with the sea. (p. 118)

Despite these experiences, the party eventually travelled on to Jersey where Fanshawe was, 'upon the seventh of June, 1646, delivered of my second child, a daughter christned Anne' (p. 119).

As the reference to 'the Prince' in the above extract reveals, travel, for Fanshawe, was bound up with political activity; she and her husband were part of the escaping Prince Charles's entourage. Thus we find, in these private autobiographical texts, women recording their participation in that most public of worlds, politics. We have already seen how Anne Clifford's personal strength of will in clinging to her claim to the Westmoreland properties led to public and political confrontation with the King and all his court. Ann Fanshawe found herself confronting a different authority when her husband was 'taken prisonner of war' (p. 135) in 1651:

> During this time of his imprisonment I failed not constantly to goe when the clock struck 4 in the morning, with a dark lanterne in my hand, all alone and on foot . . . I would goe under his window and softly call him. He, that after the first time expected me, never failed to put out his head at first call. Thus we talked together, and sometimes I was so wet with rane that it went

in at my neck and out at my heels. He directed how I should make my adresses, which I did ever to their Generall Cromwell, who had a great respect for your father and would have bought him off to his servise upon any termes. (pp. 134–5)

Her submissions to Cromwell and the Council of State were successful. The whispered conversations in the rain brought public as well as private release.

Yet political life did not always signify confrontation for those seventeenth-century women who came into contact with it. Elizabeth Delaval was given a position 'about the queen' and listed the attractions of life at court as time spent 'in dressing, in danceing, in seing and in acting of play's, in hunting, in musick, in all sorts of devertions', which with the benefit of holy hindsight she described as 'sinfull vaine pleasures' (p. 123). Anne Halkett's greatest moment of public significance was her involvement in the escape of the Duke of York in 1648. She was responsible for ordering from her own tailor a suit of women's clothes in which to disguise the Duke; when she passed on the measurements, the tailor commented that 'hee had never seene any women of so low stature have so big a wast' (p. 24), but the outfit was nevertheless prepared. Halkett, waiting with the clothes at the appointed place,

> heard a great noise of many as I thought comming up staires, which I expected to bee soldiers to take mee; butt itt was a pleasing disapointmentt, for the first that came in was the Duke, who with much joy I tooke in my armes and gave God thankes for his safe arivall. His Highnese called, 'Quickely, quickely, drese mee', and putting off his cloaths I dresed him in the wemen's habitt that was prepared, which fitted His Highnese very well and was very pretty in itt. Afftter hee had eaten some thing I made ready while I was idle, lest His Highnese should bee hungry, and having sentt for a Woodstreet cake (which I knew hee loved) to take in the barge, with as much hast as could bee His Highnese wentt crose the bridge to the staires where the barge lay. (p. 25)

There are, of course, profound ironies in this exciting episode. Halkett's contribution to the safety of a key public figure was enacted in the utmost secrecy; her public role was, necessarily, private. The Duke's initial escape came during a game of hide-and-seek, so that 'when he wentt really away they thought he was butt att the usual sport' (p. 24). Halkett's brush with political intrigue was, therefore, a rather more risky version of an ordinary domestic game. There are further ironies in the characteristically feminine role which she played even while participating in the masculine world of politics: she fed the Duke, she undressed and dressed him as though he were a child, and she enjoyed observing his prettiness in female costume. Political and sexual danger intermingle strikingly in this passage, while also being juxtaposed with homeliness and maternal care. It is, finally, deeply significant to the debate over public and private roles in this period that the all-too-public persona of the Duke was, by means of cross-dressing, thought to be safely hidden within the assumed private being of a woman.

IV

Thus we are returned to the assumed hiddenness of Renaissance women's lives. Were the public roles which these autobiographies record – from prominence in the care of the local sick to distant travel with the leading figures of the realm – an aberration, an occasional deviance from the norm? Elizabeth Delaval likens her longing for 'greatnesse and fame' in the public world of the court to the 'passion' of men for 'a mistress they dote on' (p. 132), implying an irrational and often temporary infatuation. The lives of most Renaissance Englishwomen were indeed largely filled with homely business: 'presarving quinces', an activity recorded by Margaret Hoby (p. 76), or 'working all sorts of fine works with my needle' (Ann Fanshawe, p. 110), or reading 'the Turkish History and Chaucer' (Anne Clifford, p. 54), or being in 'very sore travail, in danger of my life from that time in the morning on Wednesday, caused by the child's coming into the world with his feet first' (Alice Thornton, p. 154). In September 1653 Dorothy Osborne wrote in a letter to William Temple: 'I had the grace to goe heare a sermon upon a week day, in Earnest tis true', but though she 'listned to him at first with as much reverence and attention as if hee had bin Snt Paul', she was deeply disappointed in the quality of the sermon. Her response is unique in its wit, but perhaps typical in the privateness of a woman's reaction:

> What think you might I not preach with Mr. Marshall for a wager? but you could fancy a perfect happiness [I] heer you say. That is not much, many People doe soe, but I never heard of any body that had it more then in fancy
> ... (pp. 125–6)

The public event, the sermon, is countered and dealt with at one remove, 'in fancy', in the private world of speculation or, of course, in the autobiographical text itself.[16] Osborne's account of the sermon and its aftermath ends with her recipe for a 'good degree' of happiness: 'a faithfull friend, a Moderate fortune and a retired life' (p. 126).

There remain, however, unresolved paradoxes in this idea of a woman's 'retired life'. How accurate is it to describe the devotional and domestic occupations of Renaissance women as private? Alice Thornton's journal, which has at its heart the record of repeated personal griefs, particularly the deaths of children, is a 'Book of Remembrances' for her family, which is nevertheless motivated by an obligation to recall events for devotional purposes:

> The Lord make me truly remember his goodness and that I may never forget this above all, his mighty and stretched-out hand of deliverances to me, his poor creature, that I may extol and praise the Lord with all my soul and never let go my hope from the God of my salvation, but live the remainder of the life he gives me to his honour and glory. (p. 154)

Would such an attitude to life and to writing ever admit to a private sphere of women's piety, when God's 'goodness', though individually experienced, is to be proclaimed in praise and detailed for encouragement to other 'humblest Soules'?[17] The events recounted are particular to her family – as when, in 1632, 'there was a great fire in the next house to my father's in St. Martin's Lane in London' – but the language in which they are described tends to be archetypal, in this case proceeding to note that it was 'as if the Day of Judgment was come', causing 'great fear and trembling' (pp. 150–51). If a woman's vision of being 'led miraculously by God's Providence' (Anne Clifford, p. 47) or of being given the 'mercyfull assistance of God' (Elizabeth Delaval, p. 137) is kept secret, there is the danger, as perceived by Delaval, that a part of God's light is being kept hidden, and 'like the unprofitable servant I shou'd have nothing to answer, only behold there is thy pound which I have kept lay'd up in a napkin' (p. 137). The obligation to use the gifts of God and display the works of providence compromises the notion that women's devotional lives can be inviolably private.

Motherhood, so unavoidable an aspect of the reality and the ideal of most Renaissance women's lives, may seem to typify the personal, the 'confined', feminine sphere. Anne Clifford notes, with a certain repressed pride, that on 1 May 1617:

> I cut the Child's strings off from her Coats and made her use tags alone, so as she had 2 or 3 falls at first but had no hurt with them.
>   The 2nd the Child put on her first coat that was laced with Lace, being of Red Bays.[18]

In contrast to Clifford's marking of time through stages of her daughter's development, enjoyed through detail invested with emotional significance, Alice Thornton chronicles with appalling regularity her miscarriages, childbirths and the subsequent deaths of her children. However, she adds a sense of the universality of these trials through brief notes such as the following:

> My sister Danby died at Thorpe, September, 1645 of her sixteenth child, being a son named Francis, whom I baptized. (p. 152)

Already there is a glimpse here in Thornton's private text of an inherent paradox in this female experience: it is intensely individual and physically specific, but at the same time so communal (shared by Thornton as emblematic of all mothers and sisters) that it is hardly accurate to term it 'private'. Ann Fanshawe's record of her children challenges the idea of the privacy of motherhood in a quite different way, not suggesting its universality but highlighting the public phenomenon of children, as heirs, as separate and social beings, as recognisable public entities extending the

Figure 3.2 Lady Ann Fanshawe, C.M. Fanshawe, date unknown

family into new forms and contexts. She introduces her tally of offspring in a most revealing linguistic formula:

> My dear husband had six sons and eight daughters borne and christned, and I miscarryed of 6 more . . . (p. 106)

From the moment of successful full-term birth, the children become the heirs of her 'dear husband'; and only when a pregnancy ends in miscarriage is it directly attributable to her – a private failure. Then, in a style which is powerful in its very factuality, Fanshawe lists the locations of her children's graves:

> My eldest daughter Ann lyes buried in the parish church of Tankersley in Yorkshire, where she dyed. Elizabeth lyes in the chappell of the French Hospitall at Madrid, where she dyed of a feavor at 10 days old. My next daughter of her name lyes buryed in the parish of Fotts Cray in Kent near Frogpool, my brother Warrick's house, where she dyed, and my fourth daughter Mary lyes in my father's vault in Hartford with my first son Henry. My eldest lyes buried in the parish church of St. John's Colledge in Oxford, where he was born; my second Henry lyes in Bengey Church in Hartford-shire, and my second Richard in the Esperance in Lisbone in Portugall, he being borne 10 weeks before my time when I was in that court. (p. 107)

Once again, Fanshawe's experience is extreme – not in the number of children born and buried,[19] but in the variety of settings. However, her unique itinerary of loss stresses a general truth – that is, the separable, public outcome of the apparently private function of bearing children.

V

Where, then, is the boundary between the public and the private, the social and the personal, in the lives of such women? Their autobiographical texts are full of evidence of the blurring of these distinctions. Margaret Hoby, for instance, wrote that on 30 August 1599, she 'instructed som of my famelie' (p. 67), part of a mother's expected and private function; but only a week previously she had similarly exercised a teaching role among 'the poore and ignorant' (p. 66) in her village, representing the beginnings of a public function as bringer of wisdom which, as noted earlier, was practical as well as spiritual. Grace Mildmay – who, of all the women cited, clung the most steadfastly to the identification of women with the 'house' – found her private dwelling-place twice transformed into that most public of homes, the royal court, when the King visited Apethorpe in 1603 and 1612. It is also clear from her journal that the family table was a place where one might speak of 'high matters of state, of the Queene, her counsell', provided that such discussion was not undertaken 'un-reverently nor prophanely' (p. 124). In their lives and their texts, these women intermingled matters of domestic and national importance. Ann Fanshawe records a miscarriage (of triplets) in the same paragraph as the coronation of Charles II; she directly links the two events by tentatively blaming her personal misfortune on 'the great hurry of business I then was in, and perpetuall company that resorted to us of all qualitys' (p. 141) on account of the Restoration. Alice Thornton notes the execution of Charles I in precisely the same – apparently dispassionate – manner as the information given alongside it that her 'uncle Sir Edward Osborne died at

Kiveton of a surfeit of eating melons, being too cold for him' (p. 152). On 30 January 1676, Anne Clifford makes much of the coincidence of her birth's occurring on the same date as Charles I's death:

> The 30th Day being Sunday, I considered how this day was 86 years & then Fryday about 7 a clock in the evening was my blessed Mother with very hard labor brought to bed of mee in hier owne chamber in Skipton Castle in Craven, where she then lay. . . . But my noble father than lay in Bedford house in the Strand at London . . .
>
> And this day was 27 years [since] our then King Charles (who was borne in Scotland) was beheaded on a Scaffold in the open aire near the banqueting house at Whitehall & his dead body afterwards buried in the Chappel at Windsor in Berkshire. And when this Tragedy was performed did I lye in Baynards Castle in London and my second Lord was in his lodgings by the Cockpit at Whitehall where hee dyed about a year after. (p. 244)

The diary entry is finely poised, with each event illuminating the other in its contrasts and its parallels: birth, death; in the chamber, in the open air; the separateness of married couples, and the coincidence of suffering. This structure of opposition and similarity compensates for the lack of analysis; the juxtaposition of personal and political is message enough.

These autobiographical texts reveal, therefore, a range of public roles for Renaissance Englishwomen, while at the same time suggesting the public nature of many ostensibly private aspects of their lives and demonstrating the inseparability of these two spheres. This is nowhere truer than in the nature of the texts themselves. Autobiographical writing appears to be introverted, and these texts the most inward-looking of the genre; however, the act of inscribing a self involves the creation of a new self, a publicly accessible one, available in the shared language in spite of an absent or limited audience. Dorothy Osborne welcomes a secret letter from William Temple in 1653 and begins her reply: 'Your last letter came like a pardon to one upon the block' (p. 58). Her simile reveals how written expression contains, often ironically, the apparently intimate within an overtly political language. Autobiographical writing may thus breach the divide between private and public, and in its very essence mirror the women's lives, poised at the borderline between hiddenness and expressiveness. In their multiplicity of moods and modes – secretive, stubborn, witty, mournful, aware of both creativity and mortality – these texts resist categorisation. Equally, they deny the validity of an easy classification of the public or the private in Renaissance women's lives.

NOTES

1. Douglas G. Greene, ed., *The Meditations of Lady Elizabeth Delaval* (Gateshead: Northumberland Press, 1978; Surtees Society, vol. CXC), p. 30. All

further references are to this edition. The meditations, interspersed with auto-biographical narrative, were written between 1663 and 1671.

2. See Elaine Hobby, *Virtue of Necessity: English women's writing 1649–88* (London: Virago, 1988), pp. 26–53. Further discussion of women's auto-biographies in this period may be found in the introduction to Elspeth Graham, Hilary Hinds, Elaine Hobby and Helen Wilcox, eds, *Her Own Life: Autobiographical writings by seventeenth-century Englishwomen* (London: Routledge, 1989) and Mary Beth Rose, 'Gender, genre, and history: seventeenth-century English women and the art of autobiography', in Rose, ed., *Women in the Middle Ages and the Renaissance: Literary and historical perspectives* (Syracuse, NY: Syracuse University Press, 1986), pp. 245–78. See also Harriet Blodgett, *Centuries of Female Days* (Stroud: Alan Sutton, 1989) and Shari Benstock, ed., *The Private Self: Theory and practice of women's autobiographical writings* (London: Routledge, 1988).

3. Dorothy M. Meads, ed., *The Diary of Lady Hoby* (London: G. Routledge and Sons, 1930), p. 63. All further references are to this edition.

4. Alice Thornton, 'A book of remembrances', in Graham *et al.*, *Her Own Life*, p. 147. All further references are to this edition.

5. D.J.H. Clifford, ed., *The Diaries of Lady of Anne Clifford* (Stroud: Alan Sutton, 1990), p. 22. All further references are to this edition. Anne Clifford's early diaries were published in 1923 with an introductory note by Vita Sackville-West, and extracts appear in Graham *et al.*, *Her Own Life*, pp. 35–53.

6. John Loftis, ed., *The Memoirs of Anne, Lady Halkett and Ann, Lady Fanshawe* (Oxford: Clarendon Press, 1979), p. 101. All further references to the Halkett and Fanshawe texts are to this edition.

7. Rachel Weigall, 'An Elizabethan gentlewoman: The journal of Lady Mildmay', *Quarterly Review*, **215** (1911) pp. 119–38. All further references are to this source. Grace Mildmay's autobiographical record was written *c.* 1617; see Retha M. Warnicke, 'Lady Mildmay's journal: A study in autobiography and meditation in Reformation England', *Sixteenth Century Journal,* **20** (1989), pp. 55–68.

8. Dorothy Osborne, *Letters to Sir William Temple*, ed. Kenneth Parker (London: Penguin, 1987). All further references are to this edition.

9. Halkett's memoirs begin in devotional mode, asserting that 'there is noe sin that ever I have been guilty of in my whole life butt I repent with as much sincearity as I seeke pardon' (Loftis, ed., *Memoirs*, p. 9). However, they soon appear to warm to the creative task of recording her life story.

10. See Antonia Fraser, *The Weaker Vessel: Woman's lot in seventeenth-century England* (London: Weidenfeld & Nicolson, 1984); Ruth Kelso, *Doctrine for the Lady of the Renaissance* (Urbana: University of Illinois Press, 1956); and Suzanne W. Hull, *Chaste, Silent and Obedient: English books for women, 1475–1640* (Los Angeles: Huntington Library, 1982).

11. See Loftis, ed., *Memoirs*, p. xii. The ambiguity in the word 'affairs' sums up exactly this gendered difference between public and private worlds.

12. Ironically, the modern editions of some of these autobiographical works re-veal how prevalent this tendency still is. The biographical note in the Penguin edition of Dorothy Osborne's letters, for example, identifies her as daughter of Sir Peter Osborne and wife to William Temple, whose life then forms the basis for the remainder of the account.

13. Although Delaval does not directly identify the 'private' sphere with the feminine, there was a prevailing association in this period between Christian

retiredness and the female subject. See my discussion of this in 'Exploring the language of devotion in the English Revolution', in Tom Healey and Jonathan Sawday, eds, *Literature and the English Civil War* (Cambridge University Press, 1990), pp. 75–88.

14. Compare the role of the 'noble' Lady of the house in Jonson's 'To Penshurst'; and see p. 59, for discussion of when Grace Mildmay received royal visitors to her house.

15. For a fuller account of this incident, see Valerie Wayne, Helen Wilcox, Elspeth Graham and Vivien Jones, 'Dislocated unions: Gender and class in English Renaissance marriage', in Philip Hobsbaum, Paddy Lyons and Jim McDonald, eds, *Channels of Communication* (Glasgow: Glasgow University Press, forthcoming).

16. The mid seventeenth century marked the emergence of a number of women preachers and prophets among radical sects, but the majority of women, like Dorothy Osborne, would have regarded the public refutation of a male preacher by a female as an imagined rather than a plausible event.

17. Dedicatory poem, Alice Thornton, 'Book of Remembrances', Yale University microfilm MISC 326, p. 5.

18. Clifford, ed., *Diaries*, p. 55. The 1 May entry refers to the toddler learning to walk without walking-reins attached to her coat.

19. See Lawrence Stone, *The Family, Sex and Marriage in England 1500–1800* (London: Weidenfeld & Nicolson, 1977).

4

Queen Elizabeth in Her Speeches[1]

Frances Teague

Elizabeth I sought to shape her public image through her oratory. Despite her efforts, however, popular views of the Queen have remained distorted, both in her own time and today. Even scholarly accounts of her life and reign may show the effects of gossip and popular misconception. One consequence has been the neglect of her oratory, a central source of information about her public life. After discussing the popular misconception of Elizabeth I, I want to examine the results of that neglect.

Speaking to a Parliamentary delegation on 12 November 1584, Elizabeth commented on her public image:

> We Princes, I tell you, are set on stages, in the sight and view of all the world duly observed. The eyes of many behold our actions; a spot is soon spied in our garments, a blemish quickly noted in our doings. It behoveth us, therefore, to be careful that our proceedings be just and honorable.[2]

Self-consciousness about her public image, however, and her pains to present herself as just and honourable have had little effect on the popular perception of her character.

More interesting to the general public than the relative virtue of Elizabeth's proceedings have been the gossip and legends about her life. Like any culturally important figure, she is surrounded by tales that have little or no basis in fact. Thus, after her death, Ben Jonson retailed a packet of London gossip about her in his *Conversations with Drummond* (1619):

> Queen Elizabeth never saw herself after she became old in a true glass; they painted her, and sometimes would vermilion her nose. She had always, about Christmas evens, set dice that threw sixes or five (and she knew not they were other) to make her win and esteem herself fortunate. That she had a *membrana* on her which made her uncapable of man, though for her delight she tried many. At the coming over of Monsieur, there was a French surgeon who took in hand to cut it, yet fear stayed her, and his death. King Philip had intention by dispensation of the Pope to have married her.[3]

A more charming example of such apocrypha is the story of Sir Walter Raleigh's gallantry. Seeing Queen Elizabeth pause by a mud puddle, Raleigh whipped off his expensive plush cloak and covered over the mess so that his Queen might walk dry shod. The story even comes with a punning moral: Raleigh gained many good 'suits' by spoiling his cloak. Unfortunately, the tale comes from an unreliable source and no solid evidence confirms it, so scholars must reject it.[4] Yet even if scholars do not accept such tales and rumours, the general public certainly repeat them, and they have helped to shape Elizabeth's popular image.

Setting aside gossip, the popular view of Elizabeth has also been affected by the many fictionalised historical accounts of her reign. She is a central character in innumerable novels – ranging from serious fiction by George Garrett and Robert Nye to the murder mysteries of Leonard Tourney – and in at least ten successful films: *Queen Elizabeth* (Sarah Bernhardt as the Queen, 1912); *Mary of Scotland* (Florence Eldridge, 1936); *Fire over England* (Flora Robson, 1936); *Elizabeth and Essex* (Bette Davis, 1939); *The Sea Hawk* (Flora Robson, 1946); *Young Bess* (Jean Simmonds, 1953); *The Virgin Queen* (Bette Davis, 1955); *The Story of Mankind* (Agnes Moorehead, 1957); *The Fighting Prince of Donegal* (Catherine Lacey, 1965); and *Mary, Queen of Scots* (Glenda Jackson, 1971). None recounts history with particular accuracy. Throughout such accounts, the popular image of Elizabeth I ranges between the poles of a universal aunt named Good Queen Bess and a sexually frustrated spinster.

Neither view encourages consideration of the Queen's oratory. While verbal dexterity and the gift of a quip (jolly or bitter) is part of the public's image of Elizabeth, the sustained intellectual effort necessary to produce important speeches is not. Thus the general assumption about her oratory is that either her ministers wrote her speeches (at least the duller ones) or her overflowing emotions on beholding her subjects' love found relief in loving words.[5] Those who work with the history of Elizabeth's reign know better. Her oratory, a significant source of information about her public self, poses a complex set of questions for contemporary scholars – questions about provenance, textual variants and intentionality. Both the assumptions fostered by popular misconceptions of the Queen and the questions scholars face in analysing her work hamper consideration of her speeches.

How one answers such scholarly questions is influenced by recent studies of how Elizabeth I sought to control her public image. These investigations, centring on the image of the Virgin Queen, have produced results that may startle and fascinate those accustomed to Good Queen Bess or the Jealous Spinster. Furthermore, scholars concerned with her oratory have had to consider how her speeches helped to fashion her public image.[6] Frances Yates and Roy Strong, for example, have shown how the cult of Queen Elizabeth replaced that of the Virgin Mary, while Stephen Greenblatt has described Elizabeth's insistence upon the romantic fiction that her civil servants all adored her.[7] Such analyses of how Elizabeth appropriated ideals of religious or romantic love objects may, at first, seem to characterise her as either blasphemous or overweeningly vain. Blasphemy and vanity are uncomfortable attributes, although closer examination usually suggests that practical political considerations underlay the manipulation of her public image. Revisionist scholars studying Elizabeth's image shock anyone who depends at all on the popular notions of the Queen: political pragmatism is rarely associated with the stereotype of either spinster or aunt. Yet understanding that Queen Elizabeth used religion and romance for political ends need not lessen one's admiration for her intelligence or her use of power. Nor does her political practice diminish the reality of the intense personal loyalty she commanded.

Such revelations of political pragmatism particularly startle anyone given to traditional stereotypes of women as more concerned with love and religion than with power. These stereotypes can limit even well-meaning attempts to include Elizabeth I's oratory in the literary canon. For example, the newest edition of the popular university textbook *The Norton Anthology of English Literature* includes Queen Elizabeth as an author for the first time, though her picture has long decorated the book's cover. Now the editors print two of her six known poems: one is a love poem; the other concerns Mary Queen of Scots.[8] Such a selection may reinforce the popular image of Queen Elizabeth as a woman torn by unfulfilled love or jealousy of other women. The book also directs readers to editions of all her poems, prayers and translations, but to only *some* of her edited speeches; again, that lacuna undervalues Elizabeth's political life. Elizabeth I is, after all, of great historical importance, and her oratory contributed much more to that importance than her private poems, translations or prayers. Even that consciously feminist collection *The Norton Anthology of Literature by Women* does little to fill in that lacuna, as it includes the two poems mentioned above, but only one speech, the address to the troops at Tilbury. It still omits all her important parliamentary orations.[9] The Queen's speeches, which both help to explain English history and have literary merit, would seem suitable for anthologies, yet such collections often omit or scant her oratory, perhaps because it seems incongruent with both scholarly assumptions about Renaissance women and Elizabeth's public image.

While misconceptions about Queen Elizabeth persist, even among those who do research on her life and work, anyone who evaluates her oratory must guard against allowing those misconceptions to colour their analysis. Yet one greater problem remains. Quite apart from gossip or popular misconceptions, Elizabeth's life and work are obscured by ignorance about her canon. Scholars have not established definitive texts for some of her speeches, while the way in which she delivered those orations often remains a mystery. To some extent, Elizabeth I's oratory is left out of anthologies because well-edited texts do not exist.

Indeed, one cannot be sure how many speeches there are. The best-established texts of Elizabeth's speeches are for those that she gave or had read to Parliament. Allison Heisch estimates: 'Out of eighteen or nineteen speeches, her accession speech and thirteen others survive' (p. 31), but points out:

> Elizabeth was as careful of her cameral addresses as she was of her truly public speeches, and an assessment of those considered to be 'lost' indicates that they were either brief and spontaneous, and therefore unrecorded, or that they were intended for an immediate audience and were deliberately unrecorded. (p. 45)

J.E. Neale's *Elizabeth I and Her Parliaments* provides scrupulously edited, modernised texts for her parliamentary speeches, but excludes other oratory.[10] Some speeches made on less public occasions were deliberately suppressed by Elizabeth's government because 'not all of them were fit for public consumption' (Heisch, p. 31). Other of Elizabeth I's reported speeches (her 'cameral addresses', as Heisch calls them) and extempore remarks pose difficulties because no one knows which ones are authentic and which apocryphal:

> So far as we know there has hitherto been no attempt to set up a canon and apocrypha of stories [about Elizabeth]. The reason is simple. It would involve elaborate criticism of a hundred and one books, and even then we could say no more than 'probable' or 'improbable' about most of the stories. (Sayings, p. 215)

Thus Neale's book omits such addresses as the Tilbury speech, even though his article does accept it as part of Elizabeth's canon. George P. Rice has edited selections from her addresses and claims that his book 'represents the most complete and varied collection of speeches by Elizabeth available within the covers of a single volume', but he is sometimes careless about the texts he uses.[11] Generally he reprints versions that appear in history books from the nineteenth and twentieth centuries. In the case of Elizabeth I's Accession speech, for example, Rice uses a nineteenth-century edition of Holinshed as his source. When he does use earlier texts, he does not explain special textual problems. Thus when he uses Camden's history of Elizabeth's reign, he cites the third London edition (1675) instead of the first edition, which was written in Latin (1615, 1627) or the second, which was translated into English (1625, 1629).[12] He never explains why he has chosen the later text, nor does he point out that the English speech is a translation of Camden's original Latin. Neither does Rice's book provide information about variant readings in the speeches or the complex problems of manuscript attribution.

Even when manuscript versions of sound texts are available (as in the case of the parliamentary speeches), an editor may gloss them using untrustworthy accounts that distort the image of Elizabeth. Consequently, an editor may mistake effective propaganda for spontaneous sincerity or regard the text of a speech as well-established when its provenance is doubtful. Three of Queen Elizabeth's speeches illustrate the problems that such ignorance creates. The first is her speech at Tilbury:

> I am come amongst you, as you see, at this time, not for my recreation and disport, but being resolved in the midst and heat of the battle to live or die amongst you all, to lay down for my God, and for my kingdom, and for my people, my honor and my blood, even in the dust. I know I have the body but of a weak and feeble woman, but I have the heart and stomach of a king – and of a king of England too – and think foul scorn that Parma, or Spain, or any prince of Europe should dare to invade the borders of my realm. To which, rather than any dishonor shall grow by me, I myself will take up arms, I myself will be your general, judge, and rewarder of every one of your virtues in the field. I know already for your forwardness you have deserved rewards and crowns; and we do assure you, in the word of a prince, they shall be duly paid you.[13]

The dramatic moment and splendour of the language may obscure what happened. A reader imagines a nation in great peril, led by a warrior queen whose soldiers cheered both her and her plan to lead her troops 'in the midst and heat of the battle'. But this imagined picture is false.[14] Although no one knew it when Elizabeth went to Tilbury, the Armada had been chased away and England was out of danger. The Queen did not, in any case, intend to fight herself. Instead, she sought to raise the spirits of her army – an end she achieved, according to William Camden: 'Incredible it is how much she encouraged the Hearts of her Captains and Souldiers by her Presence and Speech to them' (p. 326). Some historians, more cynical than Camden, now think that the real reason Elizabeth's appearance encouraged her troops was that she included the promise to pay her soldiers promptly.[15] To some extent, her welcome was lukewarm. Initially, Leicester, the Tilbury commander, was reluctant for Queen Elizabeth to come near the coast, though he was certainly willing to have her visit the camp. When she reviewed the troops, he tried to persuade her to accept a heavy bodyguard in case someone tried to assassinate her. Finally, she might not have spoken those stirring words. Indeed, she might not have spoken at all to the men in her army. One eyewitness of her visit (the Mendoza letter) says nothing of her speech, while a second account (Aske) summarises what she said in verse.[16] According to her chaplain, Dr Leonel Sharp, her message was written down and read to the troops by officers and himself. The text of the speech was not published until 1651 (sixty-three years after it was given) in a book that claims Dr Sharp sent the text to the Duke of Buckingham in a letter.[17]

As Neale remarks, 'no serious reason [exists] for rejecting this speech' (Sayings, p. 227). One can even make sense of the conflicting accounts by arguing as follows: Elizabeth gave her own speech. Because the army had about 200,000 men, not everyone could hear her, so her words were repeated to the troops by the officers who received a copy of what she said from her chaplain, Dr Sharp. Imprisoned in the 1620s, Sharp sent his copy of the Queen's speech to the Duke of Buckingham, hoping to ingratiate himself; Buckingham then gave it to the anonymous collector of letters for the book *Cabala* (1651), where the speech first appeared. The problem is not an inability to construct plausible explanations, but the need for such explanations. One could, after all, argue that Sharp invented the text to help himself, or that the collector of the *Cabala* falsified the letter knowing that no one could ever prove the forgery. Despite the multiple accounts of Queen Elizabeth's visit to the Tilbury camp, no one can prove that she spoke the words that survive. A conscientious scholar must first decide whether the speech is authentic, as most historians believe, and then whether the version preserved in *Cabala* is authoritative.

A scholar who accepts the speech's authenticity must also consider authorial intent: is it an expedient public-relations ploy or a sincere and impulsive expression of royal love? Posing the question in this form, of course, creates a false disjunctive, for almost certainly Elizabeth was neither too hot- nor too cold-blooded at Tilbury. Considering these extremes does, however, highlight some common errors made in dealing with princely oratory, errors exacerbated by modern misconceptions about Elizabeth. One such mistake is to ask whether Elizabeth I wrote any of her own speeches or simply performed what Cecil wrote for her. Although William Cecil often edited what she inscribed, he wrote only a few speeches for her delivery, and these are well identified (by Neale or, more recently, by Heisch). Such a question not only offends by its sexism, but also reveals ignorance of Elizabeth's achievements. After all, the woman spoke nine languages; translated Petrarch, Boethius and Plutarch; and ran a nation. The idea that she could not write her own speeches needs to be put to rest.

A second mistake involves interpretations grounded in a twentieth-century sensibility. The following description of Elizabeth's visit exemplifies this tendency:

Perhaps an objective observer would have seen no more than a battered, rather scraggy spinster in the middle fifties perched on a fat white horse, her teeth black, her red wig slightly askew, dangling a toy sword and wearing an absurd little piece of parade-armour like something out of a theatrical property-box. But that was not what her subjects saw, dazzled as they were by more than the sun on the silver breastplate or the moisture in their eyes. They saw Judith and Esther, Gloriana and Belphoebe, Diana the virgin huntress and Minerva the wise protectress, and best of all their own beloved

Queen and Mistress, come in this hour of danger in all simplicity to trust herself among them.[18]

Admittedly this account, from Garrett Mattingly's *The Defeat of the Spanish Armada* (1959), is dated. Nor is it fair to judge the attitudes of the 1950s by the standards of the 1990s. This passage does, nevertheless, create a curious fiction about the events at Tilbury, suggesting that sensible people in the twentieth century would regard Queen Elizabeth as a foolish scarecrow and her soldiers as servile cretins. Further, Mattingly overemphasises the patriotic aspect of the trip to Tilbury. Both patriotism and morale-raising were factors in Elizabeth's visit: she did love her troops, but she also knew how to motivate them. A sentimental analysis of the speech ignores the manipulation inherent in the Queen's rhetoric.

Conversely, one may be over-clever in reading the speech and judging its influence on later events. The phrase 'I have the body but of a weak and feeble woman, but I have the heart and stomach of a king' is one that might cause intense anxiety among sixteenth-century Englishmen. Some recent critics have suggested that the English were well aware of Elizabeth's Tilbury appearance and hated the idea of an Amazon queen, a mannish-maiden warrior. Thus, Louis Montrose suggests that the Amazon, Hippolyta, must submit to and marry Theseus in *A Midsummer Night's Dream* because English society was growing restive about the sterile reign of Queen Elizabeth, another woman warrior.[19] Leah S. Marcus remarks that 'The queen's martial self-presentation at Tilbury was a glorious moment of patriotic triumph, but also . . . a spectacle that aroused distinct uneasiness among Englishmen';[20] she considers Elizabeth's appearance at Tilbury to be a potential source for Joan La Pucelle in *I Henry VI*. Both interpretations are predicated on the ability to see at a distance tensions and social disjunctions of which Renaissance commentators were probably unaware. Furthermore, such interpretations assume that Queen Elizabeth's appearance as Amazon was well enough known to have a powerfully negative influence. Yet Winifried Schleiner comments, 'If the references to Elizabeth as an Amazon are few, the main reason may be that she preferred the reputation of a peaceful ruler.'.[21] As Marcus acknowledges, 'Pictures of Elizabeth as an Amazon are all of foreign origin, or date from after her death', and 'discomfort at the "strange wonder" of the Queen's violation of sex roles was apparently not articulated, at least not in public'.[22] Such comments raise the question of how a scholar can study the influence of an appearance so poorly recorded. Examining the original sources shows that no one knows what occurred at Tilbury, whether the Queen even said she had 'the heart and stomach of a king', or how aware the public were of Elizabeth's appearance there, much less what influence her visit to the camp had.

Another well-known example of Elizabeth I's oratory is the Golden speech, which the Queen gave near the end of her reign. The speech exists in four versions, all different, and two of these seem authoritative.[23] One, which I shall call the 'parliamentary' version, exists in manuscript and was printed in D'Ewes's *Journal of Parliaments*. Her government then published another in 1601, as an official document, which I shall call the 'royal' version. The opening passages of both illustrate some differences between them:

> *Parliamentary version:* Mr. Speaker: We have heard your declaration and perceive your care of our state, by falling into the consideration of a grateful acknowledgement of such benefits as you have received; and that your coming is to present thanks unto us, which I accept with no less joy than your loves can have desire to offer such a present. I do assure you that there is no prince that loveth his subjects better, or whose love can countervail our love. There is no jewel, be it of never so rich a price, which I prefer before this jewel, I mean your love, for that we do know how to prize, but love and thanks I count inestimable. And though God hath raised me high, yet this I count the glory of my crown, that I have reigned with your loves.

> *Royal version:* Mr. Speaker, we perceive your coming is to present thanks unto Us; Know I accept them with no less joy than your loves can have desire to offer such a present, and do more esteem it than any treasure or riches, for those we know how to prize, but loyalty, love, and thanks, I account them invaluable; and though God hath raised me high, yet this I account the glory of my crown, that I have reigned with your loves.[24]

The first version tells what the parliamentary delegation recorded Queen Elizabeth as saying when she revoked certain unpopular monopolies; the second version is what her government told her citizens that she had said. The parliamentary version, probably closer to what was actually spoken, serves as part of an official record. On the other hand, the royal version is intended as a public announcement of a decision that the government knew would be popular and would increase support for the ageing Queen's policies. These multiple texts offer a rich source of information about Elizabeth's rhetorical technique. While the published texts of Renaissance speeches (especially sermons) often survive, one can rarely set what was actually *said* against what was *published* after the speech's revision.

The differences are marked.[25] Both versions cover three topics: the monarch's observation of Parliament's actions; the worth of the Parliament's gratitude; and God's elevation of Elizabeth as manifested by her people's love. The parliamentary version uses more hypotaxis and is fuller; its central section, the last half of the first sentence with the second and third sentences, elaborates on the value of Parliament's gratitude. The royal version shifts towards parataxis; it runs the four opening sentences of the parliamentary version together into three main clauses of roughly equal weight to form a single intimidating syntactical unit. This shift to concision also shifts the emphasis to Elizabeth and away from praise of Parliament. Pronoun use marks that shift in emphasis as well. In the opening passage, the parliamentary version employs eight second-person pronouns, while the royal version employs only three. Both versions shift back and forth between the plural and singular first-person pronouns. When Elizabeth speaks of her actions or duties as a monarch, she uses 'we', but when she speaks of her emotions and her values, she uses 'I'. Finally, the royal version is less wordy.

But omitting the fine jewel metaphor of the parliamentary version does not simply reduce words in the royal version. That revision may be connected to another change: the parliamentary version speaks of the love Elizabeth feels for all her subjects; the royal version speaks of the love that Parliament has shown her. In other words, Elizabeth initially emphasised the relationship between herself and Parliament. The emotional intensity of that bond is embodied in the metaphorical jewel. When the speech is revised to inform her subjects of what she has done for them and to increase their love for her, the emphasis shifts. Instead of describing a shared bond, the Queen now describes the 'loyalty, love, and thanks' that Parliament owes her. Her gift, the revocation of monopolies, is rendered greater because her debt of love to her people is diminished.

While these differences are important, so are the two versions' common elements: Queen Elizabeth's statement of concern for her subjects, the courtesy with which she treats the delegation, and her claims of ambivalence about her position. All these elements recur throughout her oratory, from her Accession speech to the Golden speech, serving as important facets of her political style. Heisch notes that this is one of four speeches in which Elizabeth evaluated her own stewardship:

> At this point, in 1601, Elizabeth must have felt that there was nothing remaining to be proved. She wished simply to sum up and to make that summation part of the public record of her reign. Neither here nor in the speeches which directly precede and follow did the queen trouble herself or her hearers with dark language or counterfeit modesty; and were it not for the existence of texts for some earlier speeches, and accounts of still others, it might be supposed that plain talk was a discovery of Elizabeth's old age. But that was not true. For even when Elizabeth was perfectly certain of her position, she was careful of what she said and to whom she said it. (p. 41)

Elizabeth I had spent a lifetime polishing the eloquence with which she expressed her care, her courtesy and her stewardship – eloquence that has won for this speech the epithet of 'Golden'. The problem remains, however, of just what the Golden speech *is* when two separate entities share that same name. One solution is a diplomatic edition that follows neither text faithfully, but instead conflates the readings of both; few scholars would welcome such an answer. A second solution is to choose between them, though the grounds for such a choice are obscure, since both versions clearly represent Elizabeth's intended text under a particular set of conditions. Most promising is the possibility of granting both texts authority, as editors sometimes do for *King Lear, The Prelude,* or *Leaves of Grass.*[26] As no scholar has yet published a scholarly edition of Elizabeth's oratory, the point is moot; however, anyone who discusses the Golden speech must acknowledge its multiple versions and take them into account, just as discussions of the Tilbury speech should acknowledge that it may not be authentic.

Providing multiple texts will not always resolve the difficulties inherent in Queen Elizabeth's oratory. The Marriage speech she gave in 1559 illustrates the problems of understanding the public and the private Elizabeth. In 1559, soon after Elizabeth I took power, her Parliament began to worry about her marriage. The House of Commons sent a delegation to the Queen, urging her to marry early. Their arguments were straightforward: a husband and children would provide her immortality, which she deserved; a husband would comfort and help her; heirs to the throne would both ornament and strengthen the realm. Finally, they told her, members of her family had always sought marriage, and to remain a virgin voluntarily was a sin.

Queen Elizabeth was not pleased. She replied to the delegation's arguments directly on 6 February 1559; four days later she sent her reply to Parliament, where John Mason read it out. As a result, two 1559 speeches exist, one cameral and one parliamentary, on the same subject (it would recur; five parliamentary speeches concern marriage and the succession [Heisch, p. 31]). The parliamentary speech presents relatively few problems: a transcript of it exists in manuscript (BM Lansdowne MSS. 94, fol. 29), though not in Elizabeth's hand. It was printed in D'Ewes's *Journal of Parliaments,* and scholars consider this text authoritative.[27] The problems lie instead with the cameral version's provenance and its relationship to the second parliamentary speech.

The first speech, which Queen Elizabeth gave impromptu to the delegation, is printed in Latin in the first part (to 1588) of William Camden's *Annals of Elizabeth* (1615); English translations of this part followed in 1625, 1630 and 1675.[28] Camden's practice is to give no source for his material. He did, however, have access to the papers of both William Cecil and the Queen and, according to MacCaffrey,

> Camden took his documentary sources very seriously and adhered closely to them . . . it is not possible to identify the source for each passage, but it is safe to say that behind every statement of fact stands some specific authority, written or oral.[29]

Other historians are more sceptical about Camden's account of the cameral speech. J.E. Neale remarks: 'I know of no text from which he could have made it, and it does not correspond with the Queen's description in her second speech.'[30] The speech's provenance is murky; Camden may work from an authoritative source to provide a Latin translation of what Elizabeth said, or he may embellish such a source, or he may invent the speech altogether. What is at stake when one questions the provenance is not simply the text but its potential usefulness as an index to Elizabeth's character and oratorical skill, as comparing the two speeches makes clear.

While the parliamentary speech is much fuller (over 800 words as opposed to about 450), the cameral is a superior piece of rhetoric by *contemporary* standards. The cameral speech does not answer the House of Commons's request topic by topic, as the parliamentary speech does. After stating her own position – she does not wish to marry – Queen Elizabeth reminds the delegation of her principal concern:

> Yea, to satisfie you, I have already joyned my self in Marriage to an Husband, namely, the Kingdom of England. And behold (said she, which I marvell ye have forgotten,) the Pledge of this my Wedlock and Marriage to my Kingdom.
> (And therewith she drew the Ring from her Finger, and shewed it, wherewith at her Coronation she had in a set form of words solemnly given her self to her Kingdom.) (MacCaffrey, *History*, p. 29)

She then assures the delegation that she will consider their petition and the will of God; she ends by telling them she hopes her epitaph will read: '*Here lieth Elizabeth, which Reigned a Virgin, and died a Virgin*'. Thus, in the cameral speech Queen Elizabeth speaks to the point, illustrating her principal argument with a telling gesture, and agrees to do whatever will please God and ensure the country's safety.

The parliamentary speech, which Mason read, is very different. Elizabeth uses similar arguments, even the same phrases, but she addresses the House of Commons's petition point by point. The style is dense and convoluted, larded with lengthy sentences and packed with parenthetical expressions. One of the more baroque passages, in which she explains that she will marry neither for ambition nor for fear, can serve as an example:

> From the which, if either ambition of high estate offered to me in marriage by the pleasure and appointment of my Prince – whereof I have some record in this presence, as you, our Treasurer, well know – or if eschewing the danger of mine enemies or the avoiding of the peril of death, whose messenger or rather a continual watchman, the Prince's indignation, was no little time daily before mine eyes (by whose means – although I know or justly may suspect – yet I will not now utter, or if the whole cause were in my sister herself, I will not now burthen her therewith because I will not charge the dead), if any of these, I say, could have drawn or dissuaded me from this kind of life, I had not now remained in this estate wherein you see me.[31]

That single sentence is almost one hundred and fifty words long and contains over ten clauses. It is not unique.

Certainly, the parliamentary speech uses phrases (such as the epitaph about virginity) and arguments that the cameral speech also employs. But the parliamentary speech is not simply a revision of the first, for its arguments, organisation and purpose differ from those of the cameral speech. If Camden's version is authentic, then Queen Elizabeth's immediate response was brief and generally negative. In Camden's text she pays lip service to the felicity of marriage in only one conditional sentence and spends most of the speech, twelve sentences, rejecting it. When she had had time to consider her answer, she wrote the second speech, which is more conciliatory towards Parliament and their desire for her marriage. The cameral speech offers an image of a queen who is dramatic and straightforward; the parliamentary speech shows a Queen who is diplomatic and ambiguous. The latter image certainly reflects Elizabeth's general strategy more reliably than the former. Most readers would like the cameral speech to be authentic, for they enjoy the dramatic gesture of Queen Elizabeth's display of the coronation ring. Yet the gesture is less effective politically than the long, tortuous syntax of the sentence from the parliamentary speech. The gesture makes Elizabeth's intent too clear: married to her kingdom, she will marry no man. The long sentence deliberately confuses with elaborate parallelism and disquiets with dark hints. The Queen may or may not marry, but anyone who questions her actions endangers her.

In 1608, many years after the occasion of these speeches, when Camden began work on the *Annals*, the marriage question was moot. Despite Parliament's anxiety about the succession, Elizabeth I had indeed 'reigned a virgin and died a virgin'. In 1603 James I had acted quickly to become her successor, and in 1615 his government sanctioned Camden's account of the first speech. If Camden's version of the speech was written after the fact, he may have been producing a pleasantly dramatic fiction that the Jacobean government found useful. In that case, James I and his officials did not censor the public image of a spirited Queen sanguine enough about her successor to ignore parliamentary matchmaking. If Camden's version *is* authentic, however, it offers fascinating evidence for Elizabeth's low opinion of marriage as well as for her self-assurance in the face of parliamentary presumption. The question of the cameral speech's authority is clearly important, but its importance should not obscure the skilfulness of the parliamentary speech. That more reliable text is less simple, less theatrical, less clear. Consequently, the parliamentary speech is the more effective piece of political rhetoric precisely because Elizabeth does not state her position forthrightly.[32]

In this last example, a central facet of Queen Elizabeth's character is obscured by her contemporary William Camden, by later writers who have treated both texts carelessly, and by herself in the rhetoric she used to achieve her political independence from Parliament. In the case of the Golden speech, a similar process may have occurred: having given the speech in one form, the Queen then altered it to achieve a political end. The Tilbury speech remains a mystery, despite claims that it reveals some aspect of her character or influenced her subjects. When one examines Queen Elizabeth's public utterances, one must recognise the folklore and romantic tales that have attached themselves to her image. One must also acknowledge and scrupulously deal with textual problems. And one must be conscious of Elizabeth I's own manipulation of her image, her politically knowing alteration of her own texts. To borrow Stephen Greenblatt's phrase, Elizabeth has fashioned herself: she invented a persona, the proud virgin Queen of England adored by her servants, and four centuries later that persona is still accepted. After a re-evaluation of Queen Elizabeth's speeches, a new image of the Queen will emerge (and I use the word 'image' advisedly). She will be more shrewd than vain, more practical than imperious, more thoughtful than fiery. Above all, she will be a superb user of language.

NOTES

1. I read earlier versions of this essay at meetings of the South Atlantic Modern Language Association and the Renaissance English Text Society; the latter paper appeared as 'Editing Elizabeth's speeches', in Suzanne Gossett, ed., *Renaissance English Text Society Proceedings* (Chicago: RETS, 1987), pp. 15–19.

2. Unless otherwise noted, I use the same texts for Elizabeth's speeches in this essay as I did in 'Elizabeth I: Queen of England', in ed. Katharina M. Wilson, *Women Writers of the Renaissance and Reformation* (Athens: University of Georgia Press, 1987), pp. 522–47, hereafter cited as Wilson; this quote on p. 541.

3. From Ian Donaldson, ed., *The Oxford Authors: Ben Jonson* (Oxford: Oxford University Press, 1985), p. 602. Herford and Simpson assess Jonson's reliability and corroborate the existence of such gossip in other accounts from the seventeenth century.

   Instances of such gossip are detailed by Carole Levin in her essay 'Power, politics, and sexuality: Images of Elizabeth I', in Jeanne R. Brink, Allison P. Coudert and Maryanne C. Horowitz, eds, *The Politics of Gender in Early Modern Europe, Sixteenth-Century Essays and Studies*, 12 (1989), pp. 95–110. Levin assesses gossip about Elizabeth's sexuality as an index to her subjects' ambivalence about her rule.

4. This tale of Raleigh's cloak was punctured by J.E. Neale, 'The sayings of Queen Elizabeth', *History*, n.s., 10 (1925), p. 222, hereafter cited as Sayings; all ensuing references will be made in the text.

5. Since I am discussing popular perceptions, I might include my own experience. Invariably, when I mention my work on Elizabeth's oratory, I am asked if she actually wrote her own speeches. This question does not come only

from laymen but also from professors of literature, history, and women's studies. If I ask what they think of her oratory, they always recall that Elizabeth gave a stirring speech when she led her army against the Armada. A few recall the Golden speech and the Marriage speeches. Hence, my choice of examples in the body of this essay.

6. Three recent articles about Elizabeth mention the work of such revisionists early on. (All ensuing references to these articles will be made in the text.) Mary Thomas Crane, ' "Video et taceo": Elizabeth I and the rhetoric of counsel', *Studies in English Literature* **28** (1988), pp. 1–15; Allison Heisch, 'Queen Elizabeth I: Parliamentary rhetoric and the exercise of power', *Signs*, 1 (1975), pp. 31–55; and John N. King, 'Queen Elizabeth I: Representations of the Virgin Queen', *Renaissance Quarterly*, **43** (1990), pp. 30–74, all begin their articles by comments on how the problem of assessing Elizabeth's image and rhetoric had been affected by the work of Frances A. Yates, *Astraea* (London: Routledge & Kegan Paul, 1975); Stephen Greenblatt, *Renaissance Self-Fashioning* (Chicago: University of Chicago Press, 1980) and Roy Strong, *The Cult of Elizabeth: Elizabethan portraiture and pageantry* (London: Thames & Hudson, 1977).

7. Yates, *Astraea*, pp. 78–9; Strong, *The Cult of Elizabeth*, p. 16; Greenblatt, *Renaissance Self-Fashioning*, pp. 165–9.

8. M.H. Abrams *et al.*, eds, *The Norton Anthology of English Literature* (New York: Norton, 1986), vol. I, pp. 973–4, 2553. The situation is, of course, complicated by the way Elizabeth 'uses male expectations about feminine behavior to protect her prerogative to circumvent those expectations' (Crane, 'Video et taceo', p. 11). Thus, modern anthologists who present Elizabeth as a woman in love, but ignore her role as a woman orator, pay unconscious tribute to the success of her tactic: appropriating patriarchal assumptions to defeat their limits. They present the persona she created to mask her real power and political skill.

    In any case, distortions caused by twentieth-century gender stereotypes are far milder than distortions of Renaissance misogny: in the article cited in Note 3 above, Levin details the rumours of Elizabeth's bastards, infanticide, and unique anatomy.

9. Sandra M. Gilbert and Susan Gubar, eds, *The Norton Anthology of Literature by Women* (New York: Norton, 1985).

10. J.E. Neale, *Elizabeth I and Her Parliaments*, 2 vols (New York: St Martin's Press, 1958); hereafter cited in the text as *E&P*. In her discussion of Elizabeth's rhetoric, Allison Heisch says that she has done an unpublished edition of the parliamentary speeches (p. 31). My thanks to Elizabeth Hageman for directing my attention to this article, and to Marianne Novy for the information that Heisch's edition was a dissertation done at Harvard. I have been unable to obtain a copy of the work.

11. George P. Rice, *The Public Speaking of Queen Elizabeth* (New York: AMS rpt of 1951 edn, 1966).

12. Wallace T. MacCaffrey gives the bibliographical history in his edition of William Camden, *The History of . . . Princess Elizabeth* (Chicago: University of Chicago Press, 1970), pp. 334–5; all ensuing references will be made in the text. I shall follow MacCaffrey's edition, a slightly modernised version of the best seventeenth-century translation, that of the 1688 edition.

13. See Note 2 above; Wilson, ed. *Women Writers*, pp. 542–3.

14. My account of the visit to Tilbury draws principally on Neale's *Queen Elizabeth I* (New York: Jonathan Cape, 1934); Miller Christy, 'Queen Elizabeth's

visit to Tilbury in 1588', *English Historical Review*, 34 (1919), pp. 43–61; and Winifried Schleiner, '*Divina virago*: Queen Elizabeth as an Amazon', *Studies in Philology* 75 (1978), pp. 163–80. Schleiner is particularly good about sorting through the various accounts of contemporary observers. Miller is sceptical about the speech text's authenticity, while Neale does accept it. I think a tentative acceptance of the speech is warranted, although I would emphasise the qualifier 'tentative'.

15. C.G. Cruickshank describes the problems of the pay system for Elizabeth's army in some detail in *Elizabeth's Army*, 2nd edn (Oxford: Clarendon Press, 1966), pp. 143–58.

16. An anonymous letter about these events was sent to the Spanish ambassador in Paris, Bernadino de Mendoza; the writer claimed to have been present in the camp, but mentions no speech; see *Calendar of Letters and State Papers Relating to English Affairs Preserved Principally in the Archives of Simancas*, ed. M.A.S. Hume (London, 1892–9). An account of the Tilbury speech is given by an eyewitness, James Aske, in his poem *Elizabetha Triumphans, with a Declaration of the Manner how her Excellency was entertained by her Souldyers into her Campe Royall, at Tilbury, in Essex* (London, 1588), 35 pp. in 4to. See also Thomas Deloney's broadside, *The Queen's visiting of the Campe at Tilsburie, with her Entertainement there* (London, 1588); Deloney was not an eye-witness, as Christy demonstrates: 'Queen Elizabeth's visit', pp. 48–51.

17. *Cabala* (microfilm; London, 1651), pp. 343–5.

18. Garrett Mattingly, *The Defeat of the Spanish Armada* (Boston, MA: Houghton Mifflin; London: Jonathan Cape, 1959), p. 349 in the American edition, 295 in the British. I learned of the passage in Schleiner's article, which quotes the passage, p. 168. Mattingly's book is still in print.

19. Louis Adrian Montrose, ' "Shaping fantasies": Figurations of gender and power in Elizabethan culture', *Representations*, 12 (1983), pp. 61–94.

20. Leah S. Marcus, *Puzzling Shakespeare: Local reading and its discontents* (Berkeley: University of California Press, 1988), pp. 51–105. Her account of what occurred at Tilbury is principally drawn from Aske. For a discussion of problems in Aske's account, see Christy, 'Queen Elizabeth's visit', pp. 55–7.

21. Schleiner, 'Divine virago', p. 179.

22. Marcus, *Puzzling Shakespeare*, pp. 62, 64–5.

23. Neale gives a thorough analysis of the problems; *E&P*, 2: pp. 391–2. The manuscript of the parliamentary version is Stowe MS. 362, fols 169–72; it was printed in Sir Simonds D'Ewes, *A Compleat Journal of the [Parliaments] . . . of Queen Elizabeth* (Wilmington, DE: Scholarly Resources rpt 1693 edn, 1974), pp. 659–60. The text of the royal version is taken from a microfilm copy of the pamphlet published in London, 1601.

24. For the purposes of this section, the texts I use are taken from D'Ewes and the 1601 pamphlet (see Note 23) rather than the text in the Wilson anthology, p. 543 (see Note 2). I have modernised spelling, punctuation, and capitalisation; 'then' is rendered as 'than' when the context demands the latter.

25. My comments on Elizabeth's rhetoric draw on ideas from Jonathan Goldberg, *James I and the Politics of Literature* (Baltimore, MD: Johns Hopkins University Press, 1983); Richard Lanham, *The Motives of Eloquence* (New Haven, CT: Yale University Press, 1983); and Marion Trousdale, *Shakespeare and the Rhetoricians* (Chapel Hill: University of North Carolina Press, 1982). Paul Corts, 'Governmental persuasion in the reign of Queen Elizabeth I, 1558–1563', PhD dissertation: Indiana University, 1971, attempts to discuss Elizabeth's rhetoric in pragmatic terms. Other discussions of Elizabeth as a writer

are listed in Elizabeth Hageman, 'Recent studies in women writers of Tudor England', *English Literary Renaissance*, **14** (1984), pp. 409–25.

26. For summaries of the textual problems involved in these works, see Gary Taylor and Michael Warren, eds, *The Division of the Kingdoms: Shakespeare's two versions of King Lear* (Oxford: Clarendon Press, 1983); Jonathan Wordsworth, M.H. Abrams and Stephen Gill, eds, *The Prelude: 1799, 1805, 1850* (New York: Norton Critical Editions, 1979); and Sculley Bradley and Harold W. Blodgett, eds, *Leaves of Grass* (New York: Norton Critical Editions, 1964, rev. 1973).

27. D'Ewes, *A Compleat Journal*, p. 549. King identifies the handwriting in the manuscript as Cecil's: 'Queen Elizabeth I', p. 38.

28. MacCaffrey, *The History of . . . Princess Elizabeth*, pp. 29–30, gives the English translation which I discuss.

29. Ibid., pp. xxiv, xxxvii–viii.

30. Neale, *E&P* vol. I, p. 47. John King says: 'The preservation of a transcript of the queen's speech among the Cecil papers makes it possible to assess Camden's accuracy. Examination of the Cecil manuscript reveals an entirely new set of problems, however, because Camden (or an unnamed intermediary) falsified the contemporary record of the queen's speech' ('Queen Elizabeth I', p. 35). This seems at first to settle the question, but unfortunately the transcript to which King refers is that of the Parliamentary speech of 10 February, not the cameral speech of 6 February. Since these are separate, though related, speeches, one must expect variation between them. To call such variation falsification seems too strong. King is quite correct, however, in questioning whether the speech is authentic, for it may not be. He also objects that Rice's claim (the Camden version is superior) is 'undocumented' and Montrose's claim (Camden worked from an official transcript) is 'unsubstantiated'; I agree completely with King on these points (King, 'Queen Elizabeth I', p. 35, note 19).

31. See Note 2; Wilson, ed., *Women Writers*, pp. 537–8.

32. What I say about Elizabeth's rhetorical tactics in the Parliamentary speech accords with Heisch's analysis (pp. 36–9) of how Elizabeth revised her 1563 parliamentary speech on marriage. That revision demonstrates conscious use of ambiguity and equivocation in 'her struggle to be gracious' (p. 37).

5

The Queen's Masque:
Renaissance Women and the
Seventeenth-Century Court
Masque

Marion Wynne-Davies

I

At Night we had the Queen's Maske in the Banquetting-House, or rather her Pagent.[1]

These are the words Dudley Carleton chose to describe 'The Masque of Blackness' (1605) in a letter to his friend Sir Ralph Winwood, who had unfortunately missed the show. Today, a glance through the catalogue of any research library would reveal that this masque is closeted neatly amongst the entries relating to the dramatist Ben Jonson. It does not appear under 'Queen Anne', the eponymous monarch of Carleton's epistle. However, closer investigation would uncover the fact that the masque titles chosen for publication by Jonson himself concur with the seventeenth- rather than the twentieth-century attribution. The titles in both the Quarto (1608) and the First Folio (1616), and the title page of the earlier text, which are contained in Herford and Simpson's eleven-volume edition of Jonson's works, refer to 'The Qveenes Masqves. The first, of Blacknesse'.[2] There is no suggestion of misplaced appropriation or textual error. Everyone knew that Ben Jonson had written the words of the masque; but like his fellow courtiers, even he complied with the persistent allocation to the Queen. The Venetian secretary, who was present at the performance, went still further, reporting that 'her Majesty [was] the authoress of the whole'.[3]

On one level, of course, we are talking about simple lexical mutation, since the word 'author' has come to mean the setting forth of written statements with a concurrent claim to the sole ownership of that text. This change was already occurring during the seventeenth century and can be seen in Jonson's alteration of the title page, which in the Quarto text referred, as we have seen, to the Queen, but became in the First Folio simply 'Masques at Court. The Author B.I.'.[4] The earlier definition was much looser, allowing the 'author' to be the initiator or instigator of a work, someone who gave existence to something in any number of ways. What the Venetian secretary is suggesting, then, is that the masque was a production by diverse people of whom the Queen was the most politically notable force.

There is an insidious acceptability about this diachronic developmental theory, which offers the seductively neat possibility of a final and complete verbal definition. But the shift of signification around the term 'author' occurs within eleven years and is caught in a much more complex web of interpretative elements. The masque allowed for an almost unique interplay of creative and imaginative faculties and these had, in turn, to jostle with the economic demands and court tensions endemic upon the genre's political identity. Rather than accepting the idea of single authorship without question, however, an archaeological analysis of the masque offers us a multidimensional discourse which opens up 'authorship' to women. As Michel Foucault writes in *The Archaeology of Knowledge*, archaeology's purpose is to diversify, not to unify, and

> to discover that whole domain of institutions, economic processes, and social relations on which a discursive formation can be articulated . . . to uncover . . . the particular level in which history can give place to definite types of discourse, which have their own type of historicity, and which are related to a whole set of various historicities.[5]

The court masque was a collective cultural construct which allowed the women of the court, and specifically the Queen, access to a politically resonant discourse. Their penetration into this exclusively masculine field disrupted the court, for the Queen's masque not only challenged the gendered preserves of authorship but questioned the legitimacy of absolute male power as symbolised by the Stuart King.

When I entitled this essay 'The Queen's Masque', however, I intended to suggest a further diversification. Not only does the term occur in early seventeenth-century discourse referring to Queen Anne, but it also suggests Ben Jonson's 'The Masque of Queens' (1609).[6] As in 'Blackness', Anne was the chief masquer of the later entertainment and her eleven attendants on stage were all ladies of the court. They included Lucy, Countess of Bedford, a well-known literary patron, Lady Anne Clifford, the diarist, and Alice Countess of Derby, a booklover and patron of several dramatists. Jonson had written the conventional panegyric to these powerful and influential women:

Penthesilea, the braue *Amazon*,
Swift-foote *Camilla*, *Queene* of *Volscia*,

Victorious *Thomyris* of *Scythia*,
Chast *Artemisia*, the *Carian* Dame,
And fayre-hayr'd *Beronice*, *Ægipts* fame,
Hypsicratea, Glory of *Asia*,
Candace, pride of *Æthiopia*
The *Britanne* honor, *Voadicea*,
The vertuous *Palmyrene Zenobia*,
The wise, and warlike *Goth*, *Amalasunta*,
And bold *Valasca* of *Bohemia*.[7]

The last masquer to be described is the Queen herself: '*Belanna* . . . alone, Possest [of] all vertues'. One element of the masque discourse as it pertains to Renaissance women must, of course, be the retention of her position as object (as opposed to subject) in the dramatic excerpts of the performance. Thus she is contained within the formal elements of the entertainment, as well as by the ideological values the masque purported to sustain.[8]

The other possible transference of signification elided by the title is 'the masque written by a Queen' and, indeed, there is such a masque. Queen Henrietta Maria composed, directed and acted in her own masque in 1626; this uncovers the possibility of women's participation in the textual composition of these court entertainments.[9] However, although a number of women were involved in the production processes, there is only one extant text written by a woman of the Jacobean court which includes masques: Lady Mary Wroth's *Urania*.[10] Through this text it is possible to locate a genuinely female voice in the discursive practices of a feminised masque.

II

In order to understand why the masque form, rather than the public theatre for example, was able to facilitate female involvement, its origins and structure must be taken into consideration. The masque was, above all, a political construct. It was developed in the Burgundian court and rapidly came to be seen by the monarchies of Renaissance Europe as an essential display of power.[11] In England these shows were imported by Henry VII as part of his propagandistic commandeering of the crown, but they reached their zenith in the Jacobean and Caroline courts.[12] The frequent involvement of noblewomen in patronage is widely documented, but the masque proffered the opportunity for personal artistic participation.[13] Not only were the ladies of the court able to commission the text they desired, they were also able to share the planning for its performance and act in its presentation. Every stage of the masque's production offered fresh possibilities for the insertion of female authorisation and creativity.

If court entertainments simply encoded a eulogy of the monarchy and his or her court, then this female involvement would be nugatory, merely reasserting the dominant order with unrestrained praise. But masques rarely succumbed to this harmonious function. Stephen Orgel and David Lindley have signalled more than adequately the more serious responses predicated by the genre, the latter writing:

> It [the masque] is at once the last expression of a full-blown Renaissance idealism in the service of a hierarchical and ordered view of the world and a form which permitted the evolution of musical and theatrical techniques that look forward to the post-Restoration era. It is at the same time an art which aspires to translate its participants into an ideal contemplative vision and a kind intimately related to the flux of political reality. Its confident celebration and triumphant assertion are couched in a literary form that is full of inner tension.[14]

It is through these fissures in the official court discourse, indicated by Lindley, that the female voice was able to escape, so that the tensions in the masque often became those of gender, replete with political as well as sexual signification.

The 'inner tension' of the masque form is manifest in its tripartite structure (the masque, the antimasque and the dance), the speaking parts of which were assigned to professional players.[15] The masque proper centred on some idealised theme such as Truth or Honour, elucidating these values through a series of speeches and songs performed by allegorical or mythical characters. The antimasque provided the antithesis to the main didactic argument, and the roles for this section of the performance, which generally occurred first, were also taken by professionals. The dance was performed at the end of the evening by the ladies and gentlemen of the court, who were always associated with the triumphant moral values espoused in the masque. These dancers did not speak; but at the conclusion of the formal performance they descended into the hall and invited the audience to dance, thereby allowing them to participate in the fulfilment of an idealised subject position. The central figure in the orchestration, however, was often the monarch. He or she rarely performed in the masque, but sat on an elevated and protruding dais to which all action on the stage was directed. The necessity for a perpetual and simultaneous recognition of the material and fictive worlds, together with the thematic antithesis of masque and antimasque, threw an almost unbearable pressure upon the supposedly harmonising function of the entertainments.

Ben Jonson's masques are prefaced by long descriptive passages, which were an essential part of the discursive practice of the masque genre and appear to elucidate the masque components already discussed. The following statement by Jonson anatomises the plan for 'The Masque of Queens':

It encreasing, now, to the third time of my being vs'd in these seruices to her Maties personall presentatio's, wth the Ladyes whom she pleaseth to honor; it was my first, and speciall reguard, to see that the Nobilyty of the Invention should be answerable to the dignity of they^r persons. For wch reason, I chose the Argument, to be, *A Celebration of honorable, & true Fame, bred out of Vertue:* obseruing that rule of the best *Artist*, to suffer no obiect of delight to passe w^thout his mixture of profit, & example.

And because her Matie (best knowing, that a principall part of life in these *Spectacles* lay in they^r variety) had commaunded mee to think on some *Daunce*, or shew, that might præcede hers, and haue the place of a foyle, or false-*Masque*; I was carefull to decline not only from others, but mine owne stepps in that kind, since the last yeare I had an *Anti-Masque* of Boyes: and therefore, now, deuis'd that twelue Women, in the habite of *Haggs* or Witches, sustayning the persons of *Ignorance, Suspicion, Credulity*, &c. the opposites to good *Fame*, should fill that part; not as a *Masque*, but a spectacle of strangenesse, producing multiplicity of Gesture, and not vnaptly sorting wth the current, and whole fall of the Deuise.[16]

There are several points worth noting: Jonson mentions that the purpose of the masque is to be an 'object of delight' as well as an 'example', thereby according with the Renaissance humanist interpretation of art as being for both pleasure and profit.[17] Set against this higher purpose of the 'best *Artist*' is the Queen's desire for 'variety', which carries the implicit condemnation of lightness as opposed to Jonson's own *gravitas*. However, the 'foyle, or false-*Masque*' which Anne requires is an essential ingredient of the whole performance, throwing virtue into sharp relief by its antic 'otherness'. In the case of 'The Masque of Queens' the contrasting show is performed by hags and witches, characterised similarly, one supposes, to those Inigo Jones also designed for William Davenant's 'Salmacidia Spolia' (1640).[18] The twelve hags supply a dialectical interpretation of the whole, opposing as they do the twelve noble ladies described earlier in this essay.

The polarisation of the hags is emphasised still further in Jonson's introduction. They are:

full of præposterous change, and gesticulation, but most applying to they^r property: who, at they^r meetings, do all thinges contrary to the custome of Men, dauncing, back to back, hip to hip, they^r handes ioyn'd and making they^r *circles* backward, to the left hand, wth strange phantastique motions of they^r heads, and bodyes.[19]

As grotesques, they present an absolute opposite to the female ideal of the court world, and especially to the lady masquers who stood immobile and speechless at the back of the stage until released towards the end of the performance for their allowed function in the formal, prescribed pattern of the dance. Thus, the courtly ladies' compound identity is located by their very difference from the hags – who are presented first – and centred upon their silence and containment, until the male voice of Heroique

Virtue sets them free. Even then, they are allowed their limited autonomy
only after Heroique Virtue has firmly reasserted the political hierarchies
of the court, by placing the Queen securely within the King's control;

> She this embracing w^{r}h a vertuous ioy,
> Farre from *selfe-loue*, as humbling all her Worth
> To him that gaue it, hath agayne brought forth
> They^r Names to Memory, and meanes this night
> To make her, once more, visible to light.
> And to that light, from whence her truth of spirit
> Confesseth all the lustre of her Merit.
> To you, most royall, and most happy King.[20]

The tenor of this speech, which affirms the gender relations in the court, is
further consolidated by the female figure of Fame, who contributes an
affirmation of the privileging of paternity in Jacobean ideology: '*Virtue*, my
Father, and my Honour; Thou/That mad'st mee good, as great'.[21] These
speeches finally conclude by reaffirming for the audience the conventional
Jacobean value system in which the King/Man dominates the Queen/
Woman; and at this point, in order to underline the already obvious power
structures, the hags are bound and led off stage. Their free movement and
challenging speech – their very actions and language – are constrained and
denied in a final reassertion of the containment of women.

Of course, the hags were given speaking parts and would therefore have
been played by boys, not women. The most authoritative writing on
women and the court masque to date is Suzanne Gossett's article 'Man-
maid, begone!: Women in masques', in which she endows this gender
substitution with great significance, although it was, after all, common
enough on the public stage.[22] But Jonson explicitly called attention to the
fact that the hags were 'twelue Women' and not 'an *Anti-Masque* of
Boyes', which he had used the previous year. Although the actors could
not alter their gender, becoming female, Jonson could suggest the feminine through them, and thereby comment, not upon gender, but upon the
social construction of women as seen in the figures of the queens. Still,
what we, as readers, appear to be left with is an overt challenge to the
ideologically acceptable formulation of woman, which can be, and is,
contained. As Jonathan Dollimore suggests in *Radical Tragedy*, what is
perceived in the dialectic of masque and antimasque might be thought of
as a 'ritual inversion'. He concludes:

> the disorder in question took many forms but dealt especially with the
> reversal of relationships of authority, sexuality and status generally – for
> example women over men, father over son [*sic*], subject over prince.

Nevertheless, the masque was also 'an ideological legitimation of the
power structure'.[23] In this commentary Dollimore is discussing a

masque-within-a-play, not the politically potent entertainments of the early modern court. Consequently, he does not take into account the dramatic origins of the court masque, which are unnecessary in an analysis of *The Revenger's Tragedy* but inevitably leave traces of a darker and more generative folk tradition in masques such as 'Queens'.

Jonson's hags belong to a weirdly mutated 'other world' which is efflorescent with bodily force and energy, and cannot be entirely circumscribed by the formal structures set against it. They may be seen in the light of the Bakhtinian 'grotesque', which

> discloses the potentiality of an entirely different world, of another order, another way of life. It leads men out of the confines of the apparent (false) unity, of the indisputable and stable.[24]

What the hags offer is not a neatly formulated dialectic but a diverse world in which Otherness is multiple, contrary and 'phantastique'.

Yet the mutual opposition implied between masque and antimasque figures is not sustained. The defeat of the hags cannot finally suppress the linguistic and physical freedom of the women in the masque, as these qualities have already emerged in the characters of the queens. A close examination of the speech – already quoted – describing the noblewomen discloses that each is endowed with a glorifying attribute – no surprises there. But of the eleven queens, only two are endowed with ideologically acceptable feminine qualities: chastity and being 'fayre-hayr'd'.[25] Two have androgynous values: virtue itself and being swift of foot (although this latter quality would have been more redolent of masculine, rather than feminine, strength). There remain seven queens who are ascribed attributes which were almost exclusively considered to be more specific to men in Jacobean ideology. These women were brave, victorious, glorious, proud, honourable and bold, while Amalsunta the Goth is said to be both wise and warlike. The qualities said to be shared by these queens are more appropriate to the traditional active public role expected of men, while the ideal of silence and immobility being visually presented appears to uphold the feminine ideal. Confronted with this dislocation between spoken text and ocular evidence, the audience must perceive the inadequacy of allowing the feminine to be determined by a single signifier, whether courtly lady or hags played by boys. The field of play which 'The Masque of Queens' opens up at this point of schism is focused upon gender, and it is through these processes of perpetuating difference that women were able to impregnate the masque with a radical feminine voice.

Like the thematic power of the masque form, women's involvement in these entertainments was essentially political. It was Queen Anne, not Ben Jonson, who instigated and enacted the negotiation between court show and court politics. The intricate diplomatic manoeuvrings about 'The Masque of Queens' is one of many examples of the international significance of the masques and the power the Queen had, or determined to have, over them. The Spanish ambassador, Don Fernandez de Girone, was in London to thank James I for helping to formulate a truce in the Netherlands war. He was favoured by Anne, and she obtained several invitations for the Spanish contingent to see 'The Masque of Queens'. This action, however, upset the French ambassador, La Boderie, who was a favourite of the King. Finally, after much negotiation, James prevailed upon Anne to wait until de Girone had left before showing the masque, and they invited La Boderie on his own. Through all of this, yet another ambassador had been offended – the Venetian, Marc Antonio Correr – and the Queen, perhaps attempting to reassert her political control, invited him to attend the masque in disguise. Correr reported to his prince:

> The Queen let it be understood that she would be pleased if I came *incognito* to the Masque, and . . . let me know that she regretted I had not been invited and pleaded that, as the King paid the bill, he desired to be the host. She says she is resolved to trouble herself no more with Masques, and that she would rather have had your Serenity's Ambassador invited than the representative of any other Prince.[26]

Far from being 'but toys', as Francis Bacon suggests in his essay 'On Masques', these entertainments were of a delicate and crucial nature in political terms. More importantly, they were not the King's lone concern.[27] The Queen used her masques to participate in foreign diplomacy, and she became annoyed with the King when her plans were thwarted. The political involvement both ran parallel to and cross-fertilised with her active participation in the imaginative authorship of the shows themselves. Moreover, Anne utilised the masque form to act contrary to the King's wishes, as surely as the hags danced 'contrary to the custome of Men'.

Queen Anne's disruptive deployment of the masque was echoed by her encouragement of political subversion in other theatrical performances at court. Another French ambassador, Beaumont, wrote in 1604:

> Consider for pity's sake what must be the state and condition of a prince, whom the preachers publicly from the pulpit assail, whom the comedians of the metropolis bring upon the stage, whose wife attends these representations in order to enjoy the laugh against her husband.[28]

A feminised discourse of political subversion and factional division between King and Queen was as evident in the plays performed before Anne as in those in which she herself participated.

III

The first decade of Jacobean rule is scattered with reports of these incidents: 'The Masque of Queens' was not, for example, the first time Anne

Figure 5.1 A Negro Nymph, daughter of Niger, Inigo Jones, 1605

had aroused a flurry of consternation through her involvement in a masque. The most sensational of the Queen's performances was in 'The Masque of Blackness', on Twelfth Night 1605, in Whitehall. The responses to it suggest that the English court was scandalised: for example, Dudley Carleton wrote to Ralph Winwood:

> At the further end was a great Shell in form of a Skallop, wherein were four Seats; on the lowest sat the Queen with my Lady *Bedford*; on the rest were placed the Ladies *Suffolk, Darby, Rich, Effingham, Ann Herbert, Susan Herbert, Elizabeth Howard, Walsingham* and *Bevil*. Their Apparell was rich, but too light and Curtizan-like for such great ones. Instead of Vizzards, their Faces and Arms up to the Elbows, were painted black, which was Disguise sufficient, for they were hard to be known; *but it became them nothing so well as their red and white, and you cannot imagine a more ugly Sight, then a Troop of lean-cheek'd Moors.*

Carleton commented again, this time to Chamberlain:

> The maske at night requires much labor to be well described; but there is a pamflet in press wch will saue me that paynes. meane time you shall onely knowe that the Actors were the Q: the Ladies Bedford, Suffolke, Darby, Rich, Harbert, Effingham Susan, El: Howard, Beuell, Walsingham and Wroth. The presentacion of the maske at the first drawing of the trauers was very fayre, and theyr apparel rich, but too light and curtisan-like; Theyr black faces, and hands wch were painted and bare vp to the elbowes, was a very lothsome sight, and I am sorry that strangers should see owr court so strangely disguised.

Lastly, Vincent wrote to Benson:

> At night was there a sumptuous shew represented by ye Q. and some dozen Ladyes all paynted like Blackamores face and neck bare and for ye rest strangely attired in Barbaresque mantells to ye halfe legge, having buskins all to be sett wth iewells, wch a waue of ye Sea as it weare very artificially made and brought to ye stage by secrett ingines cast forth of a skallop shell to performe ye residue of ye devise of dansing etc. W^ch I saw not, nor harkened after further. But tell it you only for this y^t you discerne ye humor of ye tyme.[29]

What shocked the Jacobean courtiers was that the lady masquers had painted themselves black; we have extant an Inigo Jones design as evidence of their appearance.[30] Part of the reason for the furore was that the ideal female subject was considered to be not only silent and immobile but fair in the traditional Petrarchan manner. But this was not the first time English court ladies had disguised themselves as 'Blackamores'.

On Shrove Tuesday 1510, at the court of Henry VIII, the King suddenly disappeared from the Queen's chambers, where a banquet was being held for foreign ambassadors. He then reappeared with his nobles, all disguised as Moors, and they proceeded to play at dice with the guests. When the game was over, the ladies entered:

their faces, neckes, armes & handes, couered with fyne pleasaunce blacke,
. . . so that the same ladies semed to be nygrost or blacke Mores.[31]

It is interesting to recognise the similar configuration of Queen, foreign
ambassadors and a court entertainment, suggesting that such occasions
were often held under feminine auspices. In addition, the combination of
dice and Moors in the 1510 masque gives us access to the traces of a
cultural antecedent for this 'blacking-up', which suggests a more trans-
gressive and amoral interpretation of the 1605 display.

Disguising, and a game of chance, were part of a long-standing tradition described as 'mommerie'. One of its earliest but most succinct definitions occurs in Enid Welsford's *The Court Masque* (1927):

> a procession of people disguised by masks, beast-heads, or discoloured
> faces, who enter their neighbours' houses to dance or play at dice – often in
> complete silence.[32]

Welsford goes on to describe how mommerie was a medieval ritual of a
symbolic game of chance played with demon spirits who were defeated,
and thus exorcised for the coming year.[33] But the practice also has a more
extended and diverse genealogy. Playing at dice was originally a Roman
New Year or 'Kalends' custom, which developed along several avenues.[34]
Under the Catholic Church it metamorphosed into the Feast of Fools,
which involved a symbolic role reversal between the lower and higher
clergy, and the mocking of religious celebrations by dicing on the altar. In
lay entertainments the mommers who played at dice visited their neighbours disguised as underworld spirits or demons, with blackened faces
and wild-men's costumes. By 1377 it had also become a court entertainment, for in that year the Commons of London diced with the young
Richard II, enabling him, through the use of a loaded dice, to win a golden
cup, ball and ring.[35] In each case the mommers are meant to be overcome;
they are simply allowed one day a year in which to invert hierarchies and
ridicule convention. The lower clergy, visitors and commoners, like the
hags in the Jacobean masque, are symbolically defeated, signifying the
destruction of anarchy and the restoration of the dominant ideology.
What we are confronting is a contained challenge, an acceptable form of
radicalism, which Stephen Greenblatt describes as follows:

> The subversive voices are produced by and within the affirmations of order;
> they are powerfully registered, but they do not undermine that order.
> Indeed . . . the order is neither possible nor fully convincing without both
> the presence and perception of betrayal.[36]

Greenblatt privileges the order of authority over subversion, and
while it is perfectly possible to perceive Henry VIII's delight in shock-
ing his court as within this definition, Queen Anne's masques are not
so readily fixed.

The Queen is characterised not only by her sovereignty, but also by her gender; thus, she may dislocate her royal identity from that of the King in a bilateral challenge to masculine authority. Anne's self-conscious manipulation of her subject role is evident from the history of her political intrigues and from her dominant control of the masque's thematic content. Significantly, it was her own idea that the women should be black. Jonson writes:

> (because it was her Maiesties will, to haue them *Blackmores* at first) the inuention was deriued by me, and presented thus.[37]

Moreover, Anne adopted, for her challenge to gender hierarchies, the powerfully mythical discourse of mommerie which, with its diachronic elements, denies obligations to contemporary applicability. This resistance to circumscription suggests a carnivalesque spirit, which was innate to mommerie and the antimasque. As Bakhtin writes:

> As opposed to the official feast, one might say that carnival celebrated temporary liberation from the prevailing truth and from the established order; it marked the suspension of all hierarchical rank, privileges, norms, and prohibitions. Carnival was the true feast of time, the feast of becoming, change and renewal. It was hostile to all that was immortalized and completed.[38]

By calling upon this pan-chronological symbol of blackened faces – with its magical power of complete ludic aptness – the 1605 masque breaches the ideological constructs of the Jacobean court. It becomes impossible to perceive Queen Anne's court masques as defined by a simple dialectic power structure. The web of subject relations is too complex and multidimensional for that. The masque exists at a point of convergence for many lines of interpretation: of gender, of class, of politics, of artistic construction, and of the carnivalesque. Like the signification of 'authorship', a feminised masque discourse adjusts the lens of our attention so as to focus sharply upon these threads of tension, revealing diversity rather than unity. Through an extension of the canon with texts written by women, it is now possible to perceive still more strands within the discursive practices, which have until now been invisible.

IV

The term 'voice' is used to signify a collective and cumulative discourse; yet it carries within it a subtextual assumption of a privileged literacy and orality which has often excluded women. For example, the role of women on the private stage in the Jacobean and Caroline courts has received surprisingly little attention considering that we have ample evidence for their involvement – that concerning Henrietta Maria, for example. These feminine voices of performance, although recognised, are not always 'heard'; they are muted.[39] The theory of female mutedness is discussed by Shirley Ardener:

> The theory of mutedness, therefore, does not require that the muted be actually *silent*. They may speak a great deal. The important issue is whether they are able to say all that they would wish to say, where and when they wish to say it.[40]

The material empowering of language is as important as the linguistic skill itself, and when the theory is applied to the execution of texts, what becomes startlingly apparent is the mutuality of this mutedness – a mutuality which exists between writer, text and reader/critic. The ideological suppression of voice affects the seventeenth-century court lady and the twentieth-century critic alike. Without a self-conscious recognition of our own positioning within a critical tradition, it remains impossible to acknowledge a voice which might challenge our presuppositions and, in this case, allow for the emergence of many previously muted women writers. Thus, in order to liberate the female voice from a mutedness within a theoretical discourse, it is essential to examine women writers/creators, as well as the role women played in the literature written by men.

The court's relationship with literary productivity was sometimes parental, offering the nurturing support of patronage and providing the economic facilities for dramatic, and especially masque, output. The alliance between patron and artist is a far more complex power balance than can be accommodated here, and it must suffice to indicate the importance of female patronage in early modern Europe as an acceptable way for women to participate in literary creativity.[41] But the seductive power for women of this maternal patronage system occasionally overbalanced when their involvement became more insistent – as, for example, in the case of Queen Anne and Jonson's masques. What the court masque offered aristocratic women was the 'where and when' for their own voice.

One of the women courtiers who acted in the masques of 'Blackness' and 'Queens' was Lucy Countess of Bedford, who is usually identified as the patron of John Donne, a canonical male poet.[42] Yet she had works dedicated to her by other poets (Michael Drayton, Samuel Daniel and Ben Jonson); she wrote poems herself, although none to our knowledge survives; and she organised masques. Rather than acting as an adjunct to a single male poet, she appears to have been one of the multiple centres of patronage about which Renaissance writers orbited. The two masques she directed personally are 'Cupid's Banishment' (1617), held at the Ladies' Hall in Deptford, and 'Lovers Made Men', which was presented to Lord Hay, also in 1617.[43] Other women involved in the writing of dramas or masques include the Countess of Pembroke, Elizabeth Cary and

Margaret Cavendish.[44] However, it is another of the court ladies, acting as Baryte in 'Blackness', who produced the most significant contribution to the Jacobean masque – Lady Mary Wroth.

Wroth was born into the culturally distinguished Sidney family in 1587; she was the daughter of Sir Robert Sidney, brother of the Countess of Pembroke and Sir Philip Sidney, and she was brought up at Penshurst.[45] In 1604 she married Sir Robert Wroth, even though she continued to be identified with the Sidney family. Around the same time Wroth became a close friend of Queen Anne and participated in the masques of 'Blackness' and of 'Beauty'. She was also, like Lucy Countess of Bedford, a patron, and she received dedications from Ben Jonson, John Donne, George Wither and Joshua Sylvester. Her own literary productivity was prodigious and innovative; she was the first English woman to write a full-length work of prose fiction and the first woman to write a sonnet sequence. She composed, in poetry, *Pamphilia and Amphilanthus* (1621); in prose, *Urania I* (1621) and *Urania II* (1620s); and in drama, *Love's Victory* (1620s).[46] The extent of Wroth's literary involvement was unusual for a lady of the Jacobean court, but she was hardly someone to be bound by convention, as her personal life suggests. In 1614 Robert Wroth died, leaving Lady Mary in debt. Dudley Carleton (the contemporary critic of 'The Masque of Blackness') wrote to his wife that the cause of Wroth's demise was

> a gangrene *in pudendis* [in his private parts] leaving a young widow with 1200[li] joynter, and a young sonne not a moneth old: and his estate charged with 23,000[li] debt.[47]

Wroth had to struggle to pay off this debt for the rest of her life, and the prospect of earning money from her writing must have appeared attractive. However, on the death of her son she entered into a scandalous liaison with her cousin, William Herbert Earl of Pembroke, and bore him two illegitimate children. She was forced to leave court; consequently, her performances in the masques ceased. Nevertheless, she seems to have retained a lively involvement in the masque discourse by including court entertainments in the second part of *Urania*. Wroth's life, in itself, threw the inadequacies of the court's ideological identification of women into disarray. Her literary career and her allegiance to a natal (rather than a nuptial) bond, especially through her love affair with William Herbert, disrupted the court's expectations as much as did her darkened face when she appeared on stage in 'The Masque of Blackness'.

The Countess of Montgomery's Urania was written in two parts and dedicated to Susan Herbert, who was related through marriage to the Sidney family, and a masquer in 'Blackness'. The prose romance tells the story of the constant Queen Pamphilia and her love for the fickle Emperor Amphilanthus. The main theme of both parts is the constancy of women in comparison to the inconstancy of the world; of its civil strife, political unrest and the instability of the court. Wroth draws upon the works of Sidney, Spenser and Ariosto, although it is significant that she does not transform her central character into an Amazon such as Cleophilia, Britomart and Bradamante, but combines the personal and public within the unambiguously female character of Pamphilia.[48] Rather than compounding sexuality and gender in the hermaphroditic ideal of neo-Platonism, she draws the political, poetic and romantic roles of the Queen into an exclusively feminine construct which denies conventional limitations. Pamphilia privileges her public and political duty over her personal desire. She explains that she is married to

> the kingdome of *Pamphilia* from which Husband shee could not bee di-vorced, nor ever would have other, if it might please him to give her leave, to enjoy that happinesse; and besides besought his permission, for my Lord (said shee) my people looke for me, and I must needs be with them.

Elaine V. Beilin, who quotes this passage in *Redeeming Eve*, links it to Elizabeth I's positioning herself as espoused to the Kingdom of Eng-land.[49] Wroth initiates her protagonist into the feminised discourse of autonomous rulership which had been epitomised by Elizabeth I and was revered nostalgically in the Jacobean period as a golden age of monarchy.[50]

Urania's political import extends well beyond Pamphilia, since it is a *roman à clef*. That Wroth's romance belonged to this genre was recog-nised at the time; the Earl of Rutland, for example, wrote to Lady Mary asking her to identify the characters.[51] Texts of this nature were becoming popular in the early seventeenth century: John Barclay's *Argenis* (1621) was published with just such a *clavis*, or key, as the Earl of Rutland requested.[52] Indeed, Wroth probably had to withdraw the text from pub-lication because of the libellous material in Part I, where she depicts Lord Denny, his daughter Honora, and her husband Lord Hay. The slander precipitated an insulting exchange of poems between Denny and Wroth, where he refers to her as a 'Hirmophradite in show, in deed a monster'.[53] The incident provoked condemnatory epistles against Wroth, recalling those directed against the women in 'The Masque of Blackness'. One of the recipients of Dudley Carleton's scandalised letters about 'Blackness', John Chamberlain, found time to reciprocate with further court gossip; he wrote to Carleton:

> [I enclose] certain bitter verses of the Lord Dennies upon the Ladie Marie Wroth, for that in her books of Urania she doth palpablie and grossely play upon him and his late daughter the Lady Hayes, besides many others she makes bold with, and they say takes great libertie or rather licence to traduce whom she please, and thincks she daunces in a net: I have seen an aunswer of hers to these rimes, but I thought yt not worth the writing out.[54]

Chamberlain enclosed the verses of Denny but not of Wroth, enabling an extension of the criticism not only of Wroth's traducing text but also of her very act of writing and her commandeering of a politically potent literary form.

The Denny incidents in *Urania* make for fascinating reading. Wroth refers through the allegory to 'Lord Hay's Masque' (1607), written by Thomas Campion:

> the time of marryage came, which was solemnized by the Kings command at the Court, where great tryumphs were, Masques and banquets, and such Court delights, never man with greater joy received a wife, nor any woman expressed more comfort in a match.[55]

Despite this delightful wedding, however, two years later the couple had disagreements and Wroth implied that Honora had had illicit affairs of which her husband was jealous:

> Her Cabinets hee [her husband] broke open, threatned her servants to make them confesse; letters he found, but only such as between frends might passe in complement, yet they appeared to jealousie to be amorous. He was so distemperd, as he used her ill; her father a phantastical thing, vaine as Courtiers, rash as mad-men, & ignorant as women, would needs (out of folly, ill nature, and waywardnesse, which hee cald care of his honour, and his friends quiet) kill his daughter, and so cut off the blame, or spot, this her offence may lay upon his noble bloud, as he termed it . . . the Lord, left to his pride, wherewith he pufft himself up, & was fild with it like a dropsie, or a blad[d]er blowne with wind.[56]

It seems hardly surprising that Denny, having been called a 'bladder blowne with wind', took to writing his own slanderous verses in return.

Wroth persisted in her representations of court intrigue, and also refers to the Overbury affair and to her own expectations and treatment. Lady Mary becomes Lady Lindamira, who at first was always at court,

> which indeed was the fittest place for her, being a Lady of great spirit, excellent qualities, and beautifull enough to make many in love with her.[57]

But later she loses the Queen's favour and has to retire from court because of the gossip of a 'malicious lady':

> *Lindamira* remaining like one in a gay Masque, the night pass'd, they are in their old clothes againe, and no appearance of what was.[58]

Wroth chooses the metaphor of a masque to represent the transience of the court world, its dreamlike splendour and hollow promises, and she repeats this idea later in relation to her own masque construction. There are also more international political allusions in *Urania*, such as to the downfall of King Christian III of Denmark in 1534 and the overthrow of the Italian communes in the late sixteenth and early seventeenth centuries.[59] Political and personal elements are inextricably linked, particularly through the one persistent, ominous theme of inconstancy, with the trouble and disorder that it brings.

V

There are three masques in *Urania*, all located in Part II: the central masque is presented to Pamphilia, the first to Rodomandro, who woos the Queen and finally wins her, and the last to Amphilanthus, her true love. Like Ben Jonson's masques, they are meant to teach and to delight, as well as to contain detailed instructions governing the performance. Rodomandro's masque establishes this convention. The descriptions of costumes, scenery and music are reminiscent of the Jonsonian passages quoted at the beginning of this essay. For example:

> att last Rodomandro would needs present the Court w^t a show of theire Country fashion, in manner of a maske wch indeed was very pretty and pleasant, him-selfe beeing one of the twelve maskers. And four and twenty torchbearers hee had all aparelled like horse-men in counterfett armes, bases and boots w^t great longe spurrs, faire plumes of feathers, visards they had non, the most of them having faces grim, and hard enough to bee counted visards, the maskers had a pretty kinde of visards or slight coverings of their faces, their apparell after the Tartarian fashion was all alike[.] their uper parts of a rich white clothe of gold made in fashion of an armoure and trimd w^t Gold as if the joints of the armour, ther bases of Carnation velvett laced all over w^t Gold[;] their boots white leather laced att the tops as the baces were, and spurrs of pure golde, butt nott soe longe as their torchbearers['] were, butt convenient to daunce w^t, and nott to bee offensive to the ladys when they would honor them w^t dauncing w^t them.[60]

The practical detail of the spurs, which were shorter for the masquers than for the torchbearers so that they were 'convenient to daunce w^t', suggests the material awareness of someone very familiar with the court masque. Similar conventions occur in the presentation to Pamphilia, where the enchantress Melissea appears in court surrounded by

> a strange darknes, and in that darknes a fearfull fire wch presented a chariott drawne w^t four fi[e]ry dragons, the Chariott fire, yett in the body of itt (all the parts beeing howsoever fire) satt an aged Lady. (fol. 21 iv)

This recalls numerous chariot entries in the masques, and more especially 'The Masque of Queens', where

> that wch presented it selfe was an ougly *Hell*; w^{ch}, flaming beneath, smoaked vnto the top of the Roofe.[61]

Amphilanthus' masque also recalls 'Queens' with its display of anti-masque characters, who resemble the hags with their 'strange phantas-tique motions':

rather rusht in, then came in[,] in strange habitt, and farr stranger fashion, having such scarcetie of good civilitie as little, ore non[e,] was sane in them. (fol. 28 i)

The professional ease with which Wroth commands the basic elements of the masque – her description of mechanics, entries and antimasque – defines the feminine voice within the masque discourse.

The three masques in *Urania*, however, not only prove the perfect competence of Wroth in that genre but, through their contrasting qualities, offer a perception of specifically gendered responses to the courtly shows. Rodomandro's masque sets the tone for the denial of love and the triumph of the more public virtue, honour, which is emphasised by the hierarchical allocation of ruler and ruled subject positions to Honour and Cupid:

> Honor like the brightest morne
> Shines while clowded love is worne
>   And consum'd to dust,
> Like faire flowrs long beeing pull[e]d
> Dy, and wither if nott cull[e]d
>   slightest[,] like the wurst.
> But lett harts, and voices singe
> Honor's Cupid[']s just borne kinge. (fol. 8 i)

Thematically, the dominance of political values over personal desires conforms exactly to *Urania*'s central tenet, but it belongs more exclusively to a formal masque convention where its reasserted authority is both royal and male. The entertainment's reception, by Rodomandro's court and his visitors, is one of delight and admiration. The main protagonists learn nothing, and Wroth comments ironically on their thoughtless pursuit of pleasurable adventure:

> Then for this night every one went to ther lodgings to expect what the next morning would bring forthe. (fol. 8 ii)

The masque presented to Pamphilia offers a more covert and mutable response. The witch, Melissea, who creates the fantastical masque, belongs to the literary tradition of the 'loathly lady'. She is old yet 'sage' and 'grave'; she is also capable of advising the Queen, of weaving deceptive spells and of foretelling the future.[62] The enchantress enters in a 'strange darknes'; she creates the illusion that the Queen is in the court while, in reality, the two women are engaged in a 'privatt conference'; while to Rodomandro 'she closly gave a paper telling him his beeleefe in that would make him hapyest[,] next to that whether the purpose was intended' (fol. 22 iii). All Melissea's actions are veiled in this manner, and contrary to the sage's own words – 'the more obscured the less mist' – the glimpse proffered leaves us unsatisfied and desirous for more information. Indeed, Wroth would have been well aware of the ambiguity promulgated by the word 'mist'.

The lesson of the masque fittingly combines uncertainty with sadness, for it teaches that love is an illusion; the shepherd sings:

> Love butt a phantesie light, and vaine
> Fluttering butt in poorest braine[;]
> Birds in Chimnies make a thunder
> Putting silly soules in wounder,
> Soe doth this love, this all comaunder
> To a weake poore understander[.]
>
> Slight him, and hee'le your servant bee
> Adore him, you his slave must bee,
> Scorne him, O how hee will pray you,
> Please him, and hee'lle sure beetray you[.]
> Lett nott his faulshood bee esteemd
> Least your selfe bee disesteemed[.] (fol. 2 ii)

At the conclusion of the entertainment Wroth intrudes with an authorial confirmation of Melissea's tenet, which is then echoed by Pamphilia's response:

> The instabilitie of this world is such as nott many minutes can bee left free in certaintie to any[.] noe more could itt bee to this excelling lady, who now for this instant of little twilight content, must have present troubles againe, for business of what kinde soever can have noe better name, nor any fitter. (fol. 22 iii)

Obscurity, veilings, fantasy, inconstancy – all belong to the 'twilight content', things which are half seen, not fully understood and delightful, perhaps because of that insubstantial quality, yet at the same time illusory, passing and mutable.[63] Wroth's authorial second self, Lindamira, was caught at the same point of tension between a desire for stasis and the inevitability of flux; she remained in her 'gay' clothes, even though the night had passed and there was 'no appearance of what was'. Pamphilia's response to the masque, which acts as a fulcrum in her evaluation of her own role as a royal and gendered subject, sees her accepting the political necessity of an alliance with Rodomandro, instead of her personal and sexual desire for Amphilanthus. She accepts the transience of love and asserts her public role as a responsible monarch. For her the artificial delights of the court world are over, and political manoeuvring takes their place.

Not so for Amphilanthus. In an almost stereotypical assessment of the male subject, Wroth parallels Rodomandro's staid but stable offer of love with Amphilanthus' fickle but exciting desirability. He is presented, fittingly, with an antimasque of fools, apes and a shepherd, who offer poems to the Emperor and his royal companions.[64] The epistolary message promises hope in love, which Amphilanthus finds cheering:

> entertaining hope gave the Emperour[']s dispairing hart, a little comfort, like a glorious butt setting farewell of the sun. (fol. 28 ii)

Still, Wroth emphasises the insubstantial nature of the Emperor's constancy in love by comparing him to that symbol of mutability, the moon:

> w^t this twy-light of hope Amphilanthus was as much pleased for a while as the Moone is to play w^t her owne shadow in the water[.] butt soone she is weary and soone had hee new sentiments, that thes were butt moone shine thoughts, ore (as hee never so old bee w^t-out hope) the time was nott yett come; Thus they all retired till supper. (fol. 28 iii)

The motif of twilight is repeated both lexically and in the metaphor of the setting and rising sun, yet Amphilanthus' response is very different to that of Pamphilia. He sees the prospect of change as a continual promise of hope, and throughout the narrative he remains within the construction of a pleasant and optimistic assertion of self. His personal will and desire become paramount in his formulation as a masculine subject – hedonistic, self-centred and politically expedient.

In *Urania* the masque acts as a sign of personal pleasure and political success which is simultaneously compelling and mutable. The three characters to whom these entertainments are presented offer up gender-specific responses which are applicable to the Jacobean court as well as within the confines of the narrative. Rodomandro signifies the conventional ideology with a reassertion of masculinity, royalty and public show. There is no recognition of the possible tensions endemic in a masque performance. Amphilanthus suggests another dominant masculine response, but one which is located in pleasure rather than virtue. Nevertheless, his belief in his own unassailable noble and essentially masculine subject role makes change challenging, not threatening. Both men perceive the masque as an imaginative extension of their own unquestioned and unquestioning position. For them it acts, as Dollimore suggests, as 'a ritualized ideological legitimation of the court'. Pamphilia's response to her masque is different. In itself, the narrative focuses upon powerful women – the Queen, the sage enchantress and the seductive mermaid – but it also carries a weighty narrative purpose in that it changes the direction Pamphilia will take in her choice between personal and public identities, between love as desire and love as duty, and between Amphilanthus and Rodomandro. For women, then, the masque has a potent significance which allows them active and independent involvement in the court world. It opens up a valid political purpose, and *Urania*'s genre and authorship, as befits a *roman à clef*, conform to this juxtaposing of women and politics. Still, the masque is transient, like the female voice it empowers, and indeed when Pamphilia recognises its limitations she sadly accepts the renewed conformity of her gendered role and the twilight nature of a feminised masque discourse. Female involvement in the political world was as fragile as the masque form which conveyed it; and for women like Pamphilia – Wroth, Lucy Countess of Bedford and Queen Anne – it appeared to offer only loss and a renewed containment.

VI

The interpretation of the masque form which has come to be accepted over the last twenty years suggests that it reinforces the dominant hierarchy of the power it encodes: monarch over subject, King over Queen, parent over child, man over woman, and the conservation of order over the usurping forces of chaos.[65] Although it permits inversions of this authority – the allowed subversions of hags, blackened faces and gender conflations – each time the threat is circumscribed, allowing a triumphant re-emergence of the accepted ideologies. In order for this hypothesis to be sustained, however, a basic synchronic structure has to be projected, so that the masque becomes understandable only within the double-bind of thematic dialecticism and chronological cross-sectioning. Yet it is clear that the genre draws upon diachronic material, more evocative of myth, as well as other diverse cultural discourses such as carnival, mommerie, the grotesque and misrule. Rather than privileging a hierarchy of neatly alignable pairs, each mirroring the other, we are instead presented with a mass of conflicting asymmetrical lines of power. These forces may intersect, but they can hardly be said to determine each other's existence through a mutually closeting refraction.

It sheds further light on these matters to extend the argument for a feminised masque discourse by recalling one of the interpretations of 'The Queen's Masque' – a masque written by a Queen. As I suggested earlier, there was such a composition: 'Queen Henrietta's Masque' (1626).[66] Together with Henrietta's other involvements in court performances, this work elicited the by-now-familiar litany of praise/outrage. For Salvetti, a foreign ambassador, it was 'a beautiful pastoral of her own composition', while the Stuart nobleman Henry Manners wrote:

> I heare no much honor of the Queene's maske, for, if they were not all, soome were in men's apparell.[67]

Indeed, Henrietta's appearance in William Montagu's *The Shepherd's Paradise* (1633) provoked William Prynne's infamous attack against actresses:

> S. *Paul* prohibites women to speake publikely in the Church. . . . And dare then any Christian women be so more then whorishly impudent, as to act,

to speake publikely on a Stage (perchance in mans apparell), and cut haire, here proved sinfull and abominable) in the presence of sundry-men and women?[68]

Prynne was voicing the public's growing discontent with the monarchy and succeeding in relocating Henrietta's feminised masque discourse in an explosive political arena. Wroth's bleak intuitions of instability proved surprisingly prophetic, for the Stuart Queen's masques, ironically and unconsciously, became part of the twilight of the court's dominance.

By allowing our gaze to dwell, momentarily, beyond the perimeter of the essay – that is, the Jacobean court – it becomes possible to envision the feminised masque discourse in yet another fashion. In the 1630s it provided a persistent – although at times invisible – thread of subversive power, which was woven, together with the other potent forces for change, into the destructive web of revolution. None the less this must, for the time being, remain a shadowed glimpse. The explicit focus has been the multiple diagrammatical formulations – of contained subversion or triumphant misrule – in the masques of Queen Anne and Lady Mary Wroth. As either twentieth-century readers or earlier spectators, these diverse elements draw us in through their unceasing mutability and their evocation of twilight worlds. What Wroth offers us is not simply one gendered response, but several – a reaffirmation of order, a pleasure in novelty, the fear of change. The 'Queen' and her 'masque' manoeuvred in a constantly shifting field of play, waiting for that one moment of incandescent ignition when they met. Then, like the playgoer of today who peers in the gloom of the auditorium in order to see her or his watch, they focused upon that 'phantastique' gleam – not because they wished to pre-empt the conclusion, but because they could hardly bear the pleasure of the show to end.

NOTES

1. Carleton, 'The Masque of Blackness', in C.H. Herford, Percy and Evelyn Simpson, eds, *Ben Jonson* (Oxford: Clarendon Press, 1925–52), vol. X, p. 448. Further references to the 'Queen's masque' may be found in Herford and Simpson's notes to 'Blackness', where they comment – revealingly – of 'Beauty' that 'the fiction that the Queene was "authoress of the whole" masque was well kept up' (p. 457).
2. Jonson, vol. VII, p. 164–9.
3. Ibid., vol. X, p. 457.
4. Ibid., vol. VII, p. 168.
5. Foucault, *The Archaeology of Knowledge* (London: Tavistock, 1977), pp. 164–5.
6. Jonson, vol. VII, pp. 277–317.
7. Ibid., vol. VII, p. 303. For Lucy Countess of Bedford, see Pearl Hogrefe, *Tudor Women: Commoners and Queens* (Ames: Iowa State University Press,

1975), pp. 138–9; Barbara K. Lewalski, 'Lucy Countess of Bedford: Images of a Jacobean courtier and patroness', in Kevin Sharpe and Steven N. Zwicker, eds, *Politics of Discourse* (Berkeley: University of California Press, 1987), pp. 52–77; and J.H. Wiffen, *Historical Memoirs of the House of Russell* (London: Longman, 1833), vol. II, pp. 63–123. For Lady Anne Clifford, see V. Sackville-West, ed., *The Diary of the Lady Anne Clifford* (London: Heinemann, 1923) and Retha M. Warnicke, *Women of the English Renaissance and Reformation* (Westport, CT: Greenwood Press, 1983), p. 75. On Alice Countess of Derby, see William Rees-Mogg, 'A poor player, a proud patroness and a library in California', *The Independent*, 26 April 1988; and James Knowles, 'WS MS', *Times Literary Supplement*, 25 May 1988.

8. This argument is given ample coverage by Suzanne Gossett, ' "Man-maid, begone!": Women in masques', *English Literary Renaissance*, 18 (1988), pp. 96–113.

9. A more detailed discussion of bibliographical evidence may be found in Notes 38–9 and 66; an undisputed reference to Henrietta Maria's masque may be found in Alfred Harbage, *Cavalier Drama* (New York: MLA Publications, 1936), pp. 10–21.

10. Lady Mary Wroth, *The Countesse of Montgomery's Urania*, Part I (London: John Marriott and John Grismand, 1621) and Part II (Newberry M.S. fy1565 w95).

11. Gordon Kipling, *The Triumph of Honour* (Leiden: Leiden University Press, 1977).

12. Stephen Orgel, *The Jonsonian Masque* (New York: Columbia University Press, 1967), pp. 26–32; Sidney Anglo, *Spectacle, Pageantry, and Early Tudor Policy* (Oxford: Clarendon Press, 1969).

13. David M. Bergeron, 'Women as patrons of English Renaissance drama', in Guy Lytle and Stephen Orgel, eds, *Patronage in the Renaissance* (Princeton, NJ: Princeton University Press, 1981) pp. 274–90.

14. Orgel, *The Jonsonian Masque, passim;* Lindley, *The Court Masque* (Manchester: Manchester University Press, 1984), p. 13.

15. Enid Welsford, *The Court Masque* (Cambridge: Cambridge University Press, 1927), pp. 184–6.

16. Jonson, vol. VII, p. 282.

17. For example, Jonson's own masque 'Pleasure Reconciled to Virtue' (1618), ibid., vol. VII, pp. 473–91, and theorised by Philip Sidney in *A Defence of Poetry* (c. 1579–80) in Katherine Duncan-Jones and Jan Van Dorsten, eds, *Miscellaneous Prose of Sir Philip Sidney* (Oxford: Clarendon Press, 1973), p. 99.

18. Percy Simpson and C.F. Bell, eds, *Designs of Inigo Jones For Masques and Plays at Court* (Oxford: The University Press, 1924), Plate XLIII.

19. Jonson, vol. VII, p. 301.

20. Ibid., vol. VII, pp. 304–5.

21. Ibid., vol. VII, p. 305. For a discussion of James I's attitude to women, see Juliet Dusinberre, *Shakespeare and the Nature of Women* (London: Macmillan, 1975), p. 81; and Jonathan Goldberg, 'Fatherly authority: The politics of Stuart family images', in M. Ferguson, M. Quilligan and N. Vickers, eds, *Rewriting the Renaissance* (Chicago: University of Chicago Press, 1986), pp. 3–32.

22. Gossett, ' "Man-maid, begone!" ', p. 99.

23. Dollimore, *Radical Tragedy* (Sussex: Harvester Press, 1984), pp. 26–7.

24. Mikhail Bakhtin, *Rabelais and His World*, transl. Helene Iswolsky (Bloomington: Indiana University Press, 1984), p. 48.

25. It is significant that in his annotation – conducted not under the orders of the Queen, but rather at the instigation of Prince Henry – Jonson endows Zenobia and Hypsicratea with more traditional feminine qualities: Jonson, vol. VII, pp. 309, 311.

26. Ibid., vol.X, p. 499.

27. Francis Bacon, 'Of Masques and Triumphs', in Michael Kiernan, ed., *The Essayes or Counsels, Civill and Morall* (Oxford: Clarendon Press, 1985), pp. 117–18.

28. Quoted in Ann Jennalie Cook, *The Privileged Playgoers in Shakespeare's London, 1576–1642* (Princeton, NJ: Princeton University Press, 1981), p. 115. For a more complex treatment of the royal factions at the Jacobean court, see Leeds Barroll, 'A new history for Shakespeare and his time', *Shakespeare Quarterly*, **39** (1988), pp. 441–64.

29. Jonson, vol. X, pp. 448–9. For the general condemnation of women in court masques, see also Sir John Harington in H. Harington, ed., *Nugæ Antiquæ* (London: Vernor & Hood, Poultry and Cuthell & Martin, 1804), pp. 349–52.

30. Simpson and Bell, eds, *Designs by Inigo Jones*, Plate I.

31. Edward Hall, *Chronicle* (London: J. Johnson, 1809), p. 514. The *Chronicle* was certainly known at the time, since Shakespeare uses one of the masque sequences described by Hall as the source for a scene in *King Henry the Eighth* (1613), I. iv. 53–108, which corresponds to Hall, p. 719.

32. Welsford, *The Court Masque*, pp. 81–115.

33. Ibid., pp. 20, 30–41; Richard Huizinga, *Homo Ludens* (London: Routledge, 1949), pp. 13, 56–8.

34. Welsford, *The Court Masque*, pp. 19–22; Richard Bernheimer, *Wild Men in the Middle Ages* (Cambridge, MA: Harvard University Press, 1952), pp. 59–60, 80; Elliot Tokson, *The Popular Image of the Black Man in English Drama 1550–1688* (Boston, MA: G.K. Hall, 1982), pp. 54–5.

35. Welsford, *The Court Masque*, pp. 38–40; Harleian MS. 247.

36. Stephen Greenblatt, *Shakespearean Negotiations* (Berkeley: University of California Press, 1988), p. 52.

37. Jonson, vol. vii, p. 169.

38. Bakhtin, *Rabelais and His World*, p. 10.

39. Nancy Cotton, *Women Playwrights in England c. 1363–1750* (London: Associated University Presses, 1980), which lists women acting as well as writing; for Henrietta Maria, see p. 37. I am also indebted to Sophie Tomlinson, a doctoral student at Cambridge, who gave a paper on this topic at a conference on 'Feminism and New Historicism' at Cambridge in the summer of 1988. See also Antonia Fraser, *The Weaker Vessel* (London: Weidenfeld & Nicolson, 1984), pp. 418–39.

40. Shirley Ardener, *Defining Females, The Nature of Women in Society* (London: Croom Helm, 1978), p. 21.

41. See above, Note 13. The mutual benefits, to the patron and the author, of the patronage system, and the political implications of this relationship, is discussed in Robert C. Evans, *Ben Jonson and the Poetics of Patronage* (Lewisburg, PA: Bucknell University Press, 1989), pp. 31–88.

42. See above, Note 7.

43. Wiffen, *Historical Memoirs*, pp. 74–84.

44. Mary Sidney, Countess of Pembroke: *Antonie* (1590: a translation of Garnier) and *Thenot and Piers in Praise of Astraea* (1592) in Cotton, *Women Playwrights*, p. 15. Elizabeth Cary, Viscountess Falkland: *The Tragedie of Mariam* (London: Thomas Creede for Richard Hawkins, 1613); see also David Lunn,

Elizabeth Cary (Ilford: The Royal Stuart Society, 1977) and Cotton, *Women Playwrights*, p. 15. Margaret Cavendish: 'The Claspe', in *Poems and Fancies*, a facsimile of the 1653 edition (Yorkshire, Scholar Press, 1972), pp. 155–60.

45. Lady Mary Wroth (1587–*c.* 1651–3): the biographical information comes from the few available criticisms on Wroth: Hannah Witten, 'Lady Mary Wroth's *Urania*: The work and the tradition' (unpublished PhD thesis, at University of Auckland, December 1978); Mary Nelson Paulissen, ed., *The Love Sonnets of Lady Mary Wroth* (Salzburg: Salzburg Studies in English Literature, 1982); Josephine Roberts, ed., *The Poems of Lady Mary Wroth* (Baton Rouge: Louisiana State University Press, 1983); Elaine V. Beilin, *Redeeming Eve. Women Writers of the English Renaissance* (Princeton, NJ: Princeton University Press, 1987), pp. 208–43. For the most recent investigative material I am grateful to Josephine Roberts for conversations and preliminary notes – Roberts is, at present, editing *Urania* Part II – and to Mary Beth Rose, of the Newberry Library, for her generous assistance.

There are three probable pictures of Wroth, all at Penshurst. Two of them may be seen in reproduction: (1) *Barbara Gamage, Countess of Leicester, and her children* (1596) by Marcus Gheeraerts; and (2) *Mary Sidney, Lady Wroth* (*c.* 1620), attributed to John De Critz. Both are in Roy Strong, *The English Icon* (London: Routledge & Kegan Paul, 1969), Plates 254 and 263.

46. *Pamphilia and Amphilanthus* in Roberts, *The Poems of Lady Mary Wroth*. *Urania* Parts I and II, *Love's Victorie* (Huntington MS. HM 600 f5); an edited version of the play is now available: Michael Brennan, ed., *Lady Mary Wroth's Love's Victory, The Penshurst Manuscript* (London: The Roxburghe Club, 1989). Only 250 copies were made, and the cost is a somewhat prohibitive £160.

47. Norman McClure, ed., *The Letters of John Chamberlain* (Philadelphia: American Philosophical Society, 1939), p. 519, also Beilin, *Redeeming Eve*, p. 209.

48. Sidney, in Jean Robertson, ed., *The Old Arcadia* (Oxford: Clarendon Press, 1939), pp. 26–7. Spenser, in A.C. Hamilton, *The Faerie Queene* (London: Longman, 1977), Book III. Ariosto, in Barbara Reynolds, transl. and ed., *Orlando Furioso*, I, 68–70 (Harmondsworth: Penguin, 1975).

49. Beilin, *Redeeming Eve*, pp. 211, 217, 228.

50. Ann Barton, 'Harking back to Elizabeth: Ben Jonson and Caroline nostalgia', *English Literary History*, 48 (1981), p. 715.

51. Josephine Roberts, 'An unpublished literary quarrel concerning the suppression of Lady Mary Wroth's *Urania* (1621)', *Notes & Queries*, 222 (1977), pp. 532–5; Paul Salzman, 'Contemporary references in Mary Wroth's *Urania*', *Review of English Studies*, 29 (1978), pp. 178–81; Beilin, *Redeeming Eve*, p. 211.

52. John Barclay, *Argenis* (Oxford: John Lichfield, 1634); this later edition also contains the *clavis*.

53. The MS. poem is at the Hallward Library, the University of Nottingham (Cl. Lm. 85/3). I should like to acknowledge the University of Nottingham Library and Colonel P.T. Clifton, the owner of the MS., for allowing me to quote the first line of the poem.

54. *Letters of John Chamberlain*, p. 427.

55. Thomas Campion, in Walter R. Davis, ed., *The Works of Thomas Campion* (London: Faber & Faber, 1969), pp. 203–30. Wroth depicts the masque in *Urania* I, p. 438.

56. Wroth, *Urania* I, p. 439.

57. Ibid., pp. 242, 478.

58. Ibid., p. 242.
59. Wroth, *Urania* ii, fols 37–8, 48.
60. Fol. 7 iv; all ensuing references to *Urania* II will be made in the text.
61. Jonson, vol. VII, p. 282.
62. Loathly ladies are common in medieval romances, for example in Chaucer's 'Wife of Bath's Tale' in F.N. Robinson, ed., *The Works of Geoffrey Chaucer* (Oxford: Oxford University Press, 1957), pp. 84–8. The Renaissance romance epic adopted and remodelled the figures as enchantresses – for example, Melissa in Ariosto's *Orlando Furioso* and Urganda in Edwin B. Place and Herbert C. Behm, transl. and ed, *Amadis de Gaul* (Lexington: University Press of Kentucky, 1974).
63. The use of veiling was a common device in Renaissance texts – for example in Spenser's *The Faerie Queene*, IV. x. 41, and in Sidney's *A Defence of Poetry*, p. 103. The device is given a more contemporary treatment by Michael Murrin, *The Veil of Allegory* (Chicago: University of Chicago Press, 1969).
64. This recalls Sidney, 'Certain Sonnets 28', in William A. Ringler, ed., *The Poems of Sir Philip Sidney* (Oxford: Clarendon Press, 1962), pp. 157–8.
65. Ben Jonson's masque 'Prince Oberon' (Jonson, vol. VII, pp. 336–56), participates in the dissent between father and son as it was politically, and contentiously, enacted by James I and Prince Henry.
66. Alfred Harbage, *Cavalier Drama* (New York: MLA Publications, 1936), pp. 10–21; Cotton, *Women Playwrights*, p. 37; Mary Prior, *Women in English Society 1500–1800* (London: Methuen, 1985), p. 247; W.R Streitberger, ed., *Jacobean and Court Revels Accounts* (Oxford: Malone Society, 1986), pp. 119–22; Tomlinson: see Note 39.
67. The quotations from Salvetti and Manners may be found in Harbage, *Cavalier Drama*, p. 12.
68. Montagu, *The Shepherd's Paradise;* Prynne, *Histrio-Mastix* (London: Printed by E.A. and W.I. for Michael Sparke, 1633), in Table under '*Women-Actors*'.

6

'The Chief Knot of All the Discourse': The Maternal Subtext Tying Sidney's *Arcadia* to Shakespeare's *King Lear*

Barbara J. Bono

'Nothing will come of nothing', intones Lear near the beginning of Shakespeare's play (I. i. 90).[1] Echoing Aristotle's pronouncements on the eternality of prime matter, and therefore of the world, Lear hurls down a challenge to the Christian metaphysic of creation *ex nihilo* from love that emerges tentatively from the bleak landscape of this resolutely pre-Christian drama.[2] 'Nothing will come of nothing': Lear's warning and Aristotle's dictum may also drive us back to question anew the sources of *Lear*. How have they produced it?

One traditionally accepted source is Sir Philip Sidney's heroic prose romance the *Arcadia*, where the piteous tale of the King of Paphlagonia's blinding and deposition by his bastard son Plexirtus and preservation by his legitimate son Leonatus directly influenced Shakespeare's subplot of Gloucester and his two sons Edmund and Edgar. However, it will be the burden of this essay to argue that this source relationship runs much more pervasively and deeply between the two texts. The story of the King of Paphlagonia depends upon an indissoluble narrative and sexual 'knot' or *'aporia'* that hopelessly complicates the supposedly epic teleology of Sidney's two young heroes' Asian adventures.[3] As such, it reaches out to involve other knots or *aporiae* within Sidney's text, and with them weaves a matrix of influence, a shared maternal subtext, tying together the texts of the *Arcadia* and *King Lear*. This maternal subtext expresses for Sidney and Shakespeare a masculinist anxiety about the rival reproductive power of women, inextricable from the social, political and metaphysical uncertainties of their time. Ultimately, it also expresses an enduring debate about the place of woman within metaphysical discourses of presence.

Is woman nothing? The dominant Western discourses of gender reflect the dominant Western discourses of metaphysics.[4] The pressure of binary

habits of thinking drives a masculinist metaphysics of presence to pre-
sume a negative definition of woman: she is secondary in creation – a
derivative 'woman' to his 'man' – deficient in vital heat, a spiritual principle, educational promise, formal language, a penis.[5] Yet what if these
discourses, under pressure of changing material conditions like those of
pre-capitalist early modern England, were themselves revealed to be de-
fensive responses to a perception of women's primary material role in
reproduction?[6] Then the possibility of bastard hybridisation threatens all
order. Then women's supposed 'nothing' or 'lack' or 'hole' threatens to
become her terrifying presence, an engulfing 'whole' from which the
masculinist discourse of presence cannot extricate itself.

As Coppélia Kahn's earlier book *Man's Estate: Masculine Identity in
Shakespeare* powerfully argues, Shakespeare's works enact a historically
inscribed drama of the various ages of man.[7] However, as her more recent
work, drawing on a wider range of feminist and psychoanalytic theory,
suggests, this drama of presence is enacted over a repressed fear of feminine reproductive power – what she calls, following Madelon Gohlke,
'maternal subtexts in patriarchal literature'.[8] Kahn believes these subtexts
to be 'projections' of a 'universe of masculinist assumptions' because she
understands that much of today's feminist movement wishes to free itself
from the binary essentialist model of gender that it implies, where feminine power would be identified solely with maternal reproductive function – indeed, would become but a materialist inversion of masculinist
ideology. She herself clearly favours object-relations analyses like those of
Nancy Chodorow which, while arguing the centrality of mother-figures
in the identity formation of both men and women, vary the strength and
designation of that role to imply the complexly mediated and constructed
nature of gender identity amid shifting historical and material conditions.[9] In another place I use Kahn and Chodorow extensively to argue
how Shakespeare, seeking in his romantic comedies to mutate the conventions of courtly love into those of companionate marriage, follows the
logic of role-playing through its implications for gender, revealing a consciousness of gender construction which can then be appropriated for
modern feminist ends; even in these plays, however, the goal of gender
experimentation and mutation of erotic conventions remains marriage
and reproduction, and even the most playful romantic comedies are
haunted by a fear of cuckoldry that becomes, in domestic tragedies like
Othello, the wellspring of tragic action.[10]

All Shakespeare's late Elizabethan/early Jacobean tragedies would
work well for Kahn's argument: Oedipal analysis in *Hamlet* can be
pressed back to pre-Oedipal disgust; Macbeth defines his tragic action
against his wife's urgings, and she now has no children while he can be
defeated only by someone not of woman born; Othello laments his wife's

supposed infidelity in terms that imagine her the mother of his children, the source of his serial immortality: 'The fountain from the which my current runs/ Or else dries up' (IV. ii. 58–9). However, Kahn choses *Lear* as her proof text precisely because, despite the absence of a specific mother-figure, the image of *the* Mother rises up like a dream to haunt Lear's language and action:

> O, how this mother swells up toward my heart!
> Hysterica passio, down, thou climbing sorrow,
> Thy element's below. (II. iv. 55–7)

Her analysis explores the metaphorical connections between Lear's ambivalent desire to retain control over the forms of majesty, even while crawling 'Unburthened . . . toward death' (I. i. 41) and resting on Cordelia's 'kind nursery' (I. i. 124), and the dependent child's attempts to assert its identity apart from the Mother. Kahn's analysis could also easily be extended to the play's ambivalent attitude towards a nature typified as female, which Edmund invokes in support of his bastardy ('Thou, Nature, art my goddess . . .' [I. ii. 1–22]) and which Lear initially defies (III. 1. 4–11) and which later partially heals him (IV. iv. 15–20).

In this essay I have tried to trace the presence of just such a maternal subtext in Sidney's *Arcadia* as that text's major influence on *King Lear*. At the same time, it is an influence with a profound difference. While Sidney, from the perspective of his oppositional relationship with Queen Elizabeth, cannot successfully dissociate his heroes and heroines from the negative influence of his bad mother-figures, the Jacobean Shakespeare, from a perspective after her death, tries, while reiterating the negative image of the Mother even more forcefully, also to imagine a positive one. Here, I think, object-relations theorists like Chodorow can help us to understand theoretically how this might be possible by providing us with both a positive role for the body within its representations and a revised view of woman not as 'nothing', but as the very principle of relation or mediation. The child begins as coextensive with its mother, and only gradually and partially separates him/herself from her and her representatives. In the process mothers threaten to be reduced to mere objects or bodies, the primary instance of the famous birth of language and culture *away from* woman. The child who genders himself, or is gendered, as different from the Mother – as male – does so through a more radical either/or logic, while the girl child retains the both/and position of simultaneous continuity with the Mother in gender, but differentiation from the Mother in individuality. In both cases, however, continuity in the body is never entirely lost, and the strength and intensity of these processes of differentiation and identification remain cultural variables.

The memory of the Mother, then, is something more than merely a masculinist projection – it is the very condition of our perception of materiality, which is re-encountered in particularly powerful ways at moments of bodily pleasure and stress; at the same time, it is something quite different from those particular subjectivities, those mothers, who created it, and who thus become the condition of our ability to relate critically to others as individuals. The very bodily consciousness that Sidney strains against in the *Arcadia*, Shakespeare, writing from the imagined standpoint of extreme old age, is forced to embrace in *Lear*; at the same time this embrace of creaturality becomes the condition for nascent new systems of social relationship in that play.

Recent historical scholarship has suggested that Sidney's texts are, in large part, the complex writing-out of his political frustrations in Elizabeth's court, the expression of a rebellious desire only partially rectified by the sympathetic patronage of his virtuous sister.[11] In the incomplete revised *New Arcadia* one of his new characters, Amphialus, begins to make that rebellious political desire strongly manifest, kidnapping his resistant beloved, Philoclea, from her pastoral retreat, voicing the Huguenot doctrine of subaltern magistracy which Sidney had absorbed from his continental advisers, and reluctantly serving as the agent of his mother Cecropia's overt political ambitions.[12] At the point where the revision breaks off, with Cecropia dead and Amphialus a near-suicide for love (taking Philoclea's knives, 'he stabbed himself into divers places of his breast and throat, until those wounds, with the old, freshly bleeding, brought him to the senseless gate of death' [III. 24. 575]), the tragic secondary character Queen Helen intervenes to take him away to 'the excellentest surgeon then known' (III. 25. 576).[13] Roy Strong suggestively identifies this Helen with Queen Elizabeth: however, Amphialus has scorned her all along, and there is no indication, in the incomplete text, that her healing mission will be successful.[14] Like a dimmer and more poignant version of Spenser's most attenuated mirroring of Elizabeth – Arthur's dream-quest for Gloriana – the Amphialus/Helen relationship remains forever incomplete and unsatisfied; Sidney, of course, himself died young at Zutphen, and Elizabeth did not attend his funeral.[15]

The Jacobean *Lear*, on the other hand, is a play *in extremis,* beginning as an antigenesis, ending on a note of apocalypse: Kent: 'Is this the promised end?' Edgar: 'Or image of that horror?' (v. iii. 265–6). Over eighty years old and without male heirs, Lear cannot but make his daughters his mothers, dividing his kingdom and peregrinating between them in search of some new standard of value other than the authoritarian exercise of power or its demonic opposite, extreme quantification and commodification:

LEAR: Thy fifty yet doth double five-and-twenty,
                 And thou art twice her love.

GONERIL:	Hear me, my lord.
	What need you five-and-twenty? ten? or five? . . .
REGAN:	What need one?
LEAR:	O reason not the need! (II. iv. 256–8; 260–61)

When Lear breaks down under the pressures of age, suffering and physical debility, he both acknowledges the Mother in himself and begins to re-
form the possibility of relationship:

> My wits begin to turn.
> Come on, my boy. How dost, my boy? Art cold?
> I am cold myself. (III. ii. 67–9)

The fullest analysis of *Lear* would discuss how, from a turn-of-the-
century apocalyptic anxiety exacerbated by the death of the old queen,
the *semina rerum* of things are indeed broken open so that new languages
emerge, concocted on the one hand from the appetitive rationalism of
Goneril, Regan and Edmund, and on the other from the stoic service of
Kent/Caius, the gnomic wisdom of the fool, the unaccommodated need
of Edgar as bedlam beggar, and the largely silent ministrations of Cordelia. They are, as Stephen Greenblatt notes, languages stripped of their
transcendent illusions, emptied out of their literal significance like those
many letters in the play that persistently go astray: at their worst the
language of ruthless objectification and exploitation; and at their best an
intersubjective fantasy of mutual care, a sign of the passage of the theatre,
after the largely inchoate political activism of its Elizabethan heyday, into
what Stephen Orgel has evocatively called the Jacobean 'illusion of
power'.[16] What I can hope to do in this essay is follow one literary thread
into this crisis of meaning.

The story of the King of Paphlagonia unfolds within a wintry landscape
anticipatory of the harsh heath in *Lear*, a place where supposedly lawful
authority is stripped and exposed, and bastardy thrives: ' "It was in the
kingdom of Galatia, the season being, as in the depth of winter, very cold
and as then suddenly grown to so extreme and foul a storm that never any
winter, I think, brought forth a fouler child" ' (II. 10. 275). There Sidney's
heroes, the princes Pyrocles and Musidorus, overhear a ' "disputation" '
between an ' "aged man and a young, scarcely come to the age of a man,
both poorly arrayed, extremely weather-beaten; the old man blind, and
the young man leading him" ' (II. 10. 275). The old man and the young
debate whether in their suffering they have indeed reached the depths of
human experience: the old man laments ' " 'I cannot fall worse than I
am'," ' while the young man hopefully replies, ' " 'While I have power

to do you service, I am not wholly miserable' " ' (II. 10. 276). In Shakespeare's play this hopeful colloquy will be painfully inverted by casting Edgar as the half-mad poor Tom, who optimistically declares: 'The worst returns to laughter' (IV. i. 6), only to be confronted immediately by the gruesome spectacle of his blinded father, and thus forced to confess 'the worst is not/ So long as we can say, "This is the worst" ' (IV. i. 27–8). In Sidney's heroic romance Leonatus narrates how he prevented his father's suicide attempt – ' " 'even now he would have had me to have led him to the top of this rock, thence to cast himself headlong to death' " ' (II. 10. 276) – while in Shakespeare's play Edgar, in the guise of poor Tom, will undertake the far more radical therapy of actually helping Gloucester to act out his suicide attempt, and thus experience a seemingly miraculous salvation from despair (IV. vi). None the less, although Sidney's treatment of the story is seemingly far more rational and discursively controlled – the story serves as an emblem or Sidneian 'speaking picture' of ' " 'what dutiful affection is engraffed in a son's heart' " ' (II. 10. 277) and thus supposedly as a further incitement to Pyrocles' and Musidorus' active virtue[17] – the distressed voice of the father breaks in importunately: ' " 'Ah, my son,' " said he, ' "how evil an historian are you that leave out the chief knot of all the discourse, my wickedness, my wickedness!' " ' (II. 10. 277).

What is this 'knot', this wickedly irrational centre or source of the King's dilemma? Only this:

> ' "that having had in lawful marriage, of a mother fit to bear royal children, this son . . . I was carried by a bastard son of mine (if at least I be bound to believe the words of that base woman my concubine, his mother) first to mislike, then to hate, lastly to destroy, or to do my best to destroy this son . . . undeserving destruction".' (II. 10. 277)

This 'knot', then, bound up with his illicit union to a potentially duplicitous woman, metaphorically ties Plexirtus, its production, back to the threatening winter landscape: ' "so extreme and foul a storm that never any winter, I think, brought forth a fouler child" ' (II. 10. 275). Just so does Shakespeare's Edmund –

> Who, in the lusty stealth of nature, take[s]
> More composition and fierce quality
> Than doth, within a dull, stale, tired bed,
> Go to th'creating a whole tribe of fops
> Got 'tween asleep and wake (I. ii. 11–15)

– fervently invoke his goddess Nature to 'stand up for bastards' (I. ii. 22).

The specific threat of the bastard Plexirtus and the underlying threat of the unlawfully sexual woman, with her metaphorical extension as untamed Nature, consistently disrupt the heroic pattern of the *New*

Arcadia. Sidney's original *Old Arcadia* had been a wry Terentian comedy
on the follies of love in which he deliberately eschewed any flashback
account of the princes' Asian adventures as 'work for a higher style than
mine'.[18] But in the extensive revision that became the incomplete *New
Arcadia*, he appears in Book II to have undertaken just such an epic
elaboration of the heroes' earlier activity, precisely in order to sustain his
developing distinction between their potentially elevating love for the
princesses Pamela and Philoclea and his new character Amphialus' degenerative decline. Thus, for example, Sidney prominently prefaces his account of the princes' meeting with the King of Paphlagonia with an
encomium to their superior position in the Western epic line of heroes –
' "they determined in unknown order to see more of the world . . .
thinking it not so worthy to be brought to heroical effects by fortune or
necessity, like Ulysses or Aeneas, as by one's own choice and working" '
(II. 9. 275) – and he has Pyrocles recount the triumphant conclusion of
their Asian adventures, omitting ' "many other excessive honours which
would not suffer the measure of this short leisure to describe unto you" '
(II. 23. 370).

However, this triumphant account is itself qualified from without and
undermined from within by a cumulative metaphorical portrait of male
dependence on unchecked appetitive female power. Bracketing the narrative of their Asian adventures, the princes are twice forced by crises at sea
– the first caused by a treacherous Nature (II. 7. 260–62), the second by
the bastard Plexirtus acting in collusion with the powerful sexual tempt-
ress Artaxia (II. 24. 371–75) – to deviate from their reunion with their
father/uncle Euarchus, the ultimate source of rational patriarchal authority in the work.

The first of these is described, fittingly enough for young aristocrats
embarking upon their first military and diplomatic mission, chiefly
through images of political treachery: ' "they . . . were received thereon
with so smooth and smiling a face as if Neptune had then learned falsely
to fawn on princes" '; ' "For forthwith the winds began to speak louder
and, as in a tumultuous kingdom, to think themselves fittest instruments
of commandment" '; ' "so were they carried by the tyranny of the wind
and the treason of the sea all that night" ' (II. 7. 260–62). However, the
precise turn in the account from the sea's seeming acquiescence to male
heroic control to its treachery is tellingly conveyed through a pair of
similes that anticipate the King of Paphlagonia's rueful movement from
' " 'a mother fit to bear royal children' " ' to betrayal by ' " 'that base
woman my concubine' " '. At the climax of his narrative Musidorus
apostrophises:

> 'the admirable power and noble effects of love, whereby the seeming insen-
> sible lodestone, with a secret beauty (holding the spirit of iron in it) can

draw that hard-hearted thing unto it and, like a virtuous mistress, not only make it bow itself, but with it make it aspire to so high a love as of the heavenly poles, and thereby to bring forth the noblest deeds that the children of the earth can boast of. And so the princes delighting their conceits with confirming their knowledge, seeing wherein the sea-discipline differed from land-service, they had for a day and almost a whole night as pleasing entertainment as the falsest heart could give to him he means worst to'. (II. 7. 260–61).

The lodestone, or magnet, holding ' "the spirit of iron in it" ' (as the female body holds the male seminal spirit?), orientates the iron lovingly, as ' "a virtuous mistress" ' does a man, to the most heroic deeds. But what if, as the final sentence seems to query – continuing the moralising analogy between the natural and the human realms – that ' "virtuous mistress" ' fails, or is replaced or engulfed, as the King of Paphlagonia's lawful issue was by the bastard son of ' " 'that base woman my concubine' " ', by the treacherous element – here the sea – that lies beneath?

Sidney's summarising description of the sea argues that political institutions are fragile constructs upon a monstrous motion where all distinctions threaten to be lost:

> 'Certainly there is no danger carries with it more horror than that which grows in those floating kingdoms. For that dwelling place is unnatural to mankind; and then the terribleness of the continual motion, the desolation of the far-being from comfort, the eye and the ear having ugly images before it, doth still vex the mind, even when it is best armed against it'. (II. 7. 262)

This description, which in its deliberately vague and terrifying openness could serve equally well as a description of the heath in *King Lear*, or of Lear's appalled vision of women's 'riotous appetite . . . Beneath' (IV. vi. 118–131), or of Albany's dismayed plea to Goneril for kindness, lest 'Humanity . . . perforce prey on itself/ Like monsters of the deep' (IV. ii. 50–51), anticipates the catastrophic ending of the Asian adventures, when Plexirtus' and Artaxia's treachery causes the men aboard the young heroes' ship to slay each other ' "like the children of Cadmus" ' and to conflate the perils of fire and water into a near-universal death (II. 24. 374). It is from this violent confusion of meaning and emotion that Pyrocles is in effect reborn, shipwrecked on the shores of Laconia, to begin his rebellious amorous assault upon Philoclea's virtue.

Meanwhile, within the account of the Asian adventures themselves, the authority of what the heroes manage to accomplish is undermined by the emotional intransigence of the problems they encounter. They descend from their successful political solutions of the problems of Phrygia and Pontus to the intractableness of the King of Paphlagonia's wicked 'knot' and to the miserable failure of Pyrocles' attempted rescue of Dido. The latter episode adds an intertextual dimension to the downward spiral of political action frustrated by supposedly base desire, since instead of this

Dido functioning as a tragic spur to the definition of a new epic tradition, as Virgil's Dido and her literary successors have often done, she dies meaninglessly, a pawn of her ignoble lover and her miserly father. The episode is a bitterly satiric version of Spenser's wonderful burlesque of the Trojan epic materials at the house of Malbecco in *Faerie Queene* III. ix–x, totally unrelieved by anything like Britomart's transforming romantic heroic perspective there.[19]

The account of the Asian adventures really ends with the unresolved complaint of Plangus (II. 29), like Amphialus another problematically heightened Oedipal mirror-image of the young princes. He, in his tragic lifetime, has become sexually involved with a lower-class older woman, Andromana, who even once she has become his stepmother still tries to seduce him; nearly murders his father the king; and has been unable to rescue his passively virtuous beloved, Erona, from her bondage to the memory of an unworthy husband and his vicious beloved, Artaxia. Plangus tells his tale to Basilius, King of Arcadia, who is himself dotingly in love with Pyrocles disguised as Zelmane, a supposed woman who is not his wife; Basilius records it but will do nothing actively to help him. Plangus intends to appeal to Euarchus for aid, but there is no sign in the incomplete revised *New Arcadia* that Euarchus (whose judicial presence also proves inadequate to resolve the ending of the *Old Arcadia*) will be able to help him either. This entanglement of a patriarchal line of father and son and the good woman who might redeem it in the obsessive lusts and plotting of the bad women Andromana and Artaxia hardly forms a promising re-entry into the debate about the potential morally elevating effects of loving virtuous women that forms the heart of the *New Arcadia*.

In order to move from his stance of judicial comic detachment from love in the *Old Arcadia* to his stance of romantic involvement with and heroic elevation of love in the *New Arcadia*, Sidney is at great pains to try to establish both the virtue of the heroines in the *New Arcadia* and their potentially elevating effect on Pyrocles and Musidorus. Thus, for example, in the *New Arcadia* he takes care to add to his preliminary descriptions of Philoclea precisely those neo-Platonic tropes of hyperbole that in theory make her beautiful body a means to virtue, and he heightens Pamela's majesty.[20] Meanwhile he carefully transposes the most overt signs of illicit desire in the young men to the early stages of their love, and – if we are to believe the editorial policy of his sister – himself wished the rest – the scenes of Pyrocles' consummation of his love affair with Philoclea and Musidorus' attempted rape of Pamela – bowdlerised from the revised text.[21] Both heroes and heroines are chastened by their heroic resistance during the long captivity to Cecropia and Amphialus, the mother–son pair who suddenly appear in the *New Arcadia* to absorb most of the negative potentialities of love that were broached in the *Old Arcadia*.

None the less, the clew of these negative potentialities of love remains visible even in the language and actions of Sidney's heroines in the *New Arcadia*. Following it will gradually lead us into those other 'knots', those other *'aporiae'*, in Sidney's text, and to their further entanglement with similar moments in Shakespeare's play, when the patriarchal order is stripped to reveal its dangerous dependence on a hitherto unspoken feminine maternal power. In both the *Old Arcadia* and the *New Arcadia*, Philoclea's body remains a dangerous 'ground' on which male desire seeks to inscribe itself, for instead of being merely passive matter, an innocent *tabula rasa* upon which an ideal image can be constructed, it may be motivated by its own more unstable desires. At the heart of Sidney's characterisation of Philoclea lies a subtle portrayal of the genesis of feminine desire and the dangerous extent of masculine investment in it that exposes a maternal reproductive power challenging masculine authority and redefining textual composition. This maternal subtext – recognised with trepidation by Philoclea, and with horror by her mother Gynecia, but embraced with enthusiasm by Amphialus' mother Cecropia – threatens to collapse precisely those distinctions between virtuous and vicious women upon which Sidney stakes the value of his work, and thus to undermine his control of it.

The episode (II. 4. 237–44) in which Sidney's narrator feels impelled to acknowledge the birth and outworkings of desire in Philoclea is fascinating for the subtle tension it creates between an attempted male projection of a nascent female subjectivity consonant with heterosexual desire, and its implied revelation of a maternal subtext underlying male desire. The first half is an allegorical and psychological portrait of Philoclea's movement from innocence to an aroused heterosexuality, similar in many ways to Spenser's dramatisation of Britomart's development, or Shakespeare's of Olivia's, or Milton's of Eve's. Evoking the setting of a full moon eventually clouded to suggest the dangerous passage from a strict Diana-like virginity to an active female sexuality, Sidney's narrator first recalls the stages of Philoclea's falling in love with Pyrocles disguised as Zelmane.

In the beginning, Sidney's narrator tells us:

> The sweet minded Philoclea was in their degree of well-doing to whom the not knowing of evil serveth for a ground of virtue, and hold their inward powers . . . with an unspotted simplicity . . . whose eyes and senses had received nothing but according as the natural course of each thing required, whose tender youth had obediently lived under her parents' behests, without framing out of her own will the forechoosing of any thing. (II. 4. 237–8)

She was, then – supposedly – an absolutely innocent medium, apprehending everything transparently in its 'natural' state, and, if necessary, further safeguarded by the strict control of her parents' authority. However,

Zelmane's advent gives her an admired mirroring subjectivity in which to discover and on which to exercise desire.

Like the primary mother–child dyad of psychoanalysis, Pyrocles/ Zelmane's pre-existing desire breeds desire in Philoclea, so that after a time 'her mind . . . would receive no message from her senses without that affection were the interpreter' (II. 4. 238). This revolutionary shift from a supposedly objectively guaranteed reality to an intersubjective apprehension motivated by desire encapsulates much of the metaphysical and epistemological crisis of this period and many continued theoretical debates of our own.[22] In place of a clear nature or a secure authority we now have imitative gestures destabilised by desire into a series of sliding signifiers. Philoclea begins by returning Zelmane's gazes, sighs and gestures,

> conforming herself to that which she did like, and not only wishing to be herself such another in all things, but to ground an imitation upon so much an esteemed authority; so that the next degree was to mark all Zelmane's doings, speeches, and fashions, and to take them into herself as a pattern of worthy proceeding. (II. 4. 238)

However, she soon goes beyond this mere imitation to absorbing the desirous motive behind these signs: 'ere she were aware, she accepted not only the badge but the service, not only the sign but the passion signified' (II. 4. 239).

Philoclea then exercises this desire upon greater and greater differentiation in the service of creating a stronger and stronger fantasy. Thus Sidney's narrator depicts her as moving from warm homosocial to heated heterosexual imaginings:

> First she would wish that they two might live all their lives together, like two of Diana's nymphs. . . . Then would she wish that she were her sister. . . . Then grown bolder, she would wish either herself or Zelmane a man, that there might succeed a blessed marriage betwixt them. (II. 4. 239)

Although the immediate result is her extreme perplexity and frustration, these romance tactics of dilation and delay seem ultimately designed to arouse our desire for her eventual marriage to Pyrocles, for all along we have known that 'she' is a man.

However, I want to suggest that the arousal of this desire in Philoclea also represents something subtly threatening to Sidney's patriarchal text. To begin with, it substitutes pre-linguistic desire for logocentric authority. In addition, desire is depicted as having its genesis in a supposedly female–female relationship which I have already suggested, is like the mother–child dyad of psychoanalysis, for Philoclea does not know that 'Zelmane' is in fact a man. The desire that drives the differentiating process is based, then, on a presumption of underlying intersubjective unity prior to patriarchal control. Finally, aroused female desire takes its new authority from the mother herself, for when Philoclea cannot imagine

115

how she can make her desire conform to any acceptable reality, she takes a kind of dismayed comfort from the fact that her mother, the aptly named Gynecia, seems also to love Zelmane: 'her own proof taught her to know her mother's mind, which (as no error gives so strong assault as that which comes armed in the authority of a parent) so greatly fortified her desires to see that her mother had the like desires' (II. 4. 240).[23]

In a sense, then, the movement of this central episode might be summarised as that from the clarity of nature and the assumed authority of the parents to the discovery of the maternal feminine origin of desire in general and, with it, of the signifying process. Sidney's narrator seems to recognise as much when he introduces this episode with the extraordinary interjection 'And alas, sweet Philoclea, how hath my pen till now forgot thy passions, since to thy memory principally all this long matter is intended' (II. 4. 237). In the *Old Arcadia* the narrator had frequently spoken in his own person as a way of moralistically framing the comic action; in the *New Arcadia* this strategy is almost completely abandoned as we are invited either to form our own judgements of the narrative as a whole or to involve ourselves sympathetically in the heroes' narratives. Here, however, this interjection suggests the narrator's dependence on an imagined feminine point of view: he must not forget Philoclea's 'passions', since this matter is 'intended' principally to her memory – she is its principal source and inspiration.

In much the same way Sidney's dedicatory epistle to his sister, the Countess of Pembroke, had described her desire as the source of this entire 'idle' and 'trifl[ing]' work, and himself as the dangerously desirous and effeminate medium of it. Thus 'you desired me to do it, and your desire to my heart is an absolute commandment. Now it is done only for you, only to you' – and Sidney figures himself not only as its ashamed father, but also as its monstrously fanciful mother:

> In sum, a young head, not so well stayed as I would it were (and shall be when God will) having many many fancies begotten in it, if it had not been in some way delivered, would have grown a monster; and more sorry might I be that they came in than that they gat out. (p. 57)

Rather than the more typical masculine appropriation and sublimation of the female reproductive function to arts and letters – as, for example, with the emergence of Shakespeare's sonneteer's claim for the supremacy of art over time out of the so-called 'breed sequence'[24] – we have here a virtual engulfment of the supposed masculine intellective functions by monstrous and undifferentiating female reproductive ability, as the ratiocinative 'head' becomes the deflated male sexual organ (a 'head, not so well stayed') as well as the fanciful female womb.

The only safeguard against this metaphorical slide, apart from Sidney's wistful invocation of God as remote transcendental signifier, is the virtue of his sister at the source of the work and her discretion in disseminating it, for Sidney seems to have intended it for a discerning coterie audience, largely composed of women: 'yourself or . . . such friends who will weigh errors in the balance of goodwill' (p. 57).[25] And indeed, Sidney's sister seems to have taken this responsibility very seriously. Her 1593 publication, in the wake of Sidney's friend Fulke Greville's unauthorised 1590 edition of the *New Arcadia*, of a bowdlerized 'complete' *Arcadia* made up of the incomplete revised *New Arcadia* with the ending from the *Old Arcadia* awkwardly tacked on, may be read as an attempt to contain the explosive female sexual energies released in the revised and incomplete *New Arcadia*.[26]

For within the text, Philoclea's desire, in which both Pyrocles and the narrator are so deeply invested as to fear effemination, represents the need for continual revision of the text as well as the supposed source of this linguistic instability in the female body. In the passage that follows the description of the growth of desire in Philoclea, the narrator has her come upon a white marble stone, symbolic of her former innocence, upon which she herself had written a poem vowing her eternal chastity. Now the light of the inconstant moon is insufficient for reading, and the poem is blotted and defaced. To it Philoclea seeks to append a retraction lamenting her inconstancy, 'But seeing she could not see means to join as then this recantation to the former vow, laying all her fair length under one of the trees, for a while she did nothing but turn up and down' (II. 4. 242). Her restless body now substitutes for the still marble stone as the site of writing, ensuring its discontinuities and incompleteness. Her language of aroused desire – ' "How hath the sight of this strange guest invaded my soul?" ' (II. 4. 242) – now echoes precisely that of her mother Gynecia, which in turn echoes that of Virgil's Dido, threatening epic achievement and continuity.[27] Questioning heaven, she places herself in a negative genealogy – or more precisely, a gynaecology – of feminine desire, as she mourns that ' "sin must be the mother and shame the daughter of my affection" ' (II. 4. 243) and rationalises her passion as like that of her mother. The exploration of Philoclea's desires has exposed a still more dangerous source of male dependence – the sexual mother, the reproductive rival to masculine systems of meaning.

The investment of both Sidney's narrator and his chief hero, Pyrocles, in Philoclea's desires, and her authorisation of those desires through those of her mother, ultimately expose, then, the possibility that the entire text of the *Arcadia* is unstably built upon a subtext of maternal power. Already in the *Old Arcadia* the words, gestures, character and action of Gynecia forcefully, if shamefacedly, articulate this power, and by their contiguity with other words, gestures, characters and actions communicate their disruptive influence throughout the text. Thus while they surface only intermittently, they operate in a pervasively subliminal fashion to constitute a gynaecology of this text, challenging patriarchal power, necessitating further and further revision, and establishing a link between Philoclea's subtly disturbing aroused desire and the systematic attack upon patriarchy of one of Sidney's major additions in the *New Arcadia*, Amphialus' mother Cecropia.

An examination of Philoclea's desires has led us back to an examination of those of her mother, Gynecia. Always forcefully bodily in expression, Gynecia's desires are initially described as 'working' towards some vaguely tragic end potentially disruptive of the tenor of the work as a whole. Thus she is ' "a woman of great wit, and in truth of more princely virtues than her husband; of most unspotted chastity, but of so working a mind and so vehement spirits as a man may say it was happy she took a good course, for otherwise it would have been terrible" ' (I. 3. 76), and 'she would stir up terrible tragedies rather than fail of her intent' (II. 1. 218). What are these desires, how do they work, and to what potentially 'terrible' end or intent?

Put most simply, she too is in love with Pyrocles/Zelmane. But unlike her daughter, whose initial homoerotic attraction to Zelmane supposedly offers the possibility of further and further imaginative differentiation into a potentially lawful heterosexual union, Gynecia immediately recognises that Zelmane is a young man, and that her passion for him is therefore vertiginously adulterous and even Oedipal. In so far as she interposes herself between Pyrocles and Philoclea, as she literally does near the end of Book I, she threatens to obscure potentially lawful marriage with adulterous desire; in so far as she shares her passion with Pyrocles, as she does at several degenerative moments in the text, she threatens to implicate his rebellious desires in her own. In her most frenzied ravings and disturbed dreams, the projection of these desires becomes the wish to kill both her daughter and her husband, the King. Her quasi-incestuous passion for this younger man communicates itself to the text as a whole, obscuring its distinctions and giving birth in the process of revision to a more explicitly rebellious mother-and-son pair, Cecropia and Amphialus.

For all her agonised moral compunctions (for Sidney will ultimately seek to recuperate her wifely virtue), his dominant presentation of her and her self-consciousness is as a negative impeding bodily presence, a knot beyond which his narrative cannot easily go. In that sense she is the more pervasive and powerful expression in this text of the knot of feminine reproductive power underlying the threat of bastardy which we have already encountered in our analysis of the episodic elaborations of Book II. This complication of Sidney's text begins with the intricate comparisons and interpositions of the images of Gynecia and Philoclea in

Book I. There, at first, the painting of Philoclea is declared to surpass and dim her mother's portrait:

> but in none of them all beauty seemed to speak so much as in a large table which contained a comely old man, with a lady of middle-age but of excellent beauty; and more excellent would have been deemed, but that there stood between them a young maid whose wonderfulness took away all beauty from her but that which it might seem she gave her back again by her very shadow. (I. 3. 74)

But by the end of the book the body of Gynecia steps ' "between my sight and only Philoclea" ' (I. 13. 146), blocking Pyrocles' excited view of Philoclea's body and impeding his conversation with her. In the first instance the idealising impulse casts the mother in shade, while in the second it is as though desire for the female beloved virtually conjures up the body of the mother, which then cannot be dismissed, so that ' "the terrible wit of Gynecia, carried with the beer of violent love, runs through us all" ' (I. 14. 150).

At the beginning of the second book, that 'terrible wit' begins to 'work' to produce the 'terrible tragedies' to which it is prone. Speaking strikingly in her own voice, the character of Gynecia articulates a traditionally negative sense of bodily self-consciousness, violation and shame that in desperation she is willing to turn to blasphemy and violence. Alienating herself from pastoral community, she deliberately seeks out 'the solitary places those deserts were full of, going up and down with such unquiet motions as a grieved and hopeless mind is wont to bring forth'. Echoing Virgil's Dido, she asks if ' "For nothing else have the winds delivered this strange guest to my country . . . but that only I, most wretched I, should become a plague to myself and a shame to womankind." ' Echoing St Paul on the sinful irrationality of evil, she laments that ' "imperfect proportion of reason which can too much foresee and too little prevent" ' and calls herself a ' "dust-creeping worm" '. Yet she will not deny her desire, and it causes her to question the essentiality of virtue – ' "O virtue, where dost thou hide thyself? What hideous thing is this which doth eclipse thee? Or is it true that thou wert never but a vain name and no essential thing . . . ?" ' – and to contemplate killing her daughter-rival (II. 1. 213–14).

Within the structure of the *Arcadia* as a whole, the effect of this powerful subjective passage at the very beginning of Book II is to obscure the idealistic thrust of Philoclea's later self-portrait, anchoring it instead in the sense of aroused female desire and heterodox rebellion that both Gynecia and Philoclea inherit from a character like Virgil's Dido. Furthermore, unlike Virgil's *Aeneid*, where the hero at a certain point violently differentiates himself from the heroine's illicit and vertiginous desires, constructing, as it were, his new heroic ideal upon her body, here

Gynecia's desire threatens to involve Pyrocles' desire.[28] Thus at the end of the passage we have been analysing the distraught Gynecia hears 'an extremely doleful voice' that echoes her own. Investigating, she finds the love-infected Pyrocles, and they look upon each other with a mutual recognition and astonishment that is saved from emotional collapse only by the comic entrance of the doting Basilius. Later, near the end of Book II, her even more vehement display of 'the store-house of her deadly desires' to Pyrocles is cut off by the 'confused rumour' and 'violent flood' of a lower-class rebellion, which Pyrocles, still disguised as Zelmane and himself a subtler threat to the kingdom, ambiguously puts down (II. 25. 378–9): feminine passion is displaced into lower-class rebellion, only to raise the possibility that it will be displaced yet again by a feminine power that threatens patriarchal control from within.[29]

Finally, in a passage near the resumption of the text of the *Old Arcadia* after the breaking-off of the *New Arcadia*, Pyrocles discovers a cave – traditionally symbolic of material nature – in the midst of the Arcadian landscape. Lamenting his own desire for Philoclea as dark and rebellious, he is led deeper within it by an echoic voice which claims that its passions subject it to infernal torment, and make this ' "cave, become my grave" ', ' "my state. . . . Death wrapp'd in flesh, to living grave assign'd" ' (III. 36. 633). As in the earlier passage in which the narrator had described Philoclea's discovery of her own desire, we move from hearing this voice, to discovery of a text that itself speaks of the inadequacy of writing (Pyrocles finds a poem that laments ' "No Cave, no wasting wax, no words of grief,/ Can hold, show, tell, my pains without relief" ' [p. 635]), to discovery of a female body racked by desire. Only here the body is that of Gynecia, and Pyrocles/Zelmane recoils from it 'as if she had been ready to tread upon a deadly stinging adder' (III. 36. 636). However, the conclusion of this passage is his recognition that he must deal with this snake in the Arcadian garden, this powerfully rebellious, materially rooted feminine passion, and he agrees to a later assignation in the cave with Gynecia.

Although he intends to evade this meeting – and does in fact do so, sending Basilius in his place to commit adultery with his wife while he stays behind to attempt the virtue of Philoclea – both actions are for a time read as conspiratorially enacting the same politically rebellious desire. Gynecia's love potion, the naturalistic feminine vehicle for both the crisis and the resolution of the text, throw Basilius into a deathlike trance, and Pyrocles – whether he collapses into a consummation of his desire for Philoclea, as in the original text of the *Old Arcadia*, or manages to refrain from doing so, as in the Countess of Pembroke's bowdlerised version – is none the less accused of violating her. In the scene of final judgement Pyrocles' desire for Philoclea is conflated with Gynecia's desire for Pyrocles as attempts at overthrowing patriarchal kingship, and Gynecia accepts her horrible punishment – to be buried alive with Basilius' corpse – as the apt fulfilment of her earlier regicidal dream, in which her love for Pyrocles led her through thorns to embrace only the dead and putrefying body of her husband (II. 25. 376).

The irrationally powerful character of Gynecia in the *Old Arcadia* in turn gives birth to the new character of Cecropia in the *New Arcadia*. She emerges, as it were, from Gynecia's suspicions and repressed desires, accurately intuited by Gynecia as the source of the wild animals that attack at the end of Book I, inserted as the actual source of the lower-class rebellion at the end of Book II, which I have already described as the temporary displacement of Gynecia's regicidal dream. Gynecia's repressed desire to kill her daughter Philoclea (II. 1. 214) becomes Cecropia's active violence towards the two princesses (III. 20); Gynecia's regicidal nightmare about embracing her husband's dead body (II. 25. 376) becomes Cecropia's active rebellion against Basilius; finally, her anguished language, which echoes the laments of heroines of classical tragedy and Pauline self-loathing and recrimination (II. 1. 213–14), is transformed by Cecropia into active blasphemy. Cecropia, whose name is the feminine appropriation of Cecrops, the legendary Athenian ruler who deprived women of the vote and subdued them within the patriarchal institution of marriage, now consciously seeks to undo the patriarchy on all the parallel levels of family, state and religion.[30] In the process she definitively undoes Sidney's text as well.

Cecropia emerges as the full expression of the hitherto repressed maternal subtext in Sidney's *Arcadia*. Turning upon Philoclea and Pamela, the text's representations of ideal womanhood, she tempts them to make use of their sexuality by marrying her son Amphialus; to defy the authority of their father, the King; and, finally, in Pamela's case, to blaspheme God by seeing him as merely the projection of human needs and fears, and instead to affirm the autonomous creative power of her female beauty and imagination (III. 5; III. 10).[31] Although the text explicitly refutes Cecropia by having the heroines heroically and characteristically resist her – Philoclea with 'sweet and humble dealing' and Pamela with 'majesty of virtue' (III. 6. 465) – the authenticity of their resistance is undermined for us by what we already know about their feelings and projected actions. Thus Philoclea refutes Cecropia's naturalistic arguments for marriage and children by declaring that she will ' "lead a virgin's life to my death; for such a vow I have in myself devoutly made" ' (III. 5. 460), *despite the fact that we know this vow has already been blotted by her pledge to Pyrocles*. And Pamela piously evokes God's authority as the basis for her continued obedience to her ' "peevish" ' father (III. 10. 487), *despite the fact that she has already begun to show Musidorus the favour that will later lead her to elope with him in defiance of her father's will*. Cecropia becomes the 'knot' in which hitherto heroic male desire loses itself, blocking the heroes' access to their beloveds, twisting the thwarted affections of Amphialus, in which Sidney is also so heavily invested, into ineffectual political rebellion.

Extending beyond the episodic influence of Sidney's story of the King of Paphlagonia, Cecropia also voices or enacts the *Arcadia*'s other explicit forecastings of *Lear*. At the height of her blasphemous arguments against God as a mere projection of human fear, she scoffs,

> "for else to think that those powers (if there be any such) above are moved either by the eloquence of our prayers or in a chafe at the folly of our actions carries as much reason, *as if flies should think that men take great care which of them hums sweetest, and which of them flies nimblest*". (III. 10. 488; emphasis added)

She thus articulates, as William Elton and D.P. Walker recognised long ago, those stock classical sceptical arguments against the providential care of God which were beginning to find such renewed currency in late-sixteenth- and early-seventeenth-century Europe.[32] As the blinded Gloucester laments, 'As flies to wanton boys, are we to th'gods,/ They kill us for their sport' (IV. i. 36–7). Finally, she enacts the death of any stable iconic meaning in Sidney's text, representing through her elaborately staged executions of Pamela and Philoclea the destruction of Sidney's neo-Platonic ideal of the 'speaking picture' and the realisation of his greatest fears about the vertiginous power of drama.[33] The spectacle drives Pyrocles to a blasphemous and suicidal despair – ' "O tyrant heaven, traitor earth, blind providence, no justice, how is this done?" ' (III. 22. 563–4) – unconvincingly relieved by Philoclea's mysterious 're-surrection' the next morning (III. 23). Sidney's revision stops abruptly shortly thereafter; Cecropia has taken us to the representational abyss that Shakespeare's play must overcome. Can something come from this nothing, a 'no-thing' that now extends from the 'knot/not' of women's repressed sexual power to challenge heavenly providence itself?

Lear re-enacts Cecropia's challenge fully. Centrally a play about the necessary surrender of patriarchal authority in the family, the state, religion and art, it threatens us with women who are monsters, devouring rather than nourishing their young; it invokes Nature as a harsh, cruel goddess who stands up for bastards; it suggests religion as the mere projection of human need in a world where the gods have seemingly fallen silent; it violates the ideal of the speaking picture by gouging out eyes on the stage. In compensation for what it shows and what we cannot speak about, it makes a naked appeal to maternal feeling that can support a nascent Christian theology. From the servant who applies the whites of eggs – *semina rerum* indeed – to Gloucester's bleeding sockets, to the fevered King who shepherds the Fool ahead of him into shelter, to the weeping daughter who ministers a healing kiss, to ourselves as audience in the breathless moment when, half-fearing that he will plummet, we reach out to break Gloucester's fall, *Lear* is a play that finally rests on our kind nursery, in the pre-Oedipal realm of the maternal gesture: 'and the Word was made flesh, and dwelt among us' (John 1: 14). Its final image is the pietà-like one of Lear cradling his dead daughter: the great father has now become the mother, cradling a prefiguration of love's redemptive power.

NOTES

1. All quotations from and citations of Shakespeare's works are taken from *The Complete Signet Classic Shakespeare*, gen. ed. Silvan Barnet (New York: Harcourt Brace Jovanovich, 1972) and will be noted parenthetically by act, scene and line number in the body of my text.
2. See *De generatione et corruptione*, I. iii. 317b34–319b5; *Physics* I. viii. 191a23–1. ix. 192b7; *Metaphysics* VII. vii. 1032a12–1033a23.
3. S.C. Woodhouse, *English–Greek Dictionary: A vocabulary of the Attic language* (New York: E.P. Dutton, 1910), p. 471, cites the metaphorical extension of 'knot' as '*aporia*', or narrative difficulty, quoting Sophocles' *Ajax* 1317: 'If you are here not to tighten but to help loose the knot'.
4. Thus Aristotle's discussions of form and matter in the *Physics* and *Metaphysics* find their reflection in his biological treatise, the *Generation of Animals*, I. xx. 727b34–729a33, where he states repeatedly that the male provides the form and the female the matter in the act of generation – or, as Shakespeare's Theseus argues to Hermia in *A Midsummer Night's Dream*:

   > To you your father should be as a god,
   > One that composed your beauties; yea, and one
   > To whom you are but as a form in wax
   > By him imprinted and within his power
   > To leave the figure or disfigure it. (I. i. 47–51)

5. Woman's secondary status with respect to man is assumed in either a one- or a two-sex model: in the one-sex model she is an imperfect version of man, while in the two-sex model she is his inferior. See Ian Maclean, *The Renaissance Notion of Woman: A study in the fortunes of scholasticism and medical science in European intellectual life* (Cambridge: Cambridge University Press, 1980), p. 35. The shift from the dominance of the former model to the dominance of the latter which Thomas Laqueur traces in *Making Sex: Body and gender from the Greeks to Freud* (Cambridge, MA and London: Harvard University Press, 1990) may be largely described as the further containment through differentiation of the category of woman by the category of man.
6. Lawrence Stone, for example, rehearses the economic logic of attempting to ensure female chastity – a proverbially impossible task – in *The Family, Sex and Marriage in England: 1500–1800* (New York, Hagerstown, San Francisco and London: Harper & Row, 1977), pp. 636–7.
7. Kahn, *Man's Estate: Masculine identity in Shakespeare* (Berkeley, Los Angeles and London: University of California Press, 1981).
8. See, for example, 'Excavating "those dim Minoan regions": Maternal subtexts in patriarchal literature', *Diacritics*, 12, (1982), pp. 32–41, subsequently

expanded as 'The hand that rocks the cradle: Recent gender theories and their implications', in Shirley Nelson Garner, Claire Kahane and Madelon Sprengnether, eds, *The (M)other Tongue: Essays in feminist psychoanalytic interpretation* (Ithaca and London: Cornell University Press, 1985), pp. 72–88; and 'The absent mother in *King Lear*', in Margaret W. Ferguson, Maureen Quilligan and Nancy Vickers, eds, *Rewriting the Renaissance: The discourses of sexual difference in early modern Europe* (Chicago and London: University of Chicago Press, 1986), pp. 33–49. The reference to Gohlke is to her ' "I wooed thee with my sword" ': Shakespeare's tragic paradigms', in Murray M. Schwartz and Coppélia Kahn, eds, *Representing Shakespeare: New psychoanalytic essays* (Baltimore and London: Johns Hopkins University Press, 1980), pp. 170–87.

9. Kahn, 'Excavating', p. 36. Chodorow, *The Reproduction of Mothering: Psychoanalysis and the sociology of gender* (Berkeley, Los Angeles and London: University of California Press, 1978).

10. Barbara J. Bono, 'Mixed gender, mixed genre in Shakespeare's *As You Like It*', in Barbara Keifer Lewalski, ed., *Renaissance Genres: Essays on theory, history, and interpretation, Harvard English Studies,* 14 (Cambridge, MA and London: Harvard University Press, 1986), pp. 189–212.

11. See, for example, Richard McCoy, *Sir Philip Sidney: Rebellion in Arcadia* (New Brunswick: Rutgers University Press, 1979); Arthur F. Marotti, ' "Love is not love": Elizabethan sonnet sequences and the social order', *English Literary History,* 49 (1982), pp. 396–428; Ann Rosalind Jones and Peter Stallybrass, 'Courtship and courtiership: The politics of *Astrophil and Stella*', *Studies in English Literature,* 24 (1984), pp. 53–68.

12. For the Huguenot doctrine of subaltern magistracy, see *Arcadia* III. 4, and McCoy, *Sir Philip Sidney*, pp. 11, *passim.*

13. All quotations from or citations of *The Countess of Pembroke's Arcadia* (a combination of the incomplete revised *New Arcadia* and the ending from the *Old Arcadia*) are taken from the Penguin edition, ed. Maurice Evans (Harmondsworth: Penguin, 1977) and will be noted parenthetically by book, chapter and page numbers in the body of my text.

14. Cf. Strong, *The Cult of Elizabeth* (Berkeley and Los Angeles: University of California Press, 1977), pp. 74, 147–9, especially the description of Helen in the *Arcadia*, II. 21. 351–2.

15. Edmund Spenser, *The Faerie Queene*, III. vi. 54–61. McCoy, *Sir Philip Sidney*, p. 20, quoting Paul Johnson, *Elizabeth I: A study in power and intellect* (London: Weidenfeld & Nicolson, 1974), p. 273, for how Elizabeth did not attend the funeral. For an illuminating account of the melancholy social psychology of 'the generation of 1560', see Anthony Esler, *The Aspiring Mind of the Elizabethan Younger Generation* (Durham, NC: Duke University Press, 1966).

16. 'Shakespeare and the exorcists', in Stephen Greenblatt, *Shakespearean Negotiations: The circulation of social energy in Renaissance England* (Berkeley and Los Angeles: University of California Press, 1988), pp. 94–128. Greenblatt concludes his argument about why Shakespeare would reiterate Samuel Harsnett's attempted exposure, in *A Declaration of Egregious Popish Impostures*, of 'pockets of rivalrous charisma' on the religious right (recusant Roman Catholicism) and also implicitly on the religious left (Puritanism) (pp. 96–7) with this statement of Lear's differences from Harsnett:

> Lear's sorrows are not redeemed; nothing can turn them into joy, but the forlorn hope of an impossible redemption persists, drained of its institutional signifi-

cance, empty and vain, cut off even from a theatrical realization, but like the dream of exorcism, ineradicable (p. 125)

– and he quotes Hooker on the evacuation of the letter of the Mosaic Law by Christ:

'the words which were do continue: the only difference is, that whereas before they had a literal, they now have a metaphorical use, and are as so many notes of remembrance unto us, that what they did signify in the letter is accomplished in the truth'. Both exorcism and Harsnett's own attack on exorcism undergo a comparable process of evacuation and transformed reiteration in King Lear. Whereas before they had a literal, they now have a literary use and are as so many notes of remembrance unto us, that what they did signify in the letter is accomplished – with a drastic swerve from the sacred to the secular – in the theater. (p. 126)

The positive dimension to this deconstruction of authoritarian religious illusion is the play's insistence on intersubjective need and care: in Edgar's words, 'Why I do trifle thus with the despair,/ Is done to cure it' (IV. vi. 33–4): Stephen Orgel, *The Illusion of Power: Political theater in the English Renaissance* (Berkeley: University of California Press, 1975), and for an analysis that frames the development of the Elizabethan drama as a tense discourse about potential division of the kingdom, see Franco Moretti, ' "A huge eclipse": Tragic form and the deconstruction of sovereignty,' in Stephen Greenblatt, ed., *The Power of Forms in the English Renaissance* (Norman, OK: Pilgrim Books, 1982), pp. 7–40.

17. In *An Apology for Poetry*, Sidney, of course, defines poetry as 'an art of imitation . . . that is to say, a representing, counterfeiting, or figuring forth – to speak metaphorically, a speaking picture – with this end, to teach and delight', and offers many examples of 'the speaking picture of poesy' (*An Apology for Poetry*, ed. Forrest G. Robinson [Indianapolis and New York: The Library of the Liberal Arts, 1970], pp. 18, 28–30.) And his friend and editor Fulke Greville declares that Sidney's intention in the *Arcadia* was

to limn out such exact pictures, of every posture in the minde, that any man being forced, in the straines of this life, to pass through any straights, or latitudes of good, or ill fortune, might (as in a glasse) see how to set a good countenance upon all the discountenances of adversitie, and a stay upon the exorbitant smilings of chance (*Sir Fulke Greville's Life of Sir Philip Sidney* (Oxford: Clarendon Press, 1907), p. 16).

My argument is that Sidney's character Cecropia, by staging the princesses' deaths, challenges this doctrine of the speaking picture and in the process prepares the way for Shakespeare's more extreme challenge to it in *King Lear*, where the rational perspective of sight is destroyed and we are taught, if anything, how to 'see . . . feelingly' (*Lear*, IV. vi. 149).

18. *The Old Arcadia*, ed. Katherine Duncan-Jones (Oxford and New York: Oxford University Press, 1985), Bk I, p. 10.

19. For readings of Britomart's successful transvaluation of the tradition of classical epic within a larger argument about the pivotal role of representations of woman within this process, see my *Literary Transvaluation: From Vergilian epic to Shakespearean tragicomedy* (Berkeley, Los Angeles and London: University of California Press, 1984), pp. 75–9; and Mihoko Suzuki, *Metamorphoses of Helen: Authority, difference, and the epic* (Ithaca, NY and London: Cornell University Press, 1989), pp. 150–73.

20. Cf. *NA*, I. 3. 74–7 with *OA*, Bk I, pp. 10–11.

21. For the two major passages which the Countess omitted from her 1593 edition, see Evans, *Arcadia*, pp. 865–7.
22. For one pivotal example of this shift, see Joel Fineman, *Shakespeare's Perjured Eye: The invention of poetic subjectivity in the sonnets* (Berkeley, Los Angeles and London: University of California Press, 1986).
23. In a sense I am suggesting that we need selectively to combine the argument for the intermediary role of women within a male homosocial economy as found, for example, in Eve Kosofsky Sedgwick's *Between Men: English literature and male homosocial desire* (New York: Columbia University Press, 1985) with the more negative and disruptive possibilities of the feminine argued in Patricia Parker's *Literary Fat Ladies: Rhetoric, gender, property* (London and New York: Methuen, 1987).
24. Beginning, for example, with the concluding lines of Sonnet 15: 'And, all in war with Time for love of you,/ As he takes from you, I engraft you new.'
25. See Sidney's frequent apostrophes in *The Old Arcadia* to an imagined audience of 'fair ladies', such as this which concludes Book I: 'Which accordingly was done; whereof I will repeat you a few [pastoral eclogues] to ease you, fair ladies, of the tediousness of this long discourse' (*OA*, Bk I, p. 49). Suzanne W. Hull, in *Chaste, Silent and Obedient: English books for women, 1475–1640* (San Marino, CA: Huntington Library, 1982), lists the *Arcadia* as among those English Renaissance books written for a female readership; and Mary Ellen Lamb, in *Gender and Authorship in the Sidney Circle* (Madison: University of Wisconsin Press, 1990), an important work which I read too late for incorporation into my argument here, begins the full exploration of Sidney's influence on women readers and writers.
26. For a brief account of the early editorial history of the *Arcadia*, see Evans, *Arcadia*, pp. 12–13.
27. Compare Philoclea's lament with the earlier lament of Gynecia – 'For nothing else have the winds delivered this strange guest to my country . . . but that only I, most wretched I, should become a plague to myself and a shame to womankind' (II. 1. 214) – and the lament of Virgil's Dido to her sister Anna – 'Anna soror, quae me suspensam insomnia terrent!/ quis novus hic nostris successit sedibus hospes . . .' ('Anna, my sister, what dreams thrill me with fears? Who is this stranger guest that hath entered our home?' *Aeneid* IV. 9–10, in *Virgil in Two Volumes*, transl. H. Rushton Fairclough, rev. edn. [London: Heinemann; Cambridge, MA: Harvard University Press, 1935].)
28. Compare Suzuki's suggestive discussion of the contaminating role of Amata as 'the destructive mother in the Aeneid', *Metamorphoses of Helen*, pp. 130–34.
29. In this reading I follow both McCoy, *Sir Philip Sidney*, pp. 192–4, and Stephen Greenblatt, 'Murdering peasants: Status, genre, and the representation of rebellion', *Representations*, 1 (1983), pp. 14–19, only to insist finally on the continued subversive presence of gender conflict beneath Sidney's aesthetic resolution of class conflict.
30. Cecrops is listed by ancient authorities such as Apollonius and Pausanias as the mythical first king of Athens. Augustine, following the Roman historian Varro, gives the supposed reason 'for the city's being called Athens', and hints at the ironic lessons therein for women:

> When an olive tree had suddenly appeared there, and on another spot water had gushed forth, these portents alarmed the king, and he sent to Delphic Apollo to ask what the meaning of this was and what was to be done. Apollo answered that the olive signified Minerva and the spring Neptune, and that it rested with the citizens to decide from which of the

two gods, whose symbols these were, they preferred that the city should take its name. When Cecrops received this oracle he called together all the citizens of both sexes – for at that time it was customary in that area that the women should also have a part in public deliberation – to take a vote. When therefore the multitude was consulted, the men voted for Neptune and the women for Minerva, and because the women were found to be one more, Minerva was victorious.

Then Neptune in his wrath devastated the lands of the Athenians by great floods of sea-water. . . . To appease his wrath . . . the women were subjected by the Athenians to a triple punishment, namely, that they should never vote thereafter, that none of their children should bear their mother's name and that no one should call them Athenian women . . . in the person of the women who were thus punished Minerva, though victorious, was also defeated. Nor did she defend the women who had voted for her. . . . What comments, and how lengthy, might be offered on this subject, if only my discourse were not hurrying on to other themes! (*The City of God Against the Pagans*, transl. Eva Matthews Sanford and William McAllen Green (London: Heinemann; Cambridge, MA: Harvard University Press, 1965), vol. V, XVIII. ix, pp. 391–2).

What comments might be offered indeed! Thus, as in Aeschylus' *Oresteia*, the repression of matriarchy by patriarchy is seen as the very origin of Athenian civilisation. Cecropia's arguments attempt to deconstruct this myth. I am grateful to B. Cass Clarke for first suggesting that I should explore the mythical significance of Cecropia's name.

31. ' "And see, a fair woman shall not only command without authority but persuade without speaking. . . . She is served and obeyed, which is the most notable not because the laws so command it, but because they become laws to themselves to obey her; not for her parents' sake, but for her own. . . . Beauty, beauty, dear niece, is the crown of feminine greatness which gift on whomsoever the heavens (therein most niggardly) do bestow, without question she is bound to use it to the noble purpose for which it is created, not only winning but preserving . . ." ' (III. 10. 485)

32. William R. Elton, *King Lear and the Gods* (San Marino, CA: The Huntington Library, 1966); D.P. Walker, 'Atheism, the ancient theology, and Sidney's *Arcadia*', in *The Ancient Theology: Studies in Christian Platonism from the Fifteenth to the Eighteenth Century* (Ithaca, NY: Cornell University Press, 1972), pp. 132–63.

33. The site of Pamela's and Philoclea's staged 'executions' is a great hall similar to those in which travelling players performed their plays – 'A place indeed over-fit for so unfit a matter: for being so stately made that the bottom of it being even with the ground, the roof reached as high as any part of the castle, at either end it had convenient lodgings' (III. 21. 557) – and the action performed there is repeatedly described in dramaturgic terms as 'a new play' (p. 557), 'the tragedy' (p. 557), 'their late bloody act' (p. 559).

7

'Household Kates': Chez Petruchio, Percy and Plantagenet

Laurie E. Maguire

INDUCTION

In *The Taming of the Shrew*, Christopher Sly responds to the new experience of comedy with ennui ('would 'twere done!'), while his namesake in the related *The Taming of a Shrew* reveals similar critical limitations by taking the play's title literally: 'I know now how to tame a shrew'.[1] The two Slys are not alone in their critical reactions. At the beginning of this century, Sir Arthur Quiller-Couch found Shakespeare's Petruchio plot 'tiresome' to 'any modern civilised man',[2] an opinion shared by Bernard Shaw, John Masefield and E.K. Chambers,[3] all of whom took the action announced by the title at face value: 'you can hardly refuse to shed a tear for the humiliation of Katherina'.[4] Clearly, with such approaches, *The Taming of the Shrew* was a straightforward, if unpalatable, play.

By the middle of this century, new criticism had begun to look beyond the main plot. Role playing, change of identity, illusion – all themes embodied in the induction – attracted attention, leading to a more optimistic interpretation of the relationship between Katherine and Petruchio. Thus Alexander Leggatt: '[t]he taming of Katherina is not just a lesson but a game'.[5] Whether pursuing the metaphor of play (as in Leggatt) or the psychology of behaviour modification ('Petruchio voluntarily assumes an identity . . . in order to cause Kate involuntarily to change identity')[6] or social satire ('this play satirizes not woman herself in the person of the shrew, but the male urge to control woman')[7] the critics now assumed Petruchio's former role as tamer, bringing the play 'into line with all the other Comedies in which Shakespeare gives a distinct edge to his heroine'.[8] While such approaches provided opportunities for revitalised explorations of text and performance, it was clear that one

129

form of subjugation had simply been replaced by another. The struggle was no longer to make Katherine palatable by conformity, but to make the play so.

Attempts to champion Kate, defend Shakespeare, and rehabilitate the play are understandably attractive to those of us (most of us) who wish to avoid having to view either Petruchio or Shakespeare as a chauvinist. With the development of feminist criticism, however, several critics confessed that for them the play was not, and was unlikely ever to be, palatable. Shirley Nelson Garner voices her reservations as follows:

> The play seems written to please a misogynist audience, especially men who are gratified by sexually sadistic pleasures. Since I am outside the community for whom the joke is made and do not share its implicit values, I do not participate in its humor.[9]

In a comparison of Shakespeare's shrew-taming tale with its literary predecessors, Linda Woodbridge states: 'it does not speak well of a hero that the best thing to be said in his favor is that he neither beats his wife senseless nor wraps her in a salted horsehide.' Woodbridge concludes:

> [o]ne can certainly sympathize with the 'can this play be saved?' response of those feminists who cannot bring themselves to believe that their favorite author . . . could be quite such a male chauvinist as he appears in *Taming*; . . . [b]ut feminism as we know it did not exist in Shakespeare's time, and I see little evidence that he was ahead of his time in his attitudes toward women.[10]

Clearly, the problem in determining the tone of *The Taming of the Shrew* lies in the Katherine–Petruchio relationship, which has always defied easy assessment. However, the taming of Kate Minola can best be understood in the context of the taming of two other Kates: Hotspur's wife, Kate Percy, in *I Henry IV*, and Henry V's bride-to-be, Katherine ('Kate') Valois. The husband–wife scenes in each of these three plays contain so many verbal and structural parallels, as well as links in attitudes, that the name Kate assumes an almost generic quality and becomes a synecdoche for 'woman':

> For I am he am born to tame you, Kate,
> And bring you from a wild Kate to a Kate
> Conformable as other household Kates. (*TS*, II. i. 276–8)

The near-identical manner in which all three Kates are tamed – that is, made 'conformable' – forms the subject of this essay. Examination of this triplicate wife-taming leads to a more positive view of Petruchio and to a less positive view of Hotspur and Henry V, while suggesting a cautious Shakespeare who takes a middle-of-the-road position in negotiating the tension between feminism and chauvinism.[11]

I

Katherine Minola, Lady Percy and Katherine Valois are high-spirited
women who marry martinet soldiers. On marriage a woman surrenders
her name – like her honour, her property, her identity – to her husband,
as Peter Stallybrass points out in relation to the alternative readings for
Othello, III. iii. 386: ' "Her name . . . is now begrim'd," [and] "My name
. . . is now begrim'd," make equal sense. Desdemona's "name," like her
handkerchief, is Othello's'.[12] Petruchio, Hotspur and Henry V all determine their wives' sense of identity, not merely in their (conventional)
imposition of a surname but in their idiosyncratic manipulation of the
first name 'Katherine'.

Katherine Minola is referred to by all in the play, including herself, as
Katherine.[13] On first meeting her, Petruchio, without hesitation, uses the
abbreviated form 'Kate': 'Good morrow, Kate, for that's your name, I
hear' (II. i. 182). Katherine is quick to correct his use of the diminutive,
perhaps seeing in it an attempt to diminish her, perhaps simply insisting
on her right to her own identity:

> Well have you heard, but something hard of hearing:
> They call me Katherine that do talk of me. (II. i. 183–4)

Petruchio ignores this hint, calling her Kate fifty-eight times throughout
the action of the play. Henry V follows Petruchio's example when court-
ing Katherine of France. In Holinshed's *Chronicles* Katherine is identified
by her full name throughout (usually in the form 'the ladie Katharine');[14]
but in the course of the wooing episode (v. ii. 99–374) Henry calls her
Kate thirty-one times, while addressing her as Katherine on only six
occasions. There is no reference to Lady Percy's full name in *I Henry IV*
where she is called Kate throughout; but since Kate is an abbreviated form
of Katherine, it is logical to assume that 'Kate' is Hotspur's familiar way
of addressing his Katherine. He addresses his wife by name eleven times
in their two brief encounters.[15] Katherine Percy is doubly rechristened,
by dramatist as well as husband. The historical Lady Percy was called
Elizabeth; Holinshed calls her Elinor ('Elianor'), as does Hall ('Elinor'),[16]
Shakespeare renames her Kate. What's in a name? Not a great deal,
according to Northrop Frye: 'I don't for a moment think there's any
particular significance in Kate'.[17] Unlike Frye, I think there is. This
remarkable coincidence in *The Shrew*, *I Henry IV*, and *Henry V* seems to
be a deliberate attempt by the males to re-create the Katherines as Kates:
in other words, to tame them by (re)naming them.[18]

Just as Shakespeare can rename a character he is manipulating
(Elizabeth/Elinor Percy), so Petruchio can rename a character he wishes
to control. In this *The Taming of the Shrew* shows its indebtedness to the

hierarchical theology of Creation (traditional to shrew-taming literature, yet generally considered absent from Shakespeare's version): 'So the Lord God formed from the soil every kind of animal and bird, and brought them to the man to see what he would call them; and whatever he called them, that was their name' (Genesis 2: 19–20).[19] Petruchio's wife is, like his ox and ass, part of his household stuff – a creature to name as he pleases, as Katherine herself eventually capitulates when she sanctions his right to rename more than the sun and the moon: 'What you will have it nam'd, even that it is' (IV. v. 21).

The close interrelation of name and identity in the drama of the period is evident in lines such as 'since my lord/ Is Antony again, I will be Cleopatra', 'This is I, Hamlet the Dane', and 'I am Duchess of Malfi still', statements which occur towards the end of the protagonists' careers as they are recalled to a sense of who they are.[20] In *The Taming of the Shrew* nomenclature and identity are intertwined from the outset with the verbal blunder of Sly's ancestral claim ('we came in with Richard Conqueror', Ind., I. 4–5) and the Lord's theatrical reminiscence of Soto, 'a farmer's elder son', in which the Lord tells the actor 'I have forgot your name; but sure that part/ Was aptly fitted and naturally perform'd' (Ind., I. 84; 86–7). In every Act the relationship between the name and the thing itself is tested:

> Call you me daughter? (II. i. 285)

> [Thou] feed'st me with the very name of meat (IV. iii. 32)
> [T]his is flat knavery, to take upon you another man's name. (V. i. 36–7)

In a crucial exchange in Act V, Vincentio confronts Tranio (in Lucentio's attire), while Baptista tries to smooth over the fracas:

> BAPTISTA: You mistake, sir, you mistake, sir. Pray what do you think is his name?
> VINCENTIO: His name! as if I knew not his name! I have brought him up ever since he was three years old, and his name is Tranio. (V. i. 79–83)

Vincentio clings to the belief that identity and nomenclature are fixed: to be called Tranio must mean to be Tranio. The Lord, on the other hand, privileges personality over nomenclature: Soto's fictional behaviour is more important than his fictional name. Katherine associates certain behaviour with certain names, querying her father's treatment of her as inappropriate to their named relationship.

Petruchio complicates the issue of naming. He begins by insisting on the correlation between name and identity, replacing the old Katherine–shrew equation ('Katherine the curst': I. ii. 128) with a new formation: 'a Kate/ Conformable as other household Kates' (II. i. 278). In adopting this abbreviation Petruchio may have taken his cue from Baptista's question: 'shall I send my daughter Kate to you?' (II. i. 167), the only time Baptista refers to Katherine by the abbreviated form in the course of the play. Bianca once addresses her sister as Kate ('I prithee, sister Kate, untie my hands': II. i. 21) and Hortensio calls her 'Mistress Kate' in a compassionate moment at IV. iii. 49. These are the only non-Petruchian uses of Kate in the play, and all seem to relate to moments of domestic sympathy (or, in the case of Bianca's plea, attempted domestic sympathy).

The personal associations of two of these references ('daughter Kate', 'sister Kate') are worthy of note, for one of Petruchio's tactics is to infiltrate the Minola family by using terms normally reserved for intimates: he prematurely addresses Katherine as Kate, just as he calls Baptista 'father' (II. i. 130). Although this latter title is a generic mode of address to older men (compare the greetings to Vincentio in IV. v. 45, 60–61), Petruchio's use jars with the etiquette adopted by others in the scene (II. i. 39–40, 46, 74) – including Petruchio himself, who begins formally with 'Signior Baptista' (II. i. 114) but progresses speedily to 'father'.[21] As in the later meeting with Vincentio, Petruchio uses familiar terms before he is entitled to such closeness. Conveniently, on both occasions marriage enables him to validate the title. Petruchio understands the psychological verity that to articulate something is halfway to creating it.

Not content with the simple act of renaming, Petruchio bombards Katherine with her new name:

> You lie, in faith, for you are call'd plain Kate,
> And bonny Kate, and sometimes Kate the curst;
> But Kate, the prettiest Kate in Christendom,
> Kate of Kate-Hall, my super-dainty Kate,
> For dainties are all Kates, and therefore, Kate,
> Take this of me, Kate of my consolation. (II. i. 185–90)

Christopher Sly's new identity is similarly heralded and reinforced by a new name, the repetition of which is instrumental in convincing him of his transformation. In the opening lines of the Induction, scene ii, the new style of address is stressed by three of the Lord's servingmen:

FIRST SERVINGMAN:	Will't please *your [lordship]* drink a cup of sack?
SECOND SERVINGMAN:	Will't please *your honor* taste of these conserves?
THIRD SERVINGMAN:	What raiment will *your honor* wear to-day? (Induction, ii. 2–4; emphasis added)

Sly, like Katherine, initially clings to his old name: 'I am Christophero Sly, call not me honor nor lordship' (Ind., ii. 5–6). Gradually he accepts his new identity, in which he acquires not just an ability to speak blank verse but an interest in the way to address a wife:

SLY:	What must I call her?
LORD:	Madam.
SLY:	Al'ce madam, or Joan madam?
LORD:	Madam, and nothing else, so lords call ladies. (Induction, ii. 108–11) [22]

As the Lord had earlier recognised when instructing his servants in role-playing, nomenclature is crucial to the successful transformation of identity. Not only is Sly to be called 'your honor' and 'your lordship', but Bartholomew the page is to be addressed as 'madam', and it is the escapade's change of names which the Lord anticipates with most relish: 'I long to hear him call the drunkard husband' (Ind., i. 133). *The Taming of a Shrew* (1594), plausibly a derivative version of *The Shrew*, expounds the new-name tactic more explicitly when the Lord urges 'And see you call him Lord, at everie word' (i. 46).

The difference between Sly and Katherine, as critics frequently remark, is that Sly's 'transformation' can only be temporary, while Katherine's may or may not be permanent. The question of how seriously Petruchio wants his Katherine to remain Kate is relevant here, for the text indicates that her new name, like her new cap, can be doffed with ease. Having insisted on the change to Kate, Petruchio capitulates in the final scene, when he publicly mixes the two styles of address for the first time.[23] The banter begins with a barbed comment from the widow which piques Katherine. Petruchio encourages her to retaliate: 'To her, Kate! . . . A hundred marks, my Kate does put her down' (v. ii. 33, 35). Petruchio is here urging in Kate the same behaviour he had tried to subdue in Katherine, whose spirited temperament is still recognisable. Petruchio's two apostrophic 'Katherine's come ninety lines later with the two injunctions to demonstrate uxorial subjugation – the behaviour, paradoxically, of the 'Kate' persona:

> Katherine, that cap of yours becomes you not;
> Off with that bable, throw it under-foot. (v. ii. 121–2)

> Katherine, I charge thee tell these headstrong women
> What duty they do owe their lords and husbands. (v. ii. 130–31)

Kate and Katherine can coexist, a point we should have realised in the sun/moon debate in IV. v, where 'Kate' agrees to subservience in a statement which slyly reasserts her version of her name:

> What you will have it nam'd, even that it is,
> And so it shall be so for Katherine. (IV. v. 21–2)

The woman who, in IV. iii, demanded 'leave to speak', who wanted to be 'free/ Even to the uttermost . . . in words' (73, 79–80), realises that Kate can achieve more in this respect than Katherine can. When authorised by her husband to speak, a wife can get away with the most outrageous statements. Katherine's threats to Gremio and Hortensio in I. i. 61–5 are spirited, but they pale in comparison with the hyperbole of Kate's responses to Petruchio and the imaginative freedom of her addresses to Vincentio in IV. v, or with her mind-numbing lecture to the other brides in V. ii.

What Shakespeare seems to be advocating is a two-tier standard of wifely behaviour. Petruchio and Katherine have found a mode of conjugal behaviour for public display and a mode of behaviour for private rapport. Like the cap, a conventional symbol of submission, the symbolically circumscribed identity 'Kate' must be worn in public unless otherwise decided by the husband. A detachable name was generally a threat to Renaissance males (as were all detachable items equated with honour, for detachment includes the possibility of loss).[24] But Petruchio specifically introduces the term Kate, only to let it slip. This is in accord with his earlier avowed intent, revealed in a soliloquy which concludes 'And thus I'll curb her mad and headstrong humor' (IV. i. 209). '[C]urb' is the pivotal word in this speech, for the plan is to restrain his wife, not to break her. Part of Katherine's erotic appeal must surely have been her wildness, and critics maintain that no man, then or now, would want to destroy this.[25] Again, A Shrew makes the point more explicitly; the line is padded with a paraphrase: 'To bridle [A Shrew's equivalent of 'curb'] and hold backe my headstrong wife' (ix. 43; emphasis added).

Katherine is not tamed, at least not in the sense made popular by shrew-taming tradition. She conforms to a social norm for the sake of appearance, while remaining free to be her own person in private.[26] Shakespeare's point is neither feminist nor chauvinist. He is adhering to that Renaissance sine qua non, the Great Chain of Being, which advocated a hierarchy among humans; the play's conclusion celebrates a return to hierarchical degree with father/son, master/servant, and husband/wife relationships. More significantly, Shakespeare is participating in the querelle des femmes, the heated contributions to which ranged from the long-held pejorative view that women have no souls, to the more positive compilations of historical precedents, listing women who were prudent, chaste, constant, brave and erudite.[27] Shakespeare's dialectic conclusion anticipates the argument proffered by a later participant in the debate about women, I.G., in An Apologie for Women-Kinde (1605):

> Yet did he [God] not her [Eve] cast in slauery,
> Nor any baser foule seruilitye.
> But left her guidance to her husbands will,
> Onely for order yeilding to him still.

So Abell was subiected vnto Cain,
Yet Cadets Iudge th'authoritie is vaine.
And 'tis a point that euery one can tell,
The younger borne most what doe farre excell. (sigs B3v–B4)[28]

The story of Genesis, notable for its socially expedient hierarchies, is, as we have seen, also notable for Adam's ability to determine identity through nomenclature. Such imposition of control, I.G. implies, is a useful principle for public organisation, but is privately meaningless.

It is not necessary to view the Kate/Katherine, public/private compromise as untenable, as Kahn and Bamber do. In another early play dealing with love, identity and social perceptions of masculine and feminine behaviour, Shakespeare himself tells us how to interpret Katherine's compromise. In *Romeo and Juliet* the surrender of identity is viewed as the perfect metaphor for love. Romeo tells Juliet: 'Call me but love, and I'll be new baptiz'd;/ Henceforth I never will be Romeo' (II. ii. 50–51), and in response to Juliet's question 'Art thou not Romeo, and a Montague?', he declares himself willing to deny both names: 'Neither, fair maid, if either thee dislike' (II. ii. 60–61). Later in the play, in an extraordinary parallel to the sun/moon scene in *The Taming of the Shrew*, Romeo and Juliet part after their wedding night with a debate about whether it is night or day (heralded by the nightingale or the lark). Both characters begin by asserting their own beliefs before adopting the other's terminology. Romeo's phrasing and exaggeration are particularly close to Katherine's as he asserts what he does not believe:

I'll say yon grey is not the morning's eye,
'Tis but the pale reflex of Cynthia's brow;
Nor that is not the lark whose notes do beat
The vaulty heaven so high above our heads. (III. v. 19–22)

These flamboyant verbal gestures do not receive the critical disapproval of their counterparts in *The Taming of the Shrew*, perhaps because the surrender is reciprocal.[29] In IV. v of *The Taming of the Shrew* it is clearly Katherine who is making all the verbal concessions, Petruchio who is making all the conditions. However, by v. ii Petruchio shows himself to be as 'bilingual' as his wife, using her terminology as freely as his own: the two apostrophic uses of 'Katherine' (V. ii. 121, 130) are balanced by the two of 'Kate' (V. ii. 180, 184).

In his irrational verbal demands of IV. v Petruchio is reminiscent of a great number of devoted literary husbands (beginning with Chrétien de Troyes's Erec) who tyrannise their wives with impossible demands in order to test their love, not break their spirit. Whereas Erec imposes tests of silence on his wife, Petruchio, in an unconventional test, requires Katherine to display verbal extravagance. Both Enide and Katherine resume normal discourse at the end of their respective trials, having learnt the value of appropriate speech.[30] In rejecting his extreme attitude, Petruchio both echoes the romance figure Erec and pre-echoes his romance descendant in extreme behaviour, Henry Hotspur. Hotspur insists on having the River Trent turned from its course but, having forced Glendower's compliance, drops his demand:

> I do not care. I'll give thrice so much land
> To any well-deserving friend;
> But in the way of bargain, mark ye me,
> I'll cavil on the ninth part of a hair. (*I Henry IV*, III. i. 135–8)

For him, as for Petruchio, the combat is more exciting than the victory. Petruchio can have no interest in a tamed wife, just as Hotspur eschews tamed topography.

II

Before concluding that the resolution of *The Taming of the Shrew* is reciprocally harmonious for the protagonists, we need to consider *Henry IV* and *Henry V*, for the Katherines in these plays are treated less ambiguously. The Oxford *Textual Companion* dates *I Henry IV* as 1596–7, *II Henry IV* as 1597–8, and *Henry V* as 1598–9; *The Taming of the Shrew* is placed in 1590–91.[31]

The numerous verbal and structural parallels between *The Taming of the Shrew*, *I Henry IV* and *Henry V*, as well as attitudes common to all three plays, suggest that Shakespeare had all three Katherines in mind while writing the *Henry* plays. Certainly, it would have been difficult not to have kept one eye on *Henry IV* when writing *Henry V*, and the Kate Percy/Kate Valois parallel is a natural extension of the Harry Hotspur/Harry Plantagenet equation. That Shakespeare thought back to *The Shrew*, consciously or not, when writing *I Henry IV* can be seen in pertinent verbal links. Katherine Percy berates Hotspur with 'Out, you *mad-headed* ape!/ A weasel hath not such a deal of *spleen*/ As you are toss'd with' (*I HIV*, II. iii. 77–9; see also *I HIV*, V. ii. 19: 'A *hare-brain'd* Hotspur, govern'd by a *spleen*'; emphasis added). These phrases recall Katherine Minola's description of Petruchio as a '*mad-brain* rudesby full of *spleen*' (III. ii. 10; see also *TS*, III. ii. 163: 'this *mad-brain'd* bridegroom'; emphases added). Similarly, compare the vocabulary (prompted by the idea of railing wife) in the following extracts:

> And bonny Kate, and sometimes Kate the curst;
> But Kate, the prettiest Kate in *Christendom*,

Kate of Kate-Hall, my super-dainty Kate,
For dainties are all *Kates*, (*TS*, II. i. 185–9; emphasis added)

    O, he is as tedious
As a tired horse, a railing wife,
Worse than a smoky house. I had rather live
With cheese and garlic in a windmill, far,
Than feed on *cates* and have him talk to me
In any summer house in *Christendom*. (*I HIV*. III. i. 157–62; emphasis added)

Comparison also reveals verbal links between *The Shrew* and *Henry V*. Petruchio assures Baptista that he has won Katherine's love, averring: '[s]he hung about my neck, and kiss on kiss/ She vied so fast, protesting oath on oath' (*TS*, II. i. 308–9). Henry V employs the same image when he says he will woo in French, 'which I am sure will hang upon my tongue like a new-married wife about her husband's neck, hardly to be shook off' (*HV*, V. ii. 179–81). (Compare also Lady Percy in *II Henry IV*: 'I, hanging on Hotspur's neck, . . .': II. iii. 44). Both *The Shrew* and *Henry V* use imagery of clothing to describe the husband–wife relationship ('Could I repair what she will wear in me': *TS*, III. ii. 118; 'thou shalt wear me, if thou wear me, better and better': *HV*, V. ii. 232–3), and both these plays conclude the first private encounter of wooer and Katherine with an identical warning: 'Here comes your father' (*TS*, II. i. 279; *HV*, V. ii. 279–80).

More general verbal links obtain. All three Katherines are encouraged to swear oaths to their husbands:

protesting oath on oath (*TS*, II. i. 309)

Swear me, Kate, . . ./ A good mouth-filling oath (*I HIV*, III. i. 253–4)

Then shall I swear to Kate, and you to me,
And may our oaths well kept and prosp'rous be! (*HV*, V. ii. 373–4)[32]

All three plays depend heavily on sun/moon imagery, and all introduce sustained passages of sexual innuendo in similar situations. All three relationships begin with a problem of communication, all three centre on politically or financially advantageous marriages, and all three wooers see women's function as primarily physical, perhaps because they view women as adjuncts to their relationship with their horses.[33] In *I Henry IV* and *Henry V* the relevant scenes of affection take place after war (both Hotspur and Henry V are waiting for articles to be finalised), while Petruchio turns his attention to wiving after a military career. Both Petruchio and Henry V demand that their brides kiss them in public, a request which is initially resisted as being contrary to custom. Both Katherine Minola and Katherine Percy are banished from their husband's bed. . . . These, and further parallels, will be examined shortly, but for the moment I wish simply to indicate these plays' claims to be considered together.

III

Let us consider these parallels in more detail. First, the structural similarities are marked. The Katherine–wooer scenes in each play are developed in identical fashion: all of them begin with a private encounter, followed by a public performance. In *The Taming of the Shrew*, Baptista *et al.* exit at II. i. 168, leaving Petruchio alone to await Katherine's arrival. He has time for thirteen lines of soliloquy before she appears at II. i. 181. The two then engage in a dialogue which is characterised by witty puns, bawdy, and high spirits. Petruchio embarks on his preconceived strategy with praise of Katherine's mildness, virtue and beauty, but her aggressive verbal dexterity knocks him off balance. She interrupts him with a series of quibbles, and the dialogue veers off into puns. Petruchio is forced to improvise, and it is forty-seven lines before he can resume his intended flattery: 'I find you passing gentle' (II. i. 242).

Throughout these intervening lines he has had to resort to a variety of strategies. Initially he attempts to beat Katherine at her own game by churning out wordplay as fast as she does:

PETRUCHIO:	Why, what's a moveable?
KATE:	A join'd-stool.
PETRUCHIO:	Thou hast hit it; come sit on me.
KATE:	Asses are made to bear, and so are you.
PETRUCHIO:	Women are made to bear, and so are you. (II. i. 197–200)

Unable to checkmate her here, he resorts to innuendo with retorts increasing in sexual significance until he goes too far ('What, with my tongue in your tail?': II. i. 218). He is now in danger of jeopardising the whole encounter, for Katherine is on the point of exit (he has to entreat her 'Nay, come again': II. i. 218). As Ralph Berry explains, '[t]he speed of the exchange has betrayed him into error. He knows it immediately, and "Good Kate, I am a gentleman" attempts to put things right.'[34] Having recanted, he now tries another tactic, one of deliberate misunderstanding ('Why, here's no crab, . . . Then show it me . . . What, you mean my face?': II. i. 230, 232, 234) until the exchange is interrupted by Baptista's return.

Katherine and Petruchio's first 'public' scene now follows. (Unlike the other couples under consideration, they have repeat performances in Acts IV and V, as befits their status in a play where their relationship dominates the plot.) In this first public display Petruchio actually calls attention to the difference between the private and the public Kate:

> 'Tis bargain'd 'twixt us twain, being alone,
> That she shall still be curst in company. (II. i. 304–5)

But she is in company now and, apart from her initial outburst, she is silent: she submits to Petruchio's narrative, his fictitious anecdote, and the arrangement for a wedding date. (Modern directors usually add stage business which restrains her physically to make the submission plausible.) In Act V we witness a replay of this public submission, only this time it is volunteered, not imposed. The final Act suggests that the bargain reached by Katherine and Petruchio is the opposite of the one he describes in Act II, for if Petruchio is sanctioning a public/private compromise (as he states in the above quotation), the public wife of Act V, who is clearly dutiful, must be balanced by a private wife who is independent.

Several critics, most notably Mary Beth Rose,[35] have investigated the dichotomy of Renaissance women's public versus private lives. Henderson and McManus's survey of the debate about women between 1540 and 1640 unites the issues of women's public obedience and private independence:

> Probably more than one Renaissance wife who signed her letters to her husband 'your obedient servant' saw no reason to rebel against the outward forms of submission so long as her freedom of action was intact and her real relationship with her spouse was one of mutual tolerance, affection and respect.[36]

This seems a large claim, but it can be supported by literary precedent. Chaucer's Arveragus and Dorigen reach exactly this kind of compromise:

> And for to lede the moore in blisse hir lyves,
> Of his free wyl he swoor hire as a knyght
> That nevere in al his lyf he, day ne nyght,
> Ne sholde upon hym take no maistrie . . .
> Save that the name of soveraynetee,
> That wolde he have for shame of his degree.[37]

Petruchio, I feel, simply wants outward complaisance, 'the *name* of soveraynetee', and for the same reason as Arveragus: 'for shame of his degree'. Petruchio will distinguish between public and private behaviour in his wife's life, as he apparently does in his own. This blustering, military boor in public Padua is domestic in his country house, enquiring about his dog and his cousin Ferdinand, calling for his slippers, and expressing uncertainty rather than confidence in his private moments ('And 'tis my *hope* to end successfully': IV. i. 189; emphasis added).[38]

In *I Henry IV* Katherine and Hotspur's private and public displays are independent scenic units, II. iii, and III. i. As both these scenes and their

Figure 7.1 Wedding group from *The Taming of the Shrew*, dir. Richard Monette, 1988

portrayal of the Hotspur–Katherine relationship have received scant critical attention, I wish to consider them in some detail. Hotspur is a relatively attractive figure until he is portrayed in conversation with his wife, where the flip side of military energy and passion is domestic neglect and marital disharmony. Like Petruchio, Hotspur exiles his wife from his bed. Like Petruchio, who suffers lack of sleep, food and sex while imposing these deprivations on Katherine, Hotspur denies himself quotidian domestic comforts: 'what is't that takes from thee/ Thy stomach, pleasure, and thy golden sleep?' (II. iii. 40–41). Despite his garrulity elsewhere in *I Henry IV*, Hotspur is taciturn to a fault at home, and the result is a severe problem in communication.

Hotspur announces his imminent departure ('within these two hours': II. iii. 36) and Lady Percy responds with poignant concern for her husband's mental and physical well-being. Hotspur ignores her in favour of a servant whom he questions about equestrian matters. Lady Percy strives to gain her husband's attention, but his only response is mockery:

LADY:	But hear you, *my lord*.
HOTSPUR:	What say'st thou, *my lady*? (II. iii. 73–4; emphasis added)

When she persists in soliciting information, Hotspur responds, like Petruchio, with wilful misunderstanding:

LADY:	What is it carries you away?
HOTSPUR:	Why, my horse, my love, my horse.
LADY:	Out, you mad-headed ape!
	A weasel hath not such a deal of spleen
	As you are toss'd with. In faith,
	I'll know your business, Harry, that I will.
	I fear my brother Mortimer doth stir
	About his title, and hath sent for you
	To line his enterprise, but if you go –
HOTSPUR:	So far afoot, I shall be weary, love. (II. iii. 75–84)

Despite the affectionate tone implicit in the teasing, the domestic picture revealed in Lady Percy's long speech is dispiriting. Martial thoughts not only dominate Hotspur's waking hours but disturb his slumbers:

> In thy faint slumbers I by thee have watch'd,
> And heard thee murmur tales of iron wars,
> Speak terms of manage to thy bounding steed,
> Cry 'Courage! to the field!' And thou hast talk'd
> Of sallies and retires, of trenches, tents,
> Of palisadoes, frontiers, parapets,
> Of basilisks, of cannon, culverin,
> Of prisoners' ransom, and of soldiers slain, . . . (II. iii. 47–54)

What motivates Hotspur is war: 'fighting is the one thing that does not bore him, and nothing that does not lead to fighting is worth bothering with'.[39] He does not scruple to conceal this from his wife: 'I love thee not,/ I care not for thee, Kate. This is no world/ To play with mammets and to tilt with lips./ We must have bloody noses and crack'd crowns' (II. iii. 90–93).

Editors (and directors) frequently view the dialogue in this scene as teasingly tender: 'Lady Percy's love for "my heart's dear Harry" . . . is transparently clear and in the banter they exchange one can detect his love for her.'[40] However, an almost identical husband–wife confrontation in *Julius Caesar* shows a more loving male response which reflects adversely on Hotspur. Portia challenges Brutus with his sleeplessness and secrecy, insisting, like Lady Percy, that she be allowed to share her husband's burdens. Brutus' reaction is poignant:

> You are my true and honorable wife,
> As dear to me as are the ruddy drops
> That visit my sad heart. (II. i. 288–90)
>
>   O ye gods!
> Render me worthy of this noble wife! (II. i. 302–3)

Such measured and weighty expressions of emotion show us a healthier relationship than that of the Percies. In spirit and marriage Portia is clearly a happier descendant of Lady Percy: she is, of course, Cate-O's daughter.[41]

Denied the emotional reassurance which Brutus offers Portia, Lady Percy responds to her husband in a manner which is reassuringly (if fleetingly) assertive. Using the only two techniques known to Hotspur, she resists his taciturn hegemony by verbal obstinacy and physical violence: 'Come, come, you paraquito, answer me/ Directly unto this question that I ask./ In faith, I'll break thy little finger, Harry,/ And if thou wilt not tell me all things true' (II. iii. 85–8). Her mettle avails her little. Hotspur will swear he loves her when he is on horseback, a response which serves to indicate that his public life takes precedence over his private. No Renaissance audience would find anything unorthodox in this view that marriage is subordinate to 'man's work' (even when that 'man's work' is overthrowing the state). But it is more difficult to know how to respond to the tone of III. i where, in public, Lady Percy subdues her reactions to more provocative treatment by her husband.

While Glendower, Worcester, Mortimer and Hotspur are waiting for indentures to be drawn up, Lady Percy and Lady Mortimer are admitted to the men's presence. Mortimer has made good use of his imprisonment by marrying his captor's daughter, rather than learning Welsh. The result? 'This is the deadly spite that angers me:/ My wife can speak no

143

English, I no Welsh' (III. i. 190–91). None the less, the Mortimers' relationship exudes genuine tenderness, and Lady Mortimer soothes her husband with a Welsh song. Hotspur deflates the lyric tone of this episode with a provocative double entendre: 'Come, Kate, thou art perfect in lying down./ Come, quick, quick, that I may lay my head in thy lap' (III. i. 226–7). The first comment seems to refer indecently to Lady Percy's sexual ability, but she brushes it off good-humouredly: 'Go, ye giddy goose' (III. i. 228). Shortly afterwards, Hotspur's response transforms two innocent comments by his wife ('Wouldst thou have thy head broken?' and 'be still') into *risqué* remarks: 'Neither, 'tis a woman's fault' (III. i. 237–40).[42] Hotspur then completes her inoffensive 'Now God help thee!' by adding 'To the Welsh lady's bed' (III. i. 241–2). His humour, although commencing as badinage, is becoming potentially hurtful, and Lady Percy does not let it pass: 'What's that?' (III. i. 243). But Lady Mortimer's Welsh song intervenes and prevents Lady Percy pursuing the matter.

Throughout the BBC version of this dialogue, Michelle Dotrice tried to laugh off her husband's bewildering remarks. She was unable to do this, however, when faced with lines 245 and 257. When Dotrice was presented with Hotspur's two requests, 'Come, Kate, I'll have your song too. . . . Come sing', she was visibly affronted; her reply, 'I will *not* sing' (III. i. 258; Dotrice's emphasis), was delivered with an unsteady lower jaw as she struggled to retain her dignity. This provided a perfect interpretation of an exchange which no editor has ever glossed. On one level, of course, Hotspur's request for a song is literal, as his subsequent remark shows: ''Tis the next way to turn tailor, or be redbreast teacher' (III. i. 259–60). But he has just been indulging in sexual innuendo, and Dotrice's delivery prompts one to suspect a secondary meaning of 'sing' – precisely the bawdy meaning we find in *Troilus and Cressida*:

TROILUS:	Yea, so familiar?
ULYSSES:	She will sing any man at first sight.
THERSITES:	And any man may sing her, if he can take her cliff; she's noted. (v. ii. 8–11)

Partridge, who cites this exchange, glosses 'sing' as follows: '(Of a woman) to allure, to make advances to; (of a man) to coit with'.[43] Hotspur is obviously making a lewd remark – his fifth in fifteen lines (prompted in the BBC film by Lady Mortimer leaning over to give her supine husband a lingering kiss). Hotspur does not stay to make amends to his wife – we saw earlier how Petruchio rescinded his 'tongue in your tail' joke – but leaps to his feet to see if the indentures are drawn. Military activity is imminent, and the tardy Mortimer, evidently reluctant to leave his bride, is chastised by his father-in-law: 'you are as slow/ As hot Lord Percy is on fire to go' (III. i. 263–4).

The Mortimers' relationship is obviously introduced for more than its musical value. Mortimer, like Romeo before him, vows to learn his wife's language, whereas Hotspur wrests the sense of his wife's words awry. Mortimer's predilection for private marital pleasures is viewed as reprehensible, a neglect of public, masculine duties; whereas Hotspur, in putting such duties first, avoids the censure given to kindred chivalric or military figures ranging in stature from Chrétien's Erec and Yvain to Acomat in the anonymous *Selimus* (Q 1594).

The parallel with Erec is remarkable; and, given the medieval flavour of Hotspur's character, it is closer in relevance than the early date of *Erec and Enide* (c. 1170) might suggest.[44] Erec is one of the noblest knights in Arthur's court: 'Though not yet twenty-five, he was most noble, brave, and becoming. Never had any man his age displayed such valor.'[45] His valour is amply proven in the first portion of the romance, in the course of which he meets and marries Enide; after this the private pleasures of marriage lead to his withdrawal from public, chivalric affairs:

> Erec loved Enide with such love that he cared no more for feats of arms, nor did he attend tournaments. He had no desire to joust. His only wish was to lie beside his wife, whom he made his sweetheart and his mistress. Embracing her and kissing her occupied all his attention, and he longed for no other pleasure.
> This situation saddened his companions. Often among themselves they regretted his excessive love for her.[46]

Enide, aware of the attitude of the Knights of the Round Table, regrets that she has brought shame on her husband. When Erec overhears her laments he embarks on a new series of adventures, the last of which, the Joy of the Court, offers a parallel to his own earlier marital behaviour: Maboagrain and his lady have isolated themselves from society in a 're-strictive and confining love-service' from which Erec is able to release them.[47] Indulgent, domestic love is unsuitable for a public figure, as Chrétien's Sir Yvain learns when Sir Gawain tempts him back to chivalric life in *The Knight with the Lion*:

> 'What?' Sir Gawain asks. 'Will you be like those men who are less worthy because of their wives? Holy Mary damn the man who marries and regresses!['][48]

In *Selimus*, Acomat is universally despised for his privileging of marital bliss over martial valour, but after his volte-face in scene ix, he is welcomed back to the military fold:

> that prince that follows lustfull game,
> And to fond toyes his captiue minde enclines,
> Shall neuer passe the temple of true fame,
> Whose worth is greater then the *Indian* mines.[49]

145

Hotspur is one of a sequence of protagonists who learn that uxoriousness is unhealthy. To a Renaissance audience, Hotspur's public priorities would be the right priorities.

Notwithstanding, I find the lack of conjugal communion in the Percy household disquieting. Agydas' scornful words to Zenocrate in *I Tamburlaine* could well be asked of Lady Percy:

> How can you fancy one that looks so fierce,
> Only disposed to martial stratagems?
> Who, when he shall embrace you in his arms,
> Will tell how many thousand men he slew,
> And when you look for amorous discourse,
> Will rattle forth his facts of war and blood[.][50]

I can only assume that Lady Percy loves Hotspur for the same reason that Zenocrate is attracted to Tamburlaine: he speaks well.[51]

Hotspur's matrimonial motive is presumably the same as that which prompts Petruchio and Henry V to woo their Katherines – profit (a motive shared by almost every other wooer in England in an age when marriage was a business transaction).[52] Although he is unaware of the fact, this prominent rebel is related by marriage to the man named heir by Richard II. Shakespeare confuses two historical Mortimers here (as do his sources), but it is clear that in the drama he sees Lady Percy's brother as the successor: 'was not he proclaim'd/ By Richard, that dead is, the next of blood?' (I. iii. 145–6).[53] Worcester makes this revelation in Act I, scene iii, and it is evident that Hotspur hears the news for the first time here, for he exclaims: 'But soft, I pray you, did King Richard then/ Proclaim my brother Edmund Mortimer/ Heir to the crown? (I. iii. 155–7). Shakespeare's aim in including this revelation and reaction is clearly to avoid giving Hotspur an interested motive (other than honour) in defying the King, and we can hardly take Mortimer's dynastic role very seriously when, as Alexander Leggatt points out, Mortimer himself seems not to 'notice his own importance'.[54] None the less, Hotspur's eight-line silence before responding indicates a man temporarily dumbfounded as he takes in the implications of the news. Like Mortimer, he finds that marriage has potential political advantages.

Although Mortimer seems genuinely to fall in love with Glendower's daughter, it cannot be denied that marriage into one's captor's family is a convenient way of achieving liberty. Holinshed's account, although trying to be objective, presents Mortimer as self-interested rather than romantically inclined:

> Edmund Mortimer earle of March, prisoner with Owen Glendouer, whether for irkesomnesse of cruell captiuitie, or feare of death, or for what other cause, it is vncerteine, agreed to take part with Owen, against the king of England, and tooke to wife the daughter of the said Owen.[55]

The relationship between Lady Mortimer and her husband is particularly illuminating in relation to the Percies' marriage. The New Variorum editor suggests that 'the real function of the sentimental Mortimers in this scene [is] to serve as contrast to the high-spirited Percies'.[56] But the contrast they provide works to the Percies' disadvantage. Faced with a natural language barrier larger than the artificial one erected by Petruchio's and Hotspur's casuistry, the couple communicate perfectly with kisses and tears: 'I understand thy looks . . . I understand thy kisses, and thou mine,/ And that's a feeling disputation' (III. i. 198, 202–3). Furthermore, Mortimer makes a serious effort at communication, vowing to learn his bride's mother-tongue: 'But I will never be a truant, love,/ Till I have learn'd thy language' (III. i. 204–5). Nor can we attribute the Mortimers' harmony to any feminine meekness which might make Lady Mortimer more pliable matrimonial material than Katherine Minola or Lady Percy. As her father reveals, she is as refractory and determined as they:

> She'll be a soldier too, she'll to the wars. . . .
> She is desperate here, a peevish, self-will'd harlotry,
> One that no persuasion can do good upon. (III. i. 193, 196–7)

From a private angle, the liaison is superior to that of the Percies, and David Giles made this suggestion forcefully in the final frame of III. i. in the BBC version, where Lady Mortimer glanced at a tearful Lady Percy with a look of quiet triumph.

Hotspur could learn something to his own advantage from the Mortimers' marital concord, if only as regards carefree slumber. It is, of course, 'the soldiers' life/ To have their balmy slumbers wak'd with strife', as Desdemona learns in *Othello* (II. iii. 257–8). But Mortimer is urged to lay his head on his wife's lap as a prelude to sleep:

> And she will sing the song that pleaseth you,
> And on your eyelids crown the god of sleep,
> Charming your blood with pleasing heaviness,
> Making such difference 'twixt wake and sleep
> As is the difference betwixt day and night. (III. i. 213–17)

Amor vincit insomnia – or, as Glendower says, it enables one to tell the difference betwixt day and night – that is, between the sun and the moon.

The dichotomy between sun and moon is common to all three plays under discussion. The commonplace association of females with the moon and males with the sun can be seen in a great variety of literary references. These range from Plutarch's description of Antony's and Cleopatra's twins ('a son and a daughter, [they] named [their] son Alexander and [their] daughter Cleopatra, and gave them to their surnames, the Sun to the one and the Moon to the other')[57] to Chrétien's digression about the meeting of Sir Gawain and his lady:

> I do want to say a brief word about a private meeting that took place between the sun and the moon. Do you know of whom I would speak to you? The man who was the lord of knights, renowned above all, must be called the sun. I refer to Sir Gawain. His example enhances all chivalry as the morning sun casts its rays abroad and lights all the places where it shines. And I call her the moon, for there can never be but one of such great loyalty and strong support. I call her this, however, not only because of her high reputation, but because her name was Lunete.[58]

In *The Taming of the Shrew*, Katherine and Petruchio reach agreement following a negotiation about sun and moon. We might read this as a metaphor for reaching agreement about their own natures. The female/ moon is capable of change, as is Katherine. Apologising to Vincentio, she attributes her volte-face to her 'mistaking eyes,/ That have been so dazzled with the sun' (IV. v. 45–6). But which sun? The one in the sky, or the one referred to by Petruchio earlier in the same scene: 'Now by my mother's son, and that's myself' (IV. v. 6)? Given the punning inter-changeability of language in this play, where 'rope-tricks' can mean 'rhet-oric' and 'Stoics' pun on 'stocks',[59] it is appropriate that Katherine should be dazzled by the sun/son Petruchio. However, Petruchio's victory is first illustrated in a scene which demonstrates the verbal inter-changeability of sun and moon, and hence the equivalent status of the two bodies.

Jeanne Addison Roberts has illustrated the significance of the her-maphrodite as 'a popular Elizabethan emblem for the miracle of marriage, which joined male and female'. She analyses a typical hermaphroditic emblem which features 'the sun and moon (on male and female sides respectively), reinforcing the idea of the union of these qualities in mar-riage and adding resonance to Shakespeare's scene, where the two heav-enly bodies have become interchangeable'.[60] Joel Fineman examines this iconographic tradition from a different perspective, but makes the same observations.[61] The harmonious resolution to the sun/moon debate in *The Shrew* IV. v suggests a harmonious balance of the sun–moon/male–female dialectic in Katherine and Petruchio's marriage, for if Petruchio is flexible in his approach to the nomenclature of the sun and moon, he is likely to be flexible in his approach to the male and female worlds which they represent.

This is not the case with Hotspur and Henry. After Hotspur's death Lady Percy continues to view her husband as the sun: 'For his [honour], it stuck upon him as the sun/ In the grey vault of heaven' (*II HIV*, II. iii. 18–19), and his association with the moon has been fleeting: 'By heaven, methinks it were an easy leap,/ To pluck bright honor from the pale-fac'd moon' (*I HIV*, I. iii. 201–2). Hal/Henry V is, from his first soliloquy, equated with the sun, despite his temporary alliance with Falstaff's moon-light forces. As Hotspur's sun sets, Hal's rises, and he declares his solar allegiance firmly in the wooing scene in *Henry V*: 'but a good heart, Kate, is the sun and the moon, or rather the sun and not the moon; for it shines bright and never changes, but keeps his course truly' (v. ii. 162–4). But yet (like Cleopatra, 'I do not like "but yet" ' . . .) there is something ominous in Henry's denial of a sun/moon balance. His insistence on heliacal hegemony, on overpowering the French moon with the English sun, suggests that he means to subdue Katherine's autonomy just as he has overcome her country's.[62]

After reading *The Taming of the Shrew* and *I Henry IV*, one experiences a striking sense of *déjà vu* when Katherine of France first encounters her suitor. The French and English lords exit at v. ii. 98 to survey Henry's conditions of peace, and Katherine, at Henry's request, is left behind, chaperoned by her waiting-woman, Alice. Like Katherine and Petruchio, the lovers converse in private until they are interrupted by the return of Katherine's father. The scene concludes with a public confirmation of Henry's conquest of France and a celebration of the marriage contract.

The French Katherine's behaviour is very similar to that of her Italian and Northumbrian namesakes. Alone with her suitor she displays an assertive, teasing vitality; in public she is silent and submissive. Like the earlier Katherines with their wooers, Katherine and Henry have a problem in communication, caused in this instance by the French–English language barrier.[63] Katherine quickly uses her professed ignorance to counter Henry:

HENRY: Do you like me, Kate?
KATHERINE: *Pardonnez-moi*, I cannot tell wat is 'like me'. (v. ii. 107–8)

Seizing on 'like me', Henry turns to flattery: 'An angel is like you, Kate, and you are like an angel' (v. ii. 109–10). However, Katherine is not deceived by his compliment and adroitly turns the tables on him: *'les langues des hommes sont pleines de tromperies'* (v. ii. 115–16). Henry recognises that he has been outmanoeuvred ('The Princess is the better Englishwoman': v. ii. 121), and changes tactics by changing roles. No longer the Petrarchan wooer, he adopts a naïf farm-boy role: 'I know no ways to mince it in love, but directly to say "I love you" ' (v. ii. 126–7). Katherine now resists him with logic: 'Is it possible dat I sould love de ennemie of France?' (v. ii. 169–70).

The progression of this scene is remarkably like its comic predecessor in *The Shrew*. Henry, like Petruchio, meets a woman who is easily his match in repartee, and they engage in a stimulating wit-combat. To Henry military victory is easier to achieve than amorous conquest ('If I could win a lady at leap-frog, by vaulting into my saddle . . . I should quickly leap into a wife': v. ii. 136–9). Petruchio had erroneously thought that encountering a woman, even a shrewish one, would be a trifle in comparison to his former military exploits:

> Have I not heard great ordnance in the field,
> And heaven's artillery thunder in the skies?
> Have I not in a pitched battle heard
> Loud 'larums, neighing steeds, and trumpets' clang?
> And do you tell me of a woman's tongue. (I. ii. 203–7)[64]

The only element missing that would make the wooing scene in *Henry V* a perfect partner to the wooing scene in *The Shrew* is innuendo, but this has already been supplied by the French lesson in III. iv, in which Katherine's innocent exploration of the body leads her from military vocabulary to inadvertent bawdy. The language scene and the wooing episode together create a picture of Katherine as playful, resilient and assertive.[65] Like Katherine Minola and Katherine Percy, however, Katherine Valois does a volte-face in public. When the French powers return, she is silent for the remainder of the scene, acquiescing passively to the agreement made between Charles VI and Henry V.

Despite her silence Katherine may be giddily in love, on the threshold of a lifetime of happiness; however, historical hindsight forces one to doubt this. Henry and Katherine had a brief honeymoon (two days), followed by just two years of marriage, before Henry V died of dysentery at Vincennes. Queen Katherine, three miles away in Paris and within easy reach of her husband's deathbed, was not with him when he died. Wylie and Waugh's cautious surmise that 'Henry seems to have betrayed no affection or concern for her during his last hours' is substantiated by Desmond Seward's analysis of the situation.

> [I]t was the normal custom even for medieval kings to have their wives by them when they were dying. It was not that she could not leave her baby; she had already done so and the child was in England. If her husband had summoned her she would have had to go to him. Plainly he did not summon her. The inference is that his feelings for Catherine were not quite so romantic as Shakespeare makes out.[66]

But Shakespeare does not view the relationship romantically. The three *Henry* plays are full of images of financial transaction, and Katherine is simply a pawn in an international game of exchange.[67] Henry tells Burgundy: 'you must *buy* that peace' (v. ii. 70; emphasis added), and Katherine, his 'capital demand' (v. ii. 96), has been rejected once already when her accompaniment was only '[s]ome petty and unprofitable dukedoms' (III. Chorus. 31). Lance Wilcox points out that Henry's discourse has depended heavily on images of rape throughout the play,[68] and if Henry's

French language simile in Act v is anything to go by, his view of marriage is far from romantic – 'like a new-married wife about her husband's neck, hardly to be shook off' (v. ii. 179–81). As with all good soldiers, from Petruchio and Hotspur to Claudio in *Much Ado*, warring comes before wooing. Furthermore, matrimony serves only military ends:

> Shall not thou and I, . . . compound a boy, half French, half English, that shall go to Constantinople and take the Turk by the beard? (v. ii. 206–9)

Like his father before him, who 'was thinking of civil wars when he got me' (v. ii. 225–6), or Hotspur, who tells his wife she is 'perfect in lying down' (*I HIV* III. i. 226), or Petruchio, who asserts '[w]omen are made to bear' (*TS*, II. i. 200), Henry sees woman as fulfilling a political rather than a personal need. Seward concludes: 'it is likely that the king's true feelings for her [Katherine] were essentially dynastic, and that he felt little affection for her'.[69] His wooing is accordingly pragmatic, not romantic. Henry believes that marriage with Katherine will cement current international harmony and, through procreation, ensure future *entente*. We can hardly deny the value of this approach. Theoretically it should lead, after all, to the same conclusion as *The Shrew*, in which order is established within a domestic context, while in a public sphere traditional hierarchy is celebrated. Henry V creates (albeit temporarily) domestic order and international political harmony, achieving in one scene what took Petruchio four Acts. Well might Henry say 'Thus have I politicly begun my reign'.

Any feeling of harmony is speedily undercut, however, for the Epilogue reminds us that Henry VI was 'in infant bands crown'd King' and France was lost: 'Which oft our stage hath shown' (Epilogue, 9, 13). This need not discredit Katherine and Henry's relationship – as *The Tempest* tells us, '[g]ood wombs have borne bad sons'. But at this stage Shakespeare ensures that the structural and verbal parallels with *The Shrew* and *I Henry IV* direct our attention to three matrimonial analogues – Petruchio, Hotspur, and Mortimer. We are left to ponder which course the Valois–Plantagenet alliance will take.

IV

In one respect the most obvious (and most encouraging) precedent is that provided by Katherine and Petruchio. The wooing of Katherine Minola is portrayed as a series of military assaults, and Katherine is 'starv'd for meat, giddy for lack of sleep,/ With oaths kept waking, and with brawling fed' (IV. iii. 9–10) – precisely the conditions of combat. Petruchio's victory ('the field is won': IV. v. 23) consists in winning Katherine over to his

151

side, where she is now ready to do battle on his behalf: 'To her, Kate! . . . A hundred marks, my Kate does put her down' (v. ii. 33, 35).

These elements find parallel in *Henry V*, where Katherine transfers allegiance to 'de ennemie of France'. The conventional vocabulary of Katherine Minola's long speech of obedience is especially relevant to the relationship between Henry V and Katherine Valois (I emphasise the pertinent vocabulary):

> Thy husband is thy lord, thy life, thy keeper,
> Thy head, thy *sovereign*; one that cares for thee, . . .
>
> And craves no other *tribute* at thy hands
> But love, fair looks, and true obedience –
> Too little *payment* for so great a *debt*.
> Such duty as the subject owes the *prince*,
> Even such a woman oweth to her husband; . . .
>
> I am asham'd that women are so simple
> To offer *war* where they should kneel for *peace*, . . . (v. ii. 146–7, 152–6, 161–2)

If the peace treaty negotiated by Katherine and Petruchio leads to harmony, then its vocabulary bodes well for Katherine and Henry.

But the more insistent Hotspur–Henry parallel invoked throughout the second tetralogy invites us to see the terrible irony whereby, as Marilyn Williamson points out, 'Henry has become like Hotspur and like much that as Hal he despised'.[70] We remember that the two Hotspur/Lady Percy scenes are separated by an episode in which Hal mimics his Northern rival – in particular, Hotspur's relationship with his wife:

> I am not yet of Percy's mind, the Hotspur of the north, he that kills me some six or seven dozen of Scots at a breakfast, washes his hands, and says to his wife, 'Fie upon this quiet life! I want work.' 'O my sweet Harry,' says she, 'how many hast thou kill'd to-day?' 'Give my roan horse a drench,' says he, and answers, 'Some fourteen,' an hour after; 'a trifle, a trifle'. I prithee call in Falstaff. I'll play Percy[.] (II. iv. 101–9)

At this early stage of the *Henry* sequence, Hal plays Hotspur parodically, for he is 'not yet of Percy's mind'. In the wooing scene in *Henry V* he plays Hotspur in earnest. The movement of the trilogy shows Hal rising to assume the place previously occupied by Hotspur ('think not, Percy,/ To share with me in glory any more./ Two stars keep not their motion in one sphere': *I HIV*, v. iv. 63–5). Henry's search for honour replaces Hotspur's; Henry's military prowess replaces Hotspur's; and Henry's domestic relationship likewise replaces Hotspur's.

152

Hal has played other men's roles all his life. Stephen Greenblatt points out that 'Hal's characteristic activity is playing, or, more precisely, theatrical improvisation – his parts include his father, Hotspur, Hotspur's wife, a thief in buckram, himself as prodigal and himself as penitent'.[71] To this we might add: himself as Prince John (his rejection of Falstaff parallels his brother's betrayal of the rebels at Gaultree Forest), himself as Petrarchan wooer (compare Mortimer) and himself as inept lover (compare Hotspur). The ease with which he switches roles in the wooing scene says something about the insincerity of his approach.

He begins as international litigator, with financial vocabulary reminiscent of the Lord Chief Justice in *II Henry IV*. Next he tries the Mortimer approach, emulating both his tenderness and his desire to be a language student: 'Will you vouchsafe to teach a soldier terms,/ Such as will enter at a lady's ear,/ And plead his love-suit to her gentle heart?' (v. ii. 99–101). Finally, like Hotspur, he rejects mincing poetry: 'I know no ways to mince it in love, but directly to say "I love you"; then if you urge me farther than to say "Do you in faith?" I wear out my suit' (v. ii. 126–9). We are reminded ominously of *I Henry IV*, where Lady Percy urges her husband farther, only to find that he has worn out his suit.

Like Petruchio and Hotspur before him, Henry tries to outmanoeuvre his bride with sophistry: 'in loving me, you should love the friend of France; for I love France so well that I will not part with a village of it' (v. ii. 172–4). Katherine is a possession, something he has conquered, like a French city ('the cities turn'd into a maid; for they are all girdled with maiden walls that war hath [never] ent'red': v. ii. 321–3). Katherine must learn *his* language; *her* customs are to be slighted. This is not wooing, but subjugation in disguise.

In *An Apology for Women* (1620, entered in the Stationers' Register in 1619) Christopher Newstead cites the example of Katherine of France in support of his contention that women enjoy being conquered: 'And how many *Katherines* chose rather to bee courted with conquering Launces, then Court-like Rapiers?' (sig. C3, p. 21). This is just one example of male wishful thinking, for the attractiveness of the rough wooer is a stereotype that goes hand in hand with that of the shrew. But it is interesting to note that Newstead sees Katherine as unequivocally conquered rather than wooed. He may derive his opinion from history as much as from the contemporary drama, although I view the latter source as more probable: the French career of Henry V was a popular dramatic topic in the 1590s, when the debate about women received sustained investigation.[72] Henry's romantic [*sic*] approach is even more prosaic in our only extant contemporary text, *The Famous Victories of Henry V*. The problematic state of the text complicates the issue; but Kate, like her predecessor in the problematic *A Shrew*, is given an aside in which she reveals that she is not averse to her rough suitor: 'I had best [agree to marriage] whilst he is willing,/ Least when I would, he will not' (G2v).

That *Henry V* contained material relevant to the ongoing debate about women can be seen in another Jacobean tract, Daniell Tuvill's *Asylum Veneris; or, A Sanctuary for Ladies* (1616), in which he attacks Salic law (sig. H2v, p. 110). Thus the action of *Henry V* is set in a dramatic framework which begins and ends with pertinent material concerning attitudes to women. Act I provides a lengthy explanation of why women are denied right of succession in France. The French interpretation of Pharamond's law is questioned ('the land Salique is in Germany': I. ii. 44), so Henry pursues his claim to the French throne, a claim which depends solely upon his belief in female rights in France. Yet Act V shows him denying a French woman personal rights. The topics of Salic law and the conquest of Katherine must have been of even greater relevance to Elizabethan audiences: Elizabeth derived her crown from the sequence sanctioned by Henry VIII, but she was a marginal and persecuted figure in Mary's reign, and even during her own her right to rule was debated, since her bastardy had never been revoked. The fact that the two episodes in *Henry V* which have been most criticised bear directly on the position of Katherine's independence suggests that Shakespeare was aware of the liminal and legal relevance of his material.[73]

One can only feel a sense of foreboding for Katherine's future with her conquering king if Henry's usurpation of Hotspur's role continues. But *Henry IV* also presents us with another alliance which originates, like Henry V's, in military conquest. Like the romance between Katherine and Henry, it is hindered by a language barrier; yet, unlike their relationship, it is characterised by reciprocal love. Perhaps the Mortimers' marriage provides the prototype for the Plantagenets'?

One wishes this were the case, but I think it unlikely. The parallels with Hotspur are too many and too strong throughout the *Henry IV/Henry V* plays to be assuaged by one Welsh interlude. The Mortimers' relationship gives us a picture of how the Katherine–Henry relationship might have been – or rather, how relationships could be – if one is not burdened by public duty.

Mortimer has been more than captured in battle. His better parts are all o'erthrown, and he is, in Mercutio's words, 'already dead, stabb'd with a white wench's black eye, run through the ear with a love-song, the very pin of his heart cleft with the blind bow-boy's butt-shaft' (*Romeo and Juliet*, II. iv. 13–16). Lady Mortimer's love has had the same effect on Mortimer as Juliet's on Romeo:

> Thy beauty hath made me effeminate,
> And in my temper soft'ned valor's steel! (*R&J*, III. i. 114–15)

With marriage Mortimer has lost his martial alacrity, as his father-in-law points out at III. i. 263–4.[74] Throughout this scene Mortimer functions as peacemaker between the irascible Glendower and the refractory Hotspur:

> Peace, cousin Percy, you will make him mad. (III. i. 51)

> Come, come, no more of this unprofitable chat. (III. i. 62)

> Fie, cousin Percy, how you cross my father! (III. i. 145)

When Hotspur cavils at the division of land ('Methinks my moi'ty, . . . equals not one of yours./ See how this river comes me cranking in,/ And cuts me from the best of all my land': III. i. 95–8), Mortimer attempts appeasement by pointing out that he is equally, but uncomplainingly, disadvantaged: 'Yea, but/ Mark how he bears his course, and runs me up/ With like advantage on the other side,/ Gelding the opposed continent as much/ As on the other side it takes from you' (III. i. 106–10). When Glendower exits, Mortimer further tries to palliate Hotspur by reporting Glendower's supposed high opinion of him. That Mortimer's pacifist leadership is ineffectual is revealed by the fact that Hotspur totally ignores his caution at line 51; that Mortimer's judgement is suspect can be seen in his confidence in the superstitious Glendower's alleged occult ability; and that Mortimer's good-mannered approach is useless is shown by the intervention of the hitherto silent Worcester, who reprimands Hotspur in a blunter fashion with immediate results.

'[G]ood manners be your speed' says Hotspur (half-heartedly? sarcastically?) to his brother-in-law (III. i. 188). Good manners do not bring soldiers success, and Prince John sets an example of the opposite at Gaultree Forest. Fluellen makes this connection again in *Henry V* when he compares Henry V to Alexander the Big:

> Why, I pray you, is not 'pig' great? The pig, or the great, or the mighty, or the huge, or the magnanimous, are all one reckonings, save the phrase is a little variations. (*HV*, IV. vii. 15–18)

Fluellen's Welsh accent reveals that Alexander the 'Great' became Alexander the 'Big' because he was also Alexander the 'Pig'. It is the adoption of pig-like qualities which makes Henry such a successful military leader. The man who rejects his Eastcheap friend has no difficulty in treating his bride-to-be with the same politically expedient lack of sentiment. 'I love thee cruelly' is a necessary paradox, like Alexander the pig and big. Mortimer sacrifices his military prowess for love; Hotspur does not; Henry will not.[75]

V

Because this essay is concerned with the similarities in the relationships of the three Katherines, is it now necessary to revise the conclusion about Katherine and Petruchio's marital harmony, which fits the paradigm in all but the rejection of sentiment? I think not. The significant variant in *The Taming of the Shrew* is that Petruchio is a retired soldier. He has in his time heard great ordnance in the field; but with the demise of his father, he has inherited an estate and chosen to re-enter civilian life: 'Crowns in my purse I have, and goods at home,/ And so am come abroad to see the world' (I. ii. 57–8).

Throughout the second tetralogy Shakespeare explores the high personal cost of public life. With kingship come polished perturbation and golden care. The crown is accompanied by unquiet rest: 'How many thousand of my poorest subjects/ Are at this hour asleep!': *II HIV*, III. i. 4–5). It is accompanied by mistrust ('He shall think that thou, which knowest the way/ To plant unrightful kings, wilt know again'; *RII*, v. i. 62–3); and it is accompanied by personal sacrifice (Henry IV forfeits his health; his son forfeits domestic felicity). These points apply equally to rebel leadership: Hotspur's position is accompanied by mistrust, lack of sleep, and marital rupture.

From the beginning of the second tetralogy, Shakespeare has displayed an interest in wide historical patterns. Bolingbroke, full of hope for a better world, usurps Richard II's position, only to find himself in exactly the same situation, with the blood of a kinsman on his hands. Similarly, in *Henry IV* and *Henry V* Henry takes over Hotspur's role, including the personal characteristics of his erstwhile rival. History repeats itself.

Hotspur and Henry become historical legends through military prowess. But to participate in history is to deny oneself the fullness of personal life as obtained by Mortimer and Petruchio, characters who will never attain top billing in the history books. (Indeed, Petruchio's life, like Petruchio himself, is the stuff of fiction.) In *Alarm to England* (1578) Barnabie Rich views love as incompatible with success in war:

> if all the louers that are in the world, were made in one whole armie, there is neyther Emperour, nor Monarche, but would be amazed to see such a companie of Bedlem fooles in a cluster. (sig. H2v)[76]

After describing at length the characteristics of lovers, Rich advises them to

> set aside all such trifling affaires, and vaine follies, . . . and rather to indeuour them selues, to such exercises, which haue gained Hercules, Achilles, Theseus, Caius Marius, Epaminondas, Themistocles, Alexander, Pyrrhus, Hannibal, Scipio, Pompeie, Caesar, with diuerse others, such immortall glorie, as neither the enuious rage of cruel death may blemishe, neither the

furious force of fortunes fickle wheele may diminish, neither the tracte of deuouring time shal euer be able to remoue fro[m] memorie. (sig. H4v)

Hotspur and Henry follow Rich's advice. Petruchio and Mortimer seek success in another sphere, by negotiating *ententes cordiales*. Petruchio and Mortimer thus forfeit their public careers – Petruchio through retirement and Mortimer through slackness.

The anagrammatic duality of martial and marital has particular resonance in plays which deal with the dichotomy between public and private life – not just of women, but also of men. The attempt to negotiate a compromise between personal and public identity is not a problem exclusive to women. At the end of *II Henry IV*, Henry V has to assume his public regal role – a tense moment which requires the rejection of his former private self, and the companions associated with it. Like Katherine Minola, Henry V is performing a public role in defiance of the on-stage audience's prejudgements and, also like Katherine, he realises that public order requires the adoption of a public persona. But a coronation is a one-way process. Having been renamed King Henry V, the King cannot revert to the titles Prince or Hal, or to the Eastcheap persona which accompanied them. For a ruler, taking a place in public life means forfeiting the private life unequivocally and for ever, and for the Lady or Princess who accompanies him the same is true: the private lives of Lady Percy and Katherine Valois are important only in their ability to provide a successor for public life. As Lance Wilcox reminds us, Katherine of France is both victim (martial) and bride (marital), and the same is true of Lady Percy.[77] Princess Katherine and Lady Mortimer do not become marital victims, because their husbands relinquish their martial identities. Critics of *The Taming of the Shrew* concentrate only on what Katherine appears to give up; they fail to realise how much Petruchio relinquishes in order to protect his wife from real loss.

This essay began by considering the nature of the relationship between Katherine and Petruchio in the context of the triplicate renaming of the Kates. 'What's in a name?' is the question I set out to answer. Shakespeare himself gives us the answer in a passage whose variant readings ironically illustrate stability of identity: 'That which we call a rose/ By any other [name: Q1; word: Q2] would smell as sweet' (*R&J*, II. ii. 43–4). The quiddity of a flower or a person can be disguised but not destroyed, just as the falcon can be trained but not tamed: it will perform in public only because it chooses to do so. The conclusion of *The Taming of the Shrew* gives us the illusion of conformity, in the final 'counterfeit suppose' of the play. Eve, a woman named by her husband, yielded to him '[o]nely for order', as I.G. reminds us. And if public order is served by deception and hypocrisy . . . well, illusion can have beneficial social effects (a moral *The Taming of the Shrew* propounds in many ways).[78] Ultimately, of course, names are changeable but not disposable: a Katherine can be a Kate, but she can never *not* be a Katherine. Derrida glosses a similar onomastic paradox in *Romeo and Juliet* as follows:

> Roméo est Roméo, et Roméo n'est pas Roméo. Il n'est lui-même qu'à se départir de son nom, il n'est lui-même que dans son nom. Roméo ne peut s'appeler lui-même que s'il se départit de son nom, il ne s'appelle qu'à partir de son nom.[79]

What Shakespeare shows us in the Katherine/Kate equation in *The Taming of the Shrew*, as Derrida implies, is doubling – the Elizabethan thespian ability to be two people in close succession, on different occasions, but not at the same time. The verbal doubling of Katherine with Kate proves to be a highly significant theatrical trope in a play which examines the tools of the dramatist's art: language, imagination, disguise, illusion, willing suspension of disbelief, behavioural psychology. Katherine has two names, is two people, just as the boy playing her is two people, male and female, just as the play is two plays – one for Sly and one for us. That this theatrical exploration of doubleness extends to personal names is made patently clear throughout, from the Italian significance of Lucentio's assumed name, Cambio ('change'), through Petruchio's pun on 'Bianca' at v. ii. 186 ("'Twas I won the wager, though you hit the white'), to the disappearance of the literal Sly in favour of a Katherine who, performing as Kate, becomes figuratively 'sly'.[80] The way in which the investigation of dramatic change permeates all levels of *The Taming of the Shrew* makes this a remarkably accomplished comedy for such an early date – not a crude farce about the *taming* of the shrew, but a sophisticated exploration of the *naming* of the shrew. And, as the brides (and grooms) in *Henry IV* and *Henry V* show, Shakespeare continues this theme in ways which explore names as the *sine qua non/nom* of personal and public identities.[81]

NOTES

1. All Shakespeare quotations are from G. Blakemore Evans, ed., *The Riverside Shakespeare* (Boston, MA: Houghton Mifflin, 1974), and are cited parenthetically in my text. I have expanded all speech prefixes. *The Taming of a Shrew* is quoted from Geoffrey Bullough, *Narrative and Dramatic Sources of Shakespeare*, vol. I (London: Routledge & Kegan Paul, 1957), scene xix, 15.
2. A. Quiller-Couch and John Dover Wilson, eds, *The Taming of the Shrew* (Cambridge: Cambridge University Press, 1928, reprinted 1968), p. xvi.
3. Edmund Wilson, ed., *Shaw on Shakespeare* (London: Cassell, 1961), pp. 178–82; John Masefield, *William Shakespeare* (London: Thornton Butterworth Ltd, 1911, reprinted 1928), pp. 105–9; E.K. Chambers, *Shakespeare: A Survey* (New York: Hill & Wang, 1925), pp. 40–8.
4. Chambers, *Shakespeare*, p. 40.

5. Alexander Leggatt, *Shakespeare's Comedy of Love* (London: Methuen, 1974), p. 56.
6. Robert B. Heilman, ed., *The Taming of the Shrew* (New York: New American Library, 1966), p. xxv.
7. Coppélia Kahn, *Man's Estate: Masculine identity in Shakespeare* (Berkeley, Los Angeles and London: University of California Press, 1981), p. 104.
8. Harold C. Goddard, *The Meaning of Shakespeare* (Chicago: University of Chicago Press, 1951), vol. I, p. 68.
9. Shirley Nelson Garner, '*The Taming of the Shrew*: Inside or outside of the joke', in Maurice Charney, ed., *'Bad' Shakespeare: Revaluations of the Shakespeare canon* (London and Toronto: Associated University Presses, 1988), pp. 105–19 (p. 106).
10. Linda Woodbridge, *Women and the English Renaissance* (Urbana and Chicago: University of Illinois Press, 1986), pp. 207, 222.
11. Norman Rabkin connects the three Kates, but he does not pursue the links, and relegates the subject to a note. See Norman Rabkin, *Shakespeare and the Problem of Meaning* (Chicago and London: University of Chicago Press, 1981), p. 147, note 11. A.R. Humphreys also treats the subject casually in a footnote: 'Shakespeare seems fond of "Kate" ' (A.R. Humphreys, ed., *I Henry IV* [London: Methuen, 1960, reprinted 1985], p. 51. Juliet Dusinberre connects the Kates fleetingly ('Shakespeare's Kates . . . all get the same kind of man') in *Shakespeare and the Nature of Women* (London: Macmillan, 1975), p. 289; and Muriel Bradbrook links two of them (Minola and Valois) in 'Dramatic role as social image: A study of *The Taming of the Shrew*', *Shakespeare-Jahrbuch*, **94** (1958), pp. 132–50, reprinted as Chapter VII of *The Artist and Society in Shakespeare's England: The collected papers of Muriel Bradbrook*, vol. I (Sussex: Harvester Press, 1982), pp. 106–20. Shirley Nelson Garner approaches the subject through two of the men: Petruchio is 'a comic version of Hotspur' (Garner, 'The Taming . . .', p. 117). Nevill Coghill made this connection earlier when he talked of Petruchio's 'Hotspur manners'; see 'The basis of Shakespearian comedy', in Anne Ridler, ed., *Shakespeare Criticism 1935–60* (London: Oxford University Press, 1963, reprinted 1970), pp. 201–27 (p. 208). Throughout the remainder of this essay I shall call all three women 'Katherine', reserving 'Kate' for the males' view of them.
12. Peter Stallybrass, 'Patriarchal territories: The body enclosed', in Margaret W. Ferguson, Maureen Quilligan and Nancy J. Vickers, eds, *Rewriting the Renaissance* (Chicago: University of Chicago Press, 1986), pp. 123–42 (p. 137).
13. The metrically convenient variant 'Katherina' is occasionally used; however, Katherine never refers to herself in this form. Stanley Wells points out that Katherina, although apparently authentically Italian, is in fact recorded in medieval English. See Stanley Wells and Gary Taylor with John Jowett and William Montgomery, *William Shakespeare: A textual companion* (Oxford: Clarendon Press, 1987), p. 171.
14. Raphael Holinshed, *Chronicles of England, Scotland, and Ireland* (London, 1587), vol. III. See, for example, 'the ladie Katharine' on p. 572 (twice) and 'the ladie Catharine' on p. 547; 'their daughter Katharine' appears on p. 572, and 'our most deere beloued Katharine' on p. 573.
15. According to E.G. Withycombe in *The Oxford Dictionary of English Christian Names* (Oxford: Clarendon Press, 1945, reprinted Oxford University Press, 1977) Kate was the most common diminutive of Katherine in the sixteenth and seventeenth centuries (p. 187). Berger and Bradford's *Index of Characters* lists only four plays between 1590 and 1610, besides those under

consideration, which use the name Kate (one of these is *The Taming of a Shrew*, plausibly a (modified) derivative of *The Shrew*); ten others contain a Katherine in the same period, and one has Katharina (Thomas L. Berger and William C. Bradford Jr, *An Index of Characters in English Printed Drama to the Restoration* [Englewood, CO: Microcard Editions, 1975]). Elsewhere in Shakespeare's canon we find a Katherine/Kate in *Love's Labour's Lost* and *Henry VIII*, and a 'Mistress Kate Keepdown' in *Measure for Measure* (referred to by Mistress Overdone at III. ii. 199). In *The Tempest* Stephano sings 'But none of us car'd for Kate;/ For she had a tongue with a tang' (II. ii. 49–50).

16. Holinshed, *Chronicles*, vol. III, p. 521; Edward Hall, *The Union of the Two Noble and Illustrious Families of Lancaster and York* (London, 1548), sig. C6r, p. xx.
17. Robert Sandler, ed., *Northrop Frye on Shakespeare* (New Haven, CT and London: Yale University Press, 1986), p. 72.
18. I know of no other Shakespearian female who is addressed by name so persistently. Touchstone's 'taming' of Audrey does display similar tactics in a similar situation. Trying to mould Audrey's behaviour, Touchstone insistently punctuates his speech with the vocative 'Audrey'. Although the total of his addresses does not approach those of the Kates, the principle seems to be the same.
19. *The Living Bible* (London: Coverdale House Publishers Ltd, 1971).
20. *Antony and Cleopatra*, III. xiii. 185–6; *Hamlet*, v. i. 257–8; I quote Webster from Elizabeth M. Brennan, ed., *The Duchess of Malfi* (London: Ernest Benn Ltd, 1964), IV. ii. 139.
21. In the 1988 production of the play at Stratford, Ontario, directed by Richard Monette, Colm Feore pronounced 'father' with a self-conscious silkiness, accompanied by a slightly embarrassed laugh.
22. Sly ignores the Lord's instruction and addresses his 'wife' as Petruchio does, with a name of his own: 'Madam wife' (Ind., ii. 112).
23. He has called her Katherine twice before (at their first meeting) but this was in private (II. i. 267, 280).
24. Peter Stallybrass relates this to Desdemona's strawberry-embroidered handkerchief, an item which, as Lynda Boose shows, has a long cultural history as a symbol of virginity – the red-on-white emblem of the nuptial sheets. See Stallybrass, 'Patriarchal territories'; and Boose, 'Othello's handkerchief: "The recognizance and pledge of love" ', *English Literary Renaissance*, 5 (1975), pp. 360–74.
25. Coppélia Kahn speaks about 'the most cherished male fantasy of all – that woman remain *untamed*', *Man's Estates*, p. 117). Margaret Loftus Ranald has made the most detailed study of this point of view, placing it in the context of the play's falcon-taming imagery:

> The falcon must be taught obedience to her master, but at the same time her wild and soaring nature must be preserved. This is a cardinal principle of hawk-taming. The bird must retain her hunting instinct; otherwise she is useless. But she must be taught to exercise her wild nature on command, to hunt under the government of her keeper/master. 'The manning of the haggard' or, *The Taming of The Shrew*', *Essays in Literature*, 1 (1974), pp. 149–65 (p. 153), reprinted as Chapter IV of *Shakespeare and His Social Context* (New York: AMS Press, 1987).

The most recent item I have read on falconry, an article in *The Manchester Guardian Weekly* (30 December 1990), uses vocabulary which describes Katherine's situation perfectly: '[one of the] particular pleasures in falconry . . . lies in establishing a relationship with a creature that can only be trained, not tamed' (p. 19).

26. This point is made by Linda Bamber and Coppélia Kahn, neither of whom is happy with it: 'Kate's compromise is distressing' (Bamber, *Comic Women, Tragic Men* [Stanford: Stanford University Press, 1982], p. 35); 'Kate . . . is trapped in her own cleverness. Her only way of maintaining her inner freedom is by outwardly denying it, a psychologically perilous position' (Kahn, *Man's Estate*, p. 113).

27. For good surveys of the *querelle des femmes*, see Woodbridge, *Women and the English Renaissance*; Katherine Usher Henderson and Barbara F. McManus, *Half Humankind* (Urbana and Chicago: University of Illinois Press, 1985); and Carroll Camden, *The Elizabethan Woman* (Houston, TX: Elsevier Press, 1952), pp. 241–71.

28. Quoted by Woodbridge, *Women and the English Renaissance*, p. 76 (my interpolations).

29. The issue of identity and nomenclature in *Romeo and Juliet* is complex and limitations of space preclude my pursuing it here. Jonathan Goldberg provides an illuminating approach to the topic in ' "What? in a names that which we call a Rose": The desired texts of *Romeo and Juliet*', forthcoming in Randall McLeod, ed., *Crisis in Editing: Texts of the English Renaissance* (New York: AMS Press).

30. See *Erec and Enide*, in David Staines, transl. and intro., *The Complete Romances of Chrétien de Troyes* (Bloomington and Indianapolis: Indiana University Press, 1990), pp. 1–86.

31. Wells, Taylor *et al.*, *William Shakespeare*, pp. 120–21, 109.

32. Although the 'you' of *Henry V*, v. ii. 373 may be addressed to the nobles, Q1 (1600) gives a chiastic formation which inclines one to view the line (in both Q1 and F) as a reciprocal husband/wife promise: 'Then will I swear to *Kate*, and *Kate* to mee:/ And may our vowes once made, vnbroken bee' (G4r).

Interestingly, none of the oaths takes place as described. Petruchio's description of Katherine's behaviour is part of his rhetorical fiction; Lady Percy does not obey her husband's command to swear; and King Henry's optimistic vision of the oath-swearing ('may our oaths well kept and prosp'rous be!': v. ii. 374) is contradicted both by the Epilogue and by the audience's historical knowledge. Hotspur and Henry V's view of their wives' obedience is as fictional as Petruchio's.

33. In *The Skull Beneath the Skin*, Charles R. Forker cites examples from Webster's *The White Devil*, Jonson's *The New Inn*, and Middleton's *A Mad World, My Masters* to illustrate the metaphorical connection between vaulting on to horses and sexual intercourse (p. 267; p. 559, note 13). This equine preference is repeated structurally as well as verbally in all three plays considered in this essay. In *I Henry IV* Hotspur responds to Lady Percy's love-talk with a demand for his horse; in *The Taming of the Shrew* Katherine tells Petruchio 'Now if you love me stay', to which he replies 'Grumio, my horse' (III. ii. 204); Henry V supplies both sides of the conversation in *HV*, v. ii. 132–9.

34. Ralph Berry, *Shakespeare and Social Class* (Atlantic Highlands, NJ: Humanities Press International, 1988), p. 26.

35. Mary Beth Rose, *The Expense of Spirit* (Ithaca, NY and London: Cornell University Press, 1988), *passim*, but especially pp. 34, 39, 107, 121–22, 130.

36. Henderson and McManus, *Half Humankind*, p. 81.

37. The Franklin's Tale, 744–7, 751–2, in F.N. Robinson, ed., *The Works of Geoffrey Chaucer* (Oxford: Oxford University Press, 1957).

38. The 1988 production at Stratford, Ontario made dramatic mileage out of this point. A mentally subnormal Ferdinand wandered on stage wearing pyjamas

and scratching his groin, while staring wordlessly at a clearly uncomfortable Katherine. This suggestion of Petruchio as a man who harangues women in public yet shelters the handicapped in private was subtle and effective.

39. *Northrop Frye on Shakespeare*, p. 72.

40. P.H. Davison, ed., *I Henry IV* (Harmondsworth: Penguin, 1968, reprinted 1981), p. 27.

41. I owe the point (and the pun) to George Walton Williams.

42. Puns in *Romeo and Juliet*, I. i. 22–6, *Measure for Measure*, IV. ii. 1–5, and *King Lear*, III. ii. 27–30 show the association of 'head' with 'maidenhead'. For the sexual innuendo in 'still' see Judith C. Levinson, ''Tis a woman's fault', *English Language Notes*, 11 (1973), pp. 38–40.

43. Eric Partridge, *Shakespeare's Bawdy* (London: Routledge & Kegan Paul, 1947, reprinted 1961), p. 187. There is no entry for 'sing' or 'song' in James T. Henke, *Courtesans and Cuckolds. A Glossary of Renaissance Dramatic Bawdy (Exclusive of Shakespeare)* (New York and London: Garland Publishing Inc., 1979). However, the verb is used in the sexual sense by Middleton. In *The Roaring Girl* Moll is presented to Sir Alexander Wengrave as a music teacher. Knowing the pretence, and suspecting that Moll is a whore, Sir Alexander initiates a series of bawdy double-entendres. When she mentions the proficiency of her pupils, whom she may call 'maisters', Sir Alexander replies 'I true, a company of whooremaisters; you teach to sing too?'. See *The Roaring Girl*, IV. i. 186–7, in Fredson Bowers, ed., *The Dramatic Works of Thomas Dekker*, vol. iii (Cambridge: Cambridge University Press, 1966). See also Alan Brissenden, ed., *A Chaste Maid in Cheapside* (London: Ernest Benn, 1968), II. i. 51–3: 'When I please blood,/ Merely I sing, and suck out others'; then,/ 'Tis many a wise man's fault.'

44. There is no evidence that Shakespeare knew Chrétien's romances (at least, not directly).

45. *Erec and Enide* in Staines, *Romances*, p. 2.

46. Ibid., p. 31.

47. Ibid., p. xv.

48. *The Knight with the Lion* in Staines, *Romances*, pp. 286–7.

49. W. Bang, ed., *The Tragical Reign of Selimus 1594* (MSR. Chiswick: Chiswick Press, 1908), pp. 776–9.

50. John D. Jump, ed., *Tamburlaine the Great, Parts I and II* (London: Edward Arnold, 1967), Part I, III. ii. 40–5. Barnabie Rich satirises those soldiers who (in times of peace) think only of war in *The Fruits of Long Experience* (London, 1604), pp. 28–9.

51. This is not the place to investigate Marlowe's treatment of women, but the similarities between the 'wooing' of Zenocrate and the treatment of the three Katherines are striking. Alexander Leggatt makes a particularly pertinent point when discussing Tamburlaine's refusal to grant clemency to Damascus. He writes: 'She thinks in human, personal terms . . . He thinks of patterns on maps, identifying Zenocrate not with the town where she was born *but with the towns that he will name after her*': Leggatt, 'Tamburlaine's sufferings', *Yearbook of English Studies*, 3 (1973), pp. 28–38 (pp. 30–31; emphasis added). Sara Munson Deats distinguishes between the public and private selves of Isabella in '*Edward II*: A study in androgyny', *Ball State University Forum*, 22 (1981), pp. 30–41, showing how Isabella acknowledges the conventional split but manipulates it to her own advantage.

52. G.R. Hibbard provides a good summary of the marriage market in relation to *The Taming of the Shrew* in '*The Taming of the Shrew*: A social comedy', in

Alwin Thaler and Norman Sanders, eds, *Shakespearean Essays,* Special Number II, *Tennessee Studies in Literature* (Knoxville: University of Tennessee Press, 1964), pp. 15–28.

53. Edmund, fifth Earl of March (1391–1425), is confused by Shakespeare with his uncle, Sir Edmund Mortimer (1376–1409); it was Sir Edmund who was Lady Percy's brother, and Sir Edmund who married Owen Glendower's daughter. Curiously, the historical name of Shakespeare's (and Holinshed's) nameless Lady Mortimer is Katherine. See J.H. Wylie, *The Reign of Henry the Fifth* (Cambridge: Cambridge University Press, 1914, reprinted New York: Greenwood Press, 1968), vol. I, p. 110, note 8: 'She is so called in Iss. Roll 1 H.V, Mich., Feb. 19, 22, 1414'. See also J.H. Wylie, *The History of England under Henry the Fourth* (1896; reprinted New York: AMS Press, 1969), vol. III, p. 266, note 5.

54. Alexander Leggatt, *Shakespeare's Political Drama* (London: Routledge, 1988), p. 87.

55. Holinshed, *Chronicles,* vol. III, p. 521.

56. S.B. Hemingway, ed., *New Variorum I Henry IV* (Philadelphia and London: J.B. Lippincott, 1936), p. 194.

57. T.J.B. Spencer, ed., *Shakespeare's Plutarch* (Harmondsworth: Penguin, 1964, reissued 1968), p. 222–3.

58. *The Knight with the Lion* in Staines, *Romances,* pp. 285–6.

59. See Joel Fineman, 'The turn of the shrew', in Patricia Parker and Geoffrey Hartman, eds, *Shakespeare and the Question of Theory* (New York and London: Methuen, 1985), pp. 138–59, for a discussion of interchangeable tropes and the 'problematic difference between literal and figurative language on which the sexual difference between man and woman is seen to depend' (p. 144). Tita French Baumlin also analyses language in 'Petruchio the sophist and language as creation in *The Taming of the Shrew*', *Studies in English Literature,* **29** (1989), pp. 237–57: 'Petruchio swears "by this light whereby I see thy beauty," and this very sun will later be one of his means to teach Katherina the sportive uses of an epistemic language' (p. 243).

60. Jeanne Addison Roberts, 'Horses and hermaphrodites: Metamorphoses in *The Taming of the Shrew*', *Shakespeare Quarterly,* **34** (1983), pp. 159–71 (p. 169).

61. Fineman, 'The turn of the shrew', pp. 151–3; figure 7.

62. For the feminising of the French, see Helen Ostovich, ' "Teach you our princess English?": Equivocal translation of the French in *Henry V*', a paper circulated to the seminar on 'Shakespeare's Bawdy', chaired by William Slights, at the annual meeting of the Shakespeare Association of America, Philadelphia, 1990.

63. In fact, both are better linguists than they admit. Henry has a sufficiently wide vocabulary to understand 'baiser' (v. ii. 263), and Katherine has made considerable progress since III. iv.

64. David Daniell dismisses Petruchio's claims: 'Of course he hasn't: or at least, some of it is unlikely. He has only just left home by his own confession, apparently setting off for the first time' ('The good marriage of Katherine and Petruchio', *Shakespeare Survey,* **37**, (1984), pp. 23–31 [p. 29]). But as Coppélia Kahn argues, Petruchio's military career is thematically important, for soldiership is society's legitimisation of male violence: 'Petruchio's confident references to "great ordnance in the field" . . . bespeak a lifelong acquaintance with organized violence as a masculine vocation' (Kahn, *Man's Estate,* p. 109). Women can express violence only verbally ('shrewishly'), as in Katherine Minola's threats to hit Hortensio and Gremio with a three-legged stool, or Lady Percy's threat to

break Hotspur's little finger. Katherine Valois indirectly treads on the same violent territory in the language scene of III. iv, where her English mispronunciations – 'arma', 'bilbow', 'nick', 'sin', 'mails' – provide her with the necessary military vocabulary to debate the English invasion: armour, bilbow [= sword], nick [= cut, perhaps with a reminder of neck/throat, as in Pistol's 'coup la gorge'], sin [cf. '[t]he sin upon my head': I. ii. 97], and men.

65. This is contrary to modern historical interpretation: 'One does not receive the impression of a strong personality' (Desmond Seward, *Henry V As Warlord* [London: Sidgwick & Jackson, 1987], p. 146).

66. J.H. Wylie and W.T. Waugh, *The Reign of Henry the Fifth* (Cambridge: Cambridge University Press, 1929; reprinted New York: Greenwood Press, 1968), vol. III, p. 416; Seward, *Henry V*, p. 210. Seward provides an interesting account of Katherine's vehement resistance to her wedding with Henry V (a French folksong portrays her as saying, 'I would rather have a French soldier than an English king'), and her reluctant espousal of Henry V contrasts sharply with her besotted love affair with Owen Tudor, her Clerk of the Wardrobe, after Henry's death (Seward, p. 147).

67. This point was nicely made in the English Shakespeare Company's production of *The Henries* (*I Henry IV, II Henry IV*, and *Henry V*, directed by Michael Bogdanov, 1986–9) designed to be seen in sequence. The actress who played Doll Tearsheet reappeared in *Henry V* as Katherine, and the point was unmissable: both these women were for sale; the only difference was the price. See my 'The pragmatics of politics: Casting *Henry IV* and *Henry V*', *Cahiers Elisabéthains*, **38** (1990), pp. 9–24.

68. Lance Wilcox, 'Katherine of France as victim and bride', *Shakespeare Studies*, **17** (1985), pp. 61–76.

69. Seward, *Henry V*, p. 147.

70. Marilyn L. Williamson, 'The courtship of Katherine and the second tetralogy', *Criticism*, **17** (1975), pp. 326–34 (p. 334). In becoming what he despised, Hal is even more like Hotspur than he realises: 'Hotspur is that which he thinks he despises. He professes to hate poetry, yet he uses, throughout the play, the most imaginative and intense speech' (D.J. Snider, quoted in *New Variorum I Henry IV*, p. 467).

71. Stephen Greenblatt, 'Invisible bullets: Renaissance authority and its subversion, *Henry IV* and *Henry V*', in Jonathan Dollimore and Alan Sinfield, eds, *Political Shakespeare* (Manchester: Manchester University Press, 1985), pp. 18–47 (p. 33).

72. The following references show the popularity of the Henry IV/Henry V story: (1) *Tarlton's Jests* (1637) tells how Tarlton doubled the roles of the Lord Chief Justice with that of Dericke in a version of *The Famous Victories* (Q 1598, SR 1594) performed at the Bull Inn. Doubling of these roles is not possible in the extant *FV* text. Tarlton died in 1588. (2) 1592: Thomas Nashe refers in *Pierce Penilesse* to recent performances of a *Henry V* play in which the Dauphin swears fealty to the English King. (3) 28 November 1595: Henslowe records performances of a new *Henry V* play for the Admiral's men, which can have nothing to do with Shakespeare's play and is not known to relate to *FV*. (4) Henslowe's papers include a fragment of foul papers from a *Henry IV* play written by John Day. Henslowe's *Diary* gives no indication as to which play the fragment should contribute, and no *Diary* entry records payment for such a history.

73. A.R. Humphreys describes the Archbishop's speech as '[u]nrivalled for tedium' (*Henry V* [Harmondsworth: Penguin, 1968], p. 26); and Dr Johnson

concluded that Shakespeare wrote the wooing scene simply to fill out the last act (W.K. Wimsatt Jr, ed., *Dr Johnson on Shakespeare* [New York: Hill & Wang, 1960, reprinted Harmondsworth: Penguin, 1969], p. 120).

74. Holinshed portrays the loss as pre-marital; Mortimer ‘willinglie suffered him-selfe to be taken, bicause he would not withstand the attempts of Owen Glendouer, and his complices’ (*Chronicles*, vol. III, p. 521). As this is the viewpoint offered by Henry IV – an excuse not to release the man with a claim to the throne – we should perhaps take it with a pinch of salt. In *The Fruits of Long Experience* (1604), p. 51, Barnabie Rich writes that to be conquered and not to die is the ultimate martial disgrace; Rich’s statement implies that Mortimer’s military career is over.

75. Othello, who tries to unite both, fails to achieve success in either. The conflict between public and private life, and the relationship between name and iden-tity, are both important in *Othello*. It is noteworthy that Othello plays with Desdemona’s name, reducing her to ‘Desdemon’.

76. Bardolph (who has less military credibility than Barnabie Rich) does at least know the appropriate military attitude to assume in *II Henry IV* when he reproves Shallow for his innocent domestic enquiry about Falstaff’s wife: ‘Sir, pardon, a soldier is better [accommodated] than with a wife’ (III. ii. 66–7).

77. See note 68.

78. The fact that characters’ disguises affect Vincentio, who is not impersonating anyone, suggests that the ‘real’ world can be altered by the illusory, even if one is not a participant in the illusion. The parallel with drama is obvious. Juliet Dusinberre deals with this topic in *Shakespeare and the Nature of Women*, pp. 106–8.

79. Jacques Derrida, ‘L’aphorisme à contretemps’, in *Psyché: Inventions de l’autre* (Paris: Galilée, 1987), p. 528; first quoted by Goldberg, *op. cit.*

80. See Margie Burns, ‘The ending of *The Shrew*’, *Shakespeare Studies*, 18 (1986), pp. 41–64. In a final irony unanticipated by Shakespeare, the most problematic debate in textual circles originates in a variant name, Henslowe’s significant/insignificant 1594 entry for *The Taming of a Shrew* at Newington Butts; see R.A. Foakes and R.T. Rickert, eds, *Henslowe’s Diary* (Cambridge: Cambridge University Press, 1961), p. 22.

81. While writing this essay, I have benefited greatly from conversation and corre-spondence with Thomas L. Berger, Richard Proudfoot, David Staines, George Walton Williams and the editors of this volume; all read earlier drafts and made valuable suggestions.

8

'Half a Dozen Dangerous Words'

S.P. Cerasano

In Act III, scene i of *Much Ado About Nothing*, Hero tries to encourage Beatrice's love for Benedick by staging a conversation with Ursula which she expects Beatrice to 'overhear'. During their discussion Hero dismisses the possibility of confronting Beatrice openly with Benedick's passion because Beatrice cannot be trusted to respond positively. She 'turns every man the wrong side out', Hero decides; therefore, since the match between the would-be lovers cannot end happily, Hero teasingly suggests that Benedick should be encouraged to fight against his love and ultimately to reject Beatrice. In aid of this course of action Hero contrives a plot:

> And truly I'll devise some honest slanders,
> To stain my cousin with, one doth not know
> How much an ill word may empoison liking. (III. i. 84–6)[1]

Hero's playful proposal to employ 'honest slander' brings ironic repercussions for her later in the play, for it is the 'dishonest slander' that poisons Claudio's affections, disrupts Hero's marriage, prompts Leonato's rejection of his daughter, and requires finally that Hero 'die', only to return to marry the man who earlier mistakenly condemned her to death by destroying her reputation. In this way, the possibilities presented by Hero's love game initiate the makings of a more serious matter. In the course of the play Shakespeare reveals that maintaining one's reputation is more complex than simply managing to avoid slander. The private language of 'honest slander' raised by women like Hero in order to unite lovers becomes, in the mouths of men like Don John, a publicised 'dishonest slander' by which relationships and particularly the women involved in them, can be destroyed. Moreover, *Much Ado* implicitly dramatises the plight of women and slander within the actual legal structure. Although several critics comment that the play seems to lack a final trial scene in which to absolve Hero and set things right (as, for example, occurs in *Measure for Measure*)[2] the causes and circumstances of slander – namely, the use and abuse of language – are put on trial publicly in the church scene and tested implicitly throughout the play. Finally, the language of slander is shown to be a fabrication of the social and sexual values which are mirrored and married (literally and figuratively) in the cultured discourse of the play.

The adjudication of slander suits in the Renaissance has been described by some critics (Lisa Jardine and Valerie Wayne, for instance) as following a well-established procedure and offering the possibility for the offended party to find justice under the law. Although they do not imply, for a moment, that a slander suit was a *pro forma* matter, their examples, being drawn from records of the consistory courts (which were ecclesiastical courts), do not reflect the enormous changes in the way slander was conceptualised and adjudicated during the sixteenth century. Throughout the Middle Ages, slander was construed by the Church courts as the telling of lies. It was treated as a spiritual offence and the guilty party was sentenced to do penance, which could take a variety of forms including 'humiliating [public] apology'. This conception of slander was consistent with the type of court which was addressing the offence, and the penalty was consistent with the sort of compensation that the Church courts could legally extract. Although slander was treated as a sin (capable of being ameliorated through holy acts), at some unspecified time before 1500 the courts began to allow a fee to be substituted for penance. Consequently, a blurring of the distinction between the spiritual and the civil spheres of redress occurred, and this confusion overshadowed the litigation surrounding slander suits throughout the sixteenth century.[3]

A further move from spiritual to civil in slander cases occurred with the decline of the local and ecclesiastical courts in the first half of the sixteenth century. Slander thus became actionable in the common law courts. However, the common law courts had inherited the ecclesiastical precedent that slander was a 'spiritual offence', which fell slightly outside the judicial domain that the civil law was best able to adjudicate. There was no debate among the courts at Westminster, all of which acknowledged that the telling of lies was morally wrong; but the courts were bound to specific modes of redress. Slander could not be treated as an action of trespass in the common law courts unless 'damages' could be assessed. Restricted to this criteria, the courts did not consider slander as assault, and they were reluctant to award damages for 'evanescent or indirect harm', although that was the type of damage slander most often caused.[4]

But the complications do not stop here. As a result of Henry VIII's break with the Church the ecclesiastical courts gradually began to vanish, and as they did slander suits lost their natural legal venue. In addition, there was a growing awareness that slander constituted not only a moral offence but a breach of the peace, sometimes instigating violence. In recognition of these realities the common law courts eventually found themselves in the unhappy business of trying to deal with slander in a purely civil context. By 1550 slander had become part of the everyday business of common law, in particular of the Court of King's Bench.[5] Before long – and owing in part to the allegations of conspiracy frequently accompanying slander charges – the equity courts also became involved. The Court of Star Chamber, in which assault was integral to the pleadings, became steeped in slander suits.[6] And because of its lower costs and its tradition of expediency, the Court of Requests started to deal with slander on a regular basis. By Shakespeare's day at least three major courts were forced to decide large numbers of cases, although the legal mechanisms through which they operated were ill-suited to deal with the charges at issue.

The judicial precedent established by the common law courts meant that the legal atmosphere was, in some ways, inhospitable to any claimant, and doubly inhospitable to claims by women. Perhaps the latter fact is not surprising, given the well-documented tendencies towards cultural misogyny, as well as women's general disadvantages under the law at the time. Women could not, for instance, plead for themselves without a male guardian. Yet the serious difficulty in adjudicating slander suits resided in the ephemeral nature of verbal assault. Proving that a statement was slanderous was contingent upon issues involving personal identity, and determining tangible damages caused further problems. Both factors were difficult to address and complicated to adjudicate. Then, as now, the textbook definition was clear enough. Slander was:

> a malicious defamation . . . tending either to blacken the memory of one who is dead, or the reputation of one who is alive, and thereby expose him to public hatred, contempt and ridicule.[7]

Commonly, name-calling was the precipitating activity in slander suits, such as that exemplified in the case in which Thomas Lancaster told 'diverse persons' that John Hampton was a 'cosening knave'.[8] Given the necessity of showing that Hampton had somehow suffered damages, the outcome of the lawsuit depended upon evidence demonstrating that Lancaster had wilfully spread false information about Hampton with the intention of destroying his reputation; and further, that damage to Hampton's professional or personal status (his marriage, for example) had ensued as a result of Lancaster's rumour.[9] The usual insults for which people brought suit – 'drunkard', 'quarreller', 'lewd liver', 'notorious thief', 'beggar' or 'runnegate' – might be distasteful; but legal retribution was impossible without demonstrable evidence that harm had been done.[10] And the legal process of proving that the verbal assault had taken place, such as Lancaster really calling Hampton 'a cosening knave', was often circuitous. Unless the defendant had made some egregious comments in public or performed activities such as singing songs or reciting rhymes before a large audience of reliable citizens, showing that the slanderous situation had indeed transpired was difficult. Reliable evidence had to include a number of witnesses, frequently living at a distance, who could 'document' a rumour as it spread.

Therefore, even a cursory reading of cases in a common law court, such as the Court of Requests, shows that it was easy to be violated by verbal abuse but difficult to succeed in pressing charges. Plaintiffs did sometimes manage to extract public apologies and monetary redress for their 'damages'. However, the law was fundamentally incapable of remedying losses to one's reputation. As a result, the courts do not seem to have been consulted because litigants could expect their public images to be restored through legal action. In part, the courts acted as verbal boxing rings, mediating the hostility between litigants and providing a stage whereon actors such as Thomas Lancaster and John Hampton could each audition for the role of victim, more sinned against than sinning. If, in the end, Lancaster was found guilty of slandering Hampton, then Hampton 'succeeded' in court but also had to cope with any residual damage to his reputation. If, on the other hand, Lancaster was found innocent, then he had essentially been slandered by Hampton who, by bringing charges, had implied that Lancaster was a slanderer and a criminal.

Considering the propensity of Elizabethans to take charges of slander to court, this background would have been familiar to the audience of *Much Ado About Nothing*, even though it is almost entirely unfamiliar to most twentieth-century audiences. Likewise, it is important for us to understand that the subordinate position of women during the Renaissance made them especially vulnerable to verbal abuse. Women were expected to be 'chaste, silent, and obedient', and the high social value placed upon women's chastity left them deeply susceptible to claims of whoredom.[11] In fact, virtually all slander suits involving women called into question their sexual morality. A typical case occurred in rural Shropshire in the early seventeenth century; C.J. Sisson later identified it as a provincial version of *The Old Joiner of Aldgate*.[12] In this situation two young men, Humphrey Elliot and Edward Hinkes, were charged with performing 'scandalous and infamous libelous verses, rhymes, plays, and interludes' about Elizabeth Ridge, a young woman of the same village. According to Elizabeth's account the young men hoped to characterise her as 'vile, odious, and contemptible' and, through social pressure, to force her to marry one of them. Moreover, Elizabeth laid the charge that the men conspired against her 'out of a most covetous & greedy desire to gain' her father's sizeable estate, to which she was the sole heiress. Elizabeth Ridge's reasons for taking legal action centred upon the damage done to her reputation, as did Hampton's in the former example. However, the concept of reputation was complicated by gender issues. Like other women Elizabeth was concerned that once she was labelled a 'fallen woman', no man would want to marry her. As a young woman in a small rural village she might well have perceived the opportunities for a suitable match to have been few and far between. Also, the close-knit nature of village life would have ensured that the slanderous rumours spread to most of the inhabitants of the village by the time the case came to trial. On top of these events – by which a young woman like Elizabeth Ridge would have felt violated anyway – there were the further harrowing experiences of undergoing the process of law and of demonstrating that harm had arisen. As a single woman she could not show loss of or damage to her marriage; as a young woman of her class, not engaged in meaningful work or a trade, she could not claim 'damage' to her professional life; as a woman, denied full status as a citizen, she could not easily assert that her public presence had been 'damaged'. If a woman was called a 'whore', she had little compensation to look forward to. Not surprisingly, given the personal costs involved, no woman felt that she could afford to ignore a public allegation such as slander. Even the young Elizabeth I, about whom rumours circulated to the effect that she was pregnant by Thomas Seymour in 1548–9, felt obligated to set the record straight. On 23 January 1549 she wrote to the Lord Protector:

> My lord, these are shameful slanders . . . I shall most heartily desire your lordship that I may come to the court after your just determination that I may show myself there as I am.[13]

At the same time women had to face the fact that the law was particularly inept to assist them in reclaiming such an intangible commodity as reputation, and that the potential consequences of slander for them were vastly different from those for men. The potency of language as it related to sexual status was clearly in the control of men like Elliot and Hinkes, and the process of the law favoured men, whether they were plaintiffs charging other men or defendants against complaints brought by women.

For Renaissance women, reputation, that which was synonymous with a 'good name' or a 'bad name', defined identity in an ideological, as well as in a legal, sense. A 'fair name' was essential in order for a woman to maintain her 'worthiness'; and as a woman was treated as the property of her father, husband or guardian, her name was treated as property which could be stolen, usurped or defiled. In *As You Like It*, for instance, Duke Frederick warns Celia that Rosalind 'robs thee of thy name' (I. iii. 76).[14] Related to the theme of property was an economic discourse that determined the value of a woman's name, and it was always the 'fair name' that was stolen, for the 'black name' could only be 'bought' (suggesting prostitution): 'she hath bought the name of whore, thus dearly' (*Cymbeline*,

II. iv. 128).[15] Moreover, reputation could be 'disvalued' (see, for instance, *Measure for Measure*, V. i. 220).[16] Nor was a woman's name her own property to 'sell' as she thought fit. A woman's reputation belonged to her male superior, who 'owned' her and to whom she could bring honour or disgrace. In so far as a woman was 'renamed' when she was slandered and her identity thus altered, her husband lost his good name and was rechristened with abuse – slandered by association. If the characterisation of a woman as 'loose' was true, that was all to the worse. In articulating the dual sense of *name*, signifying both 'reputation' and 'a malicious term', and in describing his wife's effect on his reputation, Frank Ford rails to the audience of *The Merry Wives of Windsor*:

> See the hell of having a false woman: my bed shall be abused, my coffers ransacked, my reputation gnawn at, and I shall not only receive this vil- lainous wrong, but stand under the adoption of abominable terms, and by him that does me this wrong. Terms! Names! Amaimon sounds well; Lucifer, well; Barbason, well: yet they are devils' additions [names], the names of fiends. But cuckold? Wittol? Cuckold! The devil himself hath not such a name. (II. ii. 280–89)[17]

The comic overtones of Ford's tirade are balanced, however, by the more severe associations of a bad name with prostitution. When Othello up- braids Montano, he remarks:

> The gravity and stillness of your youth
> The world hath noted, and your *name* is great
> In mouths of wisest censure [judgement]: what's the matter,
> That you *unlace your reputation* thus,
> And *spend your rich opinion* [reputation], for the name
> Of a *night-brawler*? (II. iii. 182–7; emphasis added)[18]

M.R. Ridley glosses 'unlace' as 'not the simple "undo" . . . but the strong- er hunting (and carving) term'. The 'undoing' of Montano is suggestive of a literal 'gutting' of his personal value. Othello implies that his unwilling- ness to 'unlace' himself and 'spend' his rich opinion is a sign not only of Montano's weakness but of his sexual vulgarity. Montano loses his repu- tation to a 'night-brawler', the disclosure of which costs him dearly in excess of what he has already 'spent' for sexual favours. For the Eliza- bethans the rhetoric was pungent. Privileging 'dishonour in thy name' makes 'fair reputation but a bawd', and slander creates 'the wound that nothing healeth' (*The Rape of Lucrece*, ll. 621–3, 731).[19] The language of a sullied reputation – whether or not that reputation belonged to a man or a woman – was constantly associated with female sexuality gone amiss, as if no Montano would ever go astray were it not for the presence of a bawd to tempt him and rob him of his wealth.

The church scene in *Much Ado About Nothing* is replete with just these sorts of legal and ideological associations. At its opening Claudio first breaks the terms of the pre-marital agreement that Don Pedro had arranged for him. He then explicitly rejects Hero and openly refuses to accept her as his property: 'There, Leonato, take her back again' (IV. i. 30). After Claudio's dispossession of Hero he calls her 'rotten orange' (IV. i. 31) and 'an approved wanton' (IV. i. 44), but he waits until he has dissociated himself from her completely so that her reputation and moral state cannot sully his own. In a particularly brutal and unambiguous manner he states that he does not wish: 'to knit my soul/ To an approved wanton' (IV. i. 43–4). Claudio's choice of language identifies Hero with prostitution, a suggestion that acts as a powerful verbal cue inciting the other men in the scene to join in his abuse of her. Don Pedro casts her as 'a common stale [whore]' (IV. i. 65). Leonato declares that she is 'fallen' (IV. i. 139), her very flesh is 'foul-tainted' (IV. i. 143), that her sin 'appears in proper nakedness' (IV. i. 175). To destroy Hero's identity further, Claudio attempts to reduce her image, her very being to 'nothingness':

> Would you not swear,
> All you that see her, that she were a maid,
> By these exterior shows? But she is *none*: (IV. i. 37–40; emphasis added)

In Claudio's eyes Hero has dissolved from a façade of 'seeming' to 'none' ('no one' – that is, nothingness). The tactics that reduce Hero's status and deny her humanity creep in throughout Claudio's speech in this scene. His language becomes increasingly insidious as he first appeals to the others (primarily the men) to believe that Hero bears a false front, and then turns directly against Hero herself. Intriguingly, he tries to make her name potent and worthless at the same time:

HERO:	O God defend me, how am I beset!
	What kind of catechizing call you this?
CLAUDIO:	To make you answer truly to your name.
HERO:	Is it not Hero? Who can blot that name
	With any just reproach?
CLAUDIO:	Marry, that can Hero;
	Hero itself can blot out Hero's virtue. (IV. i. 77–82)

While Hero seeks an explanation as to 'who' ('what person') can blot her name with just cause, Claudio replies that 'Hero itself' can stain her honour. On his rhetorical terms, she cannot possibly win. But whether he means that her tainted name 'itself' can dishonour Hero, or whether she is being symbolically reduced to a genderless object ('Hero *itself*'), Claudio's response is tempered with the sexual values of his society. He would not call a man 'wanton' because it is so explicitly a male term of opprobrium for a woman.

When Claudio slanders Hero in such an extreme manner his rhetoric has the effect of uniting part of the male community behind him, with the exception of Benedick (who, with Beatrice, stands outside the rhetorical and social codes to which Claudio and the others subscribe) and the Friar (who immediately takes steps to attempt to turn slander to 'remorse': (IV. i. 211). Nevertheless, Leonato, Don Pedro and Don John all take an active verbal role in Hero's persecution, knowing that Claudio's slander could well lead to grievous injury. Leonato, in fact, demands Hero's extinction, even her death, as a justifiable retribution for her presumed digression and for jeopardising his name. When Hero swoons, Leonato responds:

> O Fate, take not away thy heavy hand!
> Death is the fairest cover for her shame
> That may be wished for. . . .
>
> Do not live, Hero, do not ope thine eyes;
> For did I think thou wouldst not quickly die,
> Thought I thy spirits were stronger than thy shames,
> Myself would on the rearward of approaches
> Strike at thy life. (IV. i. 115–17; 123–7)

Slander and death are familiar bedfellows throughout Shakespeare's plays. The slandered victim, spoken of in terms that relate to discredit, sexual defilement and disease, was finally described as an outcast. Slander, popularly thought of as 'the transient murderer', if not actually the cause of literal death, was thought to lead to public alienation and metaphorical death. As Antony succinctly points out concerning his political opponents:

> These many men shall die; their names are prick'd.
>
> He shall not live. Look, with a spot I damn him. (*Julius Caesar*, IV. i. 1, 6).[20]

The urgency of the Friar's proposal to turn slander into remorse recognises the price Hero will have to pay for Claudio's slander. Her alternatives are to be reborn ('a greater birth': IV. i. 213) and to begin anew with a pure reputation (possibly to be slandered again at some future time) or to be hidden away 'in some reclusive and religious life' (IV. i. 242). But finally, the Friar urges that death and resurrection is the best course – 'Come, lady, die to live' (IV. i. 253) – regardless of the fact that Hero initially 'died upon his [Claudio's] words' (IV. i. 223) and that Claudio makes no attempt to repair her shattered emotions at the end of the scene, simply going off and leaving her for dead.

In describing the violation of Hero as the conspiracy of 'eyes, tongues, minds, and injuries' (IV. i. 243), Friar Francis reminds us of the other ways in which those in Messina are slandered and violated, and of the covert strategies that stand in the way of the characters' ability to negotiate meaningful interactions. Chief among these undercurrents is that presented by the atmosphere of Messina itself, an environment which revolves around tale-telling, eavesdropping and spying, all purportedly performed in the name of some legitimate purpose. From the opening of the play, where Beatrice asks for 'news' of Benedick, the characters seem caught up in a web of gossip and surface appearances. Marriages are arranged by proxy, while men and women woo and wed behind masks – literal face-coverings and social expectations alike. This tendency towards doubling encourages naive young men like Claudio to cling to the traditional male sphere of war in public, and to accept the less-than-gratifying pose of Petrarchan lover in his private life.

As long as conversations are witty and frivolous, Messina's social code is attractive; but as soon as serious issues are at stake, the community opens itself up to misrepresentation and slander.[21] As much as Hero is slandered by Claudio's words she is also slandered by his eyes, by his predisposition to distrustfulness, and by his need to spy on her in order to test her virtue. And because the men in Messina are so willing to accept what they (mis)perceive and (mis)hear, they easily become impulsive and abusive. Leonato and Claudio will trust each other through a process of male bonding, but they will equally trust impersonal and unsubstantiated 'report'. As a result, they condemn Hero on the basis of slight evidence without allowing her to defend herself. The natural tendency of the residents of Messina is towards gullibility, inconstancy, unpredictability and slander; and also towards giving short shrift to personal identity, individual circumstances or motivations, patience and constancy.

The ways in which characters identify each other in public give another indication of their reduced status as individuals. This is especially true of women and others, such as foreigners, who are disadvantaged by their social role, and all of whom are categorised by the term 'none'. The gentlemen killed in the war before the play opens are described as 'none of name' (I. i. 6); and although Beatrice asks about the well-being of 'Signor Montanto', the messenger knows 'none of that name' (I. i. 30). It is only when Hero interposes, identifying Beatrice's enquiry as that concerning 'Signor Benedick of Padua' (therefore an alien: I. i. 33), that the messenger recognises the man to whom Beatrice refers. Likewise, after Claudio's first meeting with Hero he initially identifies her by everything other than her name, thereby renaming her. She is 'the daughter of Signor Leonato' (I. i. 150–51), 'a modest young lady' (I. i. 153), 'a jewel' (I. i. 168) and 'the sweetest lady' (I. i. 174). It is at the moment when he wishes to acquire Hero that he finally names her: 'if Hero would be my wife' (I. i. 182). And like the name-calling in the church scene, other men are quick to pick this up. Subsequently, Don Pedro privileges Hero's name and her identity at a point that involves acquisition: 'Claudio, I have wooed in thy name, and fair Hero is won' (II. i. 280–81). Interestingly, when Hero is defamed her name is used repeatedly and made an object of mockery (as is her identity):

> DON JOHN: The lady is disloyal.
> CLAUDIO: Who, Hero?
> DON JOHN: Even she, Leonato's Hero, your Hero, every man's Hero. (III. ii. 93–6)

Sadly but predictably, Hero herself ends up condoning this practice – that which encourages women to exchange or surrender their identity willingly – when she interprets her restoration in Act V, scene iv:

> One Hero dies defiled, but I do live
> And surely as I live, I am a maid. (V. iv. 63–4)

Indeed, Hero's act of giving up her name to restore her relationship with Claudio metaphorically prefigures the time when she will actually relinquish it – when they marry and she takes his name.

In contrast with Hero, the male characters of the main plot have firmly fixed names and identities, and they spend a fair amount of time using their names and reassuring themselves of their identities. When their names are exchanged for titles ('Don Pedro' for 'the prince', for instance) it is to enhance their status. There are two intriguing exceptions to this generalisation, however, and both relate to men bearing dishonourable names. One is the character of Don John, a social outcast who cannot hide his bastard status or his melancholy temperament behind the mask of an honourable name: 'I cannot hide what I am: I must be sad when I have cause, and smile at no man's jests' (I. iii. 12–14). (The name 'john' was coterminous with 'waiter', 'footman', or other subservient at the time.) The other exception occurs in Act IV, scene ii, when Dogberry tries to get Conrade and Borachio to answer for their offences by taking on the name and identity of 'false knaves' (false names, although surely a pun is intended here). Every time Dogberry challenges them with this label, one or the other counters: 'we are none' (IV. ii. 23, 28). But both instances occur in the subplot; the main male characters in the play appear to have more control, both over their own names and over the names they apply to others. Moreover, the speed with which they confer and change nomenclature to suit whatever they hope to accomplish allows them to take a cavalier approach to identity – and a cavalier approach, as well, to the harm that an individual suffers when misidentified and slandered. While the women are defending the names of the men (Hero: ‘Indeed he [Benedick] hath an excellent good name’: III. i. 98) the men jest about slandering inanimate things (Balthasar: ‘Oh, good my lord, tax not so bad a voice,/ To slander music any more than once’: II. ii. 44–5). Their power resides in the choice they maintain – and take for granted – to determine their own identities. Even in the game-playing–teasing between Antonio and Ursula at the dance, Antonio guards his name as the ultimate signifier of his reputation. Ursula identifies Antonio by the wagging of his head, but his recourse is verbal. He refuses to accept her label: ‘At my word, I am not [Antonio]’ (II. i. 110).

Janice Hays concludes that when Hero faints in the church scene she is exhibiting a distinctly feminine sort of power. The ‘going down in order to come up’ imitates ‘the Demeter–Persephone pattern of responding to experience’. In psychological terms Hays explains Hero’s faint as suggestive of the power of giving birth, but also as replicating the coping mechanism that women have developed in order to be care-takers. In other words, it is another testimony to the way in which women are socially expected, and conditioned to put themselves in a position of weakness in order to maintain their femininity.[22] Were this not enough of a sacrifice, Hero’s response is complicated by what can be demonstrated through lawsuits to have been the severity of the legal-cum-social code of the times. The danger of slanderous language, as it affected women, expands upon David L. Stevenson’s sense that *Much Ado* is marked by ‘mimetic realism’ – what he aptly describes as ‘the natural, this-worldly atmosphere’, especially as regards the ‘potency of language’ used in the play.[23] Not only does the play imitate the quality of everyday language used during Shakespeare’s day. More than this, it reflects the real threat of the language of conflict, with all its sexual and erotic overtones. Therefore Hero faints not only from shock and because the violence of Claudio’s rhetoric is akin to a physical assault, but also because she realises that neither the legal process, her father’s position in Messina, the force of her own argument, nor the testimony of her friends can ultimately exonerate her.

The violence of war in foreign parts, alluded to at the beginning of the play, becomes the violence of rhetoric at home. Aggression becomes domesticated. Perhaps because the nature of war forbids it, the men in the main plot seem unaccustomed to verbal communication, so that too often they respond in silence, in excess, or in ways inappropriate for times of peace. For example, when Leonato grants his permission for Hero to marry Claudio and asks for everyone’s ‘amen’, Claudio is strangely silent and has to be prodded by Beatrice: ‘Speak, Count, ’tis your cue’ (II. i. 286). Claudio doesn’t really know what to say, so unaccustomed is he to the intercourse of peace, so he ends up clumsily offering what he thinks is a compliment, but is finally an oddly self-reflexive transaction:

> Silence is the perfectest herald of joy; I were but little happy, if I could say how much. Lady as you are mine, I am yours; I give away myself for you and dote upon the exchange. (II. i. 288–91)

What he is doting on is obviously himself. Not fully understanding language, Leonato is dismissive of words, convinced that words are air, that they are totally without substance: 'Charm ache with air, and agony with words' (v. i. 26). It is partly this insensitive disregard for language that motivates the men's careless use of language throughout the play, despite the fact that they are effusive, and that *Much Ado About Nothing* is largely a play about men talking to one another. Antonio would like to pin the responsibility for slander on the young men:

> God knows I lov'd my niece,
> And she is dead, slander'd to death by villains,
> That dare as well answer a man indeed
> As I dare take a serpent by the tongue.
> Boys, apes, braggarts, Jacks, milksops! . . .
>
> What, man! I know them, yea,
> And what they weigh, even to the utmost scruple,
> Scrambling, outfacing, fashion-monging boys,
> That lie, and cog, and flout, deprave, and slander,
> Go anticly, and show outward hideousness,
> And speak off half a dozen dangerous words,
> How they might hurt their enemies, if they durst,
> And this to all. (v. i. 87–91, 92–9)

Yet it is not a fault limited to young men. After Hero faints, Leonato continues to rail for almost forty lines before he loses steam. In a play in which words are so very cheap, language is superfluous. Echoing the play's title, Leonato's abundant rhetoric is essentially 'much ado' and worth 'nothing'.

Beatrice cries: 'Sweet Hero, she is wronged, she is slandered, she is undone' (v. i. 299). The language of the church scene places the audience as witnesses of the misogynist ends to which language could be – and was, at times – put. It also shows the way in which men use language to set up the law for their own advantage, and how they continually use language to diminish women to nothingness. Claudio, knowing 'nothing' of Hero as an individual and only inaccurate gossip about her behaviour (itself 'nothing'), metaphorically condemns her to death and symbolically to 'nothingness'. By the last scene he seems to have changed but little. Although the epitaph on Hero's monument is blatant ('Done to death by slanderous tongues,/ Was the Hero that here lies': v. iii. 3–4), he asks for pardon from the goddess of the night, herself a symbol of darkness, absence, 'nothingness'.

Claudio cannot, of course, create something from nothing; but the 'honest slander' of the subplot involving Beatrice and Benedick does. This is the point at which I believe that those critics who argue that Hero's 'honest slander' does not raise the same issues as Claudio's slander are in error. To begin with, the Beatrice–Benedick subplot displaces the Claudio–Hero plot through the sharp juxtaposition of reality and fiction, for Beatrice and Benedick show a healthy distrust for the conventions of idealised love. In this way they know how to 'name' themselves, how to deal with the pitfalls of language, and how to stand back from romantic conventions:

BENEDICK: The savage bull may [bear the yoke]; but if ever the sensible Benedick bear it, pluck off the bull's horns and set them in my forehead, and let me be vilely painted, and in such great letters as they write, 'Here is food horse to hire,' let them signify under my sign, 'Here you may see Benedick, the married man.' (I. i. 243–8)

BEATRICE: And, Benedick, love on, I will requite thee,
Taming my wild heart to thy loving hand.
If thou dost love, my kindness shall incite
  thee
To bind our loves up in a holy band;
For others say thou dost deserve, and I
Believe it better than reportingly. (III. i. 111–16)

In one sense 'honest slander' complements the other forms of reconciliation in the play, helping to explain why the Beatrice–Benedick subplot is rhetorically richer than the main plot. Claudio's 'malicious slander' is balanced out by the 'honest slander' that helps to bring Beatrice and Benedick together, as Claudio's fantasised love is balanced out by the more genuine, mature love of Beatrice and Benedick. Similarly, Claudio's 'nothingness' is countered by the avowal of the love shared by Beatrice and Benedick, which is brought on by Claudio's denunciation of Hero in the church scene:

BENEDICK: I do love nothing in the world so well as you – is that not strange?
BEATRICE: As strange as the thing I know not. It were as possible for me to say I loved nothing so well as you, but believe me not; and yet I lie not; I confess nothing, nor I deny nothing. I am sorry for my cousin. (IV. i. 266–72)

However, Beatrice's verbal potency is limited. Later in the same scene, when she bids Benedick to kill Claudio and the former refuses, she realises that as a woman she has only language – not action – within her power, and that is not always effective:

179

But manhood is melted into curtsies, valour into compliment, and men are only turned into tongue, and trim ones too: he is now as valiant as Hercules that only tells a lie and swears it. I cannot be a man with wishing, therefore I will die a woman with grieving. (IV. ii. 316–23)

The fact that 'honest slander' is a concept created by one of the women in the play, and it is implemented by women, prompts questions about language and 'real' slander in the 'real' world – or rather, about slander in the world that men have constructed. In Act III, scene i, Hero and Ursula toy with the invention of 'honest slanders' because they realise how ambiguous language (and slander) can be. Language, they think, can exist on two levels: one serious, and one in which potentially serious values such as truth and falsehood, may be determined in a game-like fashion; and as the women fabricate their account of Benedick's love they believe that they are playfully creating truth from a fiction:[24]

> HERO: Our talk must only be of Benedick.
> When I do name him, let it be thy part
> To praise him more than ever man did merit:
> My talk to thee must be how Benedick
> Is sick in love with Beatrice. Of this matter
> Is little Cupid's crafty arrow made,
> That only wounds by hearsay. (III. i. 17–23)

The women, however, understand well the profound distinction between 'honest' and 'dishonest' slander, and they realise that it is more a matter of language creating reality than creating illusion. Some critics find the solution of *Much Ado* an unsatisfactory one: in the words of Roger Sale, 'the apparent triumph of this dishonest illusion'. But the play's conclusion is not so simply paraphrased as 'Tricking into marriage is honest, whereas tricking out of marriage is dishonest'.[25] Don John – the bastard without legitimate name – reveals, by his fictional account of Hero's transgressions, that to name things is to make them real. Yet concurrently, while language can slander it can also be chaste:

> Fie, fie, they are not to be nam'd, my lord,
> Not to be spoken of!
> There is not chastity enough in language
> Without offence to utter them. (IV. i. 95–8)

Much Ado's resolution might be temporary and fictional, but the fictions that language creates are consequential. The power of language to bring about order or chaos is treated throughout the play; and whether we observe Margaret, called 'Hero' by Borachio at the chamber window, or Hero, called 'wanton' by Claudio, it is the preservation of 'chastity in language' by women and Hero's vision of 'honest slander' that bring about the resolution of the play. For if there was 'dishonest slander' alone, the play could not end as it does. Carol Neely observes: 'patriarchal marriage customs conveniently coalesce with romantic rhetoric, enabling him [Claudio] to maintain Hero as object of social exchange and possession.' Claudio's slander, then, is an expression of masculine anxieties about marriage and about male sexuality.[26] But Hero – by presenting the possibility of 'honest slander' – offers the vision of a different rhetoric. Claudio essentially becomes trapped in his own language; by his slander he loses Hero. And through the 'honest slander' used by women we learn that honest interaction can exist in Messina. In creating an alternative rhetoric, Hero suggests that the female characters can empower themselves through language within the patriarchal system that confines them. Hence, her final 'naming' is a naming of doubles, of alternatives that subvert the notion and the process of 'dishonest slander'. In this she is also seeing possibilities that promise to free both women and men from the rhetoric that contains them and simultaneously distances them from each other. Here her gesture and her language come together strongly as she 'unmasks' (literally and symbolically) by offering alternatives:

HERO [*unmasking*]: And when I liv'd, I was your other wife;
And when you lov'd, you were my other husband.
(v. iv. 60–61)

If Claudio is thought to have become at all enlightened in the final moments of the play, the conclusion of *Much Ado* suggests that the deceived can be led to a new understanding. But what of the central deception of the play itself – that 'honest slander' can exist? Following Hero's path, if men choose to slander women on the basis of 'nothing', then they deserve to be manipulated with the language of their own fictions. And women must accept that they will be controlled by men until they create their own rhetoric (fictions). Conversely, as the members of the audience are eavesdroppers on the play, they end up falling in with Claudio as he spies on Hero, however much they might think that they emphasise with Hero. Shakespeare himself knew the workings of the law,[27] and to raise the ghost of slander at all before his audience was to present a situation that, in reality, disallowed a comic ending. Hero's 'honest slander' is a fantasy that resists the social and legal realities of the time. Thus, when the official (legal and social) discourses on the issue of slandering women break down, they can be taken up only by dramatic discourse, as the theatre allows for greater latitude in ideology. The members of the audience might be cheered by the play's altruism, but they also have to accept Hero's language in order for the play to end on so unlikely a note; and language, as *Much Ado* shows us, is fickle. 'Honest slander' is created at a price. Hero's 'renaming' is not really a vindication of the truth or the affirmation of her former self but an unmasking of men's 'truth' through the creation of a second reality. As she states:

> One Hero died defil'd, but I do live,
> And surely as I live, I am a maid. (v. iv. 63–4)

Finally, Hero invents the personal language she needs to survive the fiction of Claudio's idealism, its dangerous consequences, and the failure of a public legal system to redress violations on women. Hero puts Claudio's language on trial. In so doing she demonstrates that 'dishonest' slander is every bit as fictional as the play itself. And also, in so doing, she bankrupts the patriarchal power of language to hold sway over women.

NOTES

1. All quotations are from *Much Ado About Nothing*, ed. A.R. Humphreys (London and New York: Methuen, 1981).
2. See, for instance, Karen Newman, *Shakespeare's Rhetoric of Comic Character* (New York and London: Methuen, 1985), pp. 111 ff. It is in the context of deciding whether the play is a comedy, a dark comedy, or a romance that most discussion about its conclusion arises. Carol Neely also touches on the issue of the absence of a trial scene in *Broken Nuptials in Shakespeare's Plays* (New Haven, CT and London: Yale University Press, 1985), p. 39.
3. Lisa Jardine and Valerie Wayne restrict themselves to evidence drawn from the consistory courts, for example, in Valerie Wayne, ed., *The Matter of Difference* (Hemel Hempstead: Harvester Wheatsheaf, 1991), p. 161. Here, Valerie Wayne is drawing on Jardine's forthcoming essay about *Othello* in particular. It should be noted that the commentary on slander in Renaissance literature is fast-growing, and not all of it can be cited here. However, readers should see Joyce Hengerer Sexton, 'The theme of slander in *Much Ado about Nothing* and Garter's *Susanna*', *Philological Quarterly*, **54** (1975), pp. 419–33. For information on slander and the law, see J.H. Baker, *An Introduction to Legal History* (London: Butterworth, 1979); W.S. Holdsworth, *History of English Law* (London: Methuen, 1922–6), vol. VIII, pp. 333–78; David M. Walker, *The Oxford Companion to Law* (Oxford: Clarendon Press, 1980); J.A. Sharpe, *Defamation and Sexual Slander in Early Modern England: The Church Courts at York* (York: Borthwick Institute, 1980); Paul Hair, ed., *Before the Bawdy Court: Selections from Church Courts and other records relating to the correction of moral offenses in England, Scotland and New England, 1300–1800* (New York: Barnes & Noble, 1972).
4. Baker, *An Introduction to Legal History*, pp. 364–5.
5. Ibid., p. 368.
6. C.J. Sisson, *Lost Plays of Shakespeare's Age* (London: Frank Cass, 1970), p. 10.
7. Sir Thomas Edlyne Tomlins, *The Law Dictionary* (London: n.p., 1820). The term 'spoken libel' was coterminous with slander, as cases such as PRO, STAC8/71/15 show.
8. PRO, REQ2/220/8. I have modernised spelling and punctuation throughout my quotations from lawsuits.

2 2

9. A.K.R. Kiralfy, *Potter's Historical Introduction to English Law and Its Institutions* (London: Sweet & Maxwell, 1958), pp. 430–35.
10. Some cases in which common insults are recorded are (all REQ2): 53/16, 156/3, 220/8, 402/25.
11. Standard sources discussing the social place of women during the Renaissance include the now-outdated Carroll Camden, *The Elizabethan Woman* (London: Cleaver-Hume, 1952) and Wallace Notestein, 'The English woman, 1580 to 1650', in J.H. Plumb, ed., *Studies in Social History* (London: Longman, 1955).
12. PRO, STAC8/250/31. See also Sisson, *Lost Plays*, pp. 140 ff.
13. As quoted in Maria Perry, *The Word of a Prince* (Woodbridge, Suffolk: The Boydell Press, 1990), pp. 61–2.
14. *As You Like It*, ed. Agnes Latham (London: Methuen, 1975).
15. *Cymbeline*, ed. J.M. Nosworthy (London: Methuen, 1965).
16. *Measure for Measure*, ed. J.W. Lever (London: Methuen, 1965).
17. *The Merry Wives of Windsor*, ed. H.J. Oliver (London: Methuen, 1971).
18. *Othello*, ed. M.R. Ridley (London: Methuen, 1959).
19. *The Rape of Lucrece*, in F.T. Price, ed., *Shakespeare's Poems* (London: Methuen, 1960).
20. *Julius Caesar*, ed. T.S. Dorsch (London: Methuen, 1958).
21. See also Barbara Everett, ' "Something of great constancy" ' in John Russell Brown, ed., *'Much Ado About Nothing' and 'As You Like It'* (London: Macmillan, 1979), pp. 102–3; and Paul and Miriam Mueschke, 'Illusion and metamorphosis', pp. 130–48 in the same volume.
22. 'Those "soft and delicate desires": *Much Ado* and the distrust of women', in Carolyn Lenz, Gayle Green and Carol Neely, eds, *The Woman's Part* (Urbana: University of Illinois Press, 1980), pp. 79–99; this material is from pp. 88–9.
23. David L. Stevenson, ed., The Signet Edition of *Much Ado About Nothing* (New York: New American Library, 1964), p. xxiii.
24. Ruth Nevo, *Comic Transformations in Shakespeare* (London and New York: Methuen, 1980), p. 171.
25. Roger Sale, *'Much Ado About Nothing'* (London: Penguin Books, 1990), pp. 98–9.
26. Neely, *Broken Nuptials*, p. 44.
27. S. Schoenbaum, *William Shakespeare: A compact documentary life* (New York: Oxford University Press, 1977), p. 289, cites the lawsuit of Susanna Shakespeare Hall against John Lane Jr for slander in 1613. This case, of course, postdates *Much Ado* by quite a few years. I offer it only by way of historical example.

9

'Their Testament at Their Apron-strings': The Representation of Puritan Women in Early-Seventeenth-Century England

Akiko Kusunoki

I

Compared with many other religions, Christian doctrine in general seems to give women more room; it certainly seems so to a person like myself, brought up in the religious climate of Buddhism and Shintoism, whose doctrines make no specific reference to the existence of women. For all the emphasis on the necessity of woman's self-effacement in Pauline doctrine, the creation story in Genesis at least offers an explanation of the creation of woman as well as that of man. It also gives a definition not just of man, but of woman, though it identifies woman merely as a helpmate for man, not as an independent being. Feminists today may find these explanations deficient, but still, the fact that women's existence is recognised by biblical authority was of great significance in the process of women's efforts to establish their autonomy in earlier periods of history.

However, the biblical explanations of the relationship between man and woman contain some ambiguities and contradictions. For instance, although the concept of male authority and female inferiority is explicitly established in the Scriptures, the creation story in Genesis identifies the material from which God formed Eve as Adam's rib, a material which may suggest the possibility of women's refusal of subjection. For example, detractors of women had insisted since medieval times that the rib is crooked, and therefore women are not submissive by nature. The fact that the rib is located in the central part of the body may indicate – as indeed some writers (including women) in the early seventeenth century argued – the spiritual equality of the two sexes.[1] Furthermore, the whole episode may after all imply female superiority for, as defenders of women often pointed out, woman was made from a part of Adam's body, the Divine creation, whereas man was made from dust. It is interesting to note how differently people in Western culture have interpreted these ambiguities and contradictions implicit in the Scriptures, and to examine what impact these different interpretations have made upon social behaviour in specific periods.

A notable example of this impact can be seen in the relationship between women and Puritanism in early-seventeenth-century England. Returning to the anecdote of 'the rib', for instance, we may observe direct contradictions in the interpretation of the biblical story among Puritan men and women at that time. Thus Thomas Adams, a formidable Puritan preacher, inveighed against contemporary women's fondness for fine ornaments in his sermon 'Mystical Bedlam', asserting that the cause of their offence originated in the material from which they were made, Adam's rib, which was less substantial and authentic than the dust from which man was made.[2] On the other hand, Rachel Speght, a Puritan, tried to vindicate her belief that 'the rib' illustrated the integrity of women in a tract which will be discussed later in this essay.[3] In the light of the impact of Puritanism upon early-seventeenth-century English women, what is particularly noteworthy is the transformation of the representation of female Puritans on stage in the late Jacobean and Caroline periods, especially in terms of their speech.

II

The Reformation introduced a new perspective on marriage into England by proposing the ideal of chastity in marriage; this was in direct opposition to the medieval elevation of celibacy. Matrimony came to be regarded as a divinely ordained unity, 'an hie, holye and blessed order of life',[4] instead of the necessary evil required for the production of posterity or the release of sexual frustration. In this new view of marriage, love and affection are emphasised and partnership is considered the cornerstone of the relationship between husband and wife. From the 1580s to the 1630s, this view was disseminated throughout England in Puritan preachers' sermons and writings. However, the Puritan emphasis on mutual affection between spouses also contains a contradiction. This 'blessed order of life' is actually maintained only through wives' submission to their husbands' authority. Puritans derived the sanction for man's controlling power over his wife from biblical authority:

> Wives, submit yourselves unto your own husbands, as unto the Lord. For the husband is the head of the wife, even as Christ is the head of the church: and he is the saviour of the body. (Ephesians 5: 22–3)

What Puritan divines advocated, therefore, was a patriarchal form of marriage based on wives' willing subjection to their husbands' authority. Drawing on biblical examples, Puritan preachers developed a role model for women in which they fulfil their function, as wives, through voluntary submission to their husbands' will. William Gouge, one of the most influential Puritan preachers at the time, delivers a typical view: 'though husband and wife may mutually serve one another through love: yet the Apostle suffereth not a woman to rule over the man.'[5] As R. Valerie Lucas argues, Puritan preachers' sermons and writings in fact create the illusion of partnership by proposing male authority and female submission as duties to God in marriage.[6] The Puritan notion of partnership thus concealed the repressive aspect of the power relations in patriarchal marriage. Through ingenious rhetorical strategies, Puritan divines persuaded female congregations to accept their subjection in the household.

Because of the stress on the necessity of wives' submission to their husbands' authority, the Puritan view of marriage denied women subjectivity in a true sense. In consequence, language – as a means of expressing independent thought – was not attributed to women. A basis for male authority and female silence is firmly established in the Scriptures:

> Let your women keep silence in the churches: for it is not permitted unto them to speak; but they are commanded to be under obedience, as also saith the law. And if they will learn anything, let them ask their husbands at home: for it is a shame for women to speak in the church. (1 Corinthians 14: 34–5)

John Dod and Robert Cleaver, in *A Godlie Forme of Householde Government*, elaborate on this doctrine:

> Now silence is the best ornament of a woman, and therefore the law was given to the man, rather then to the woman, to shew that he should be the teacher, and she the hearer; and therefore shee is commanded to learne of her husband.[7]

However, some Puritan women in the late Elizabethan and Jacobean periods interpreted this seemingly obvious injunction to female silence in ways that were incompatible with the orthodox view. Already in the early years of the Jacobean period (long before the 1640s, when large numbers of women started preaching) there were Puritan women who had not only been teaching their husbands but had also been preaching in public. Their activities become visible in the criticism and complaints of contemporary writers, which was also the case with the female preachers of the later period. William Heale, for instance, expresses his disapproval of these Puritan women in *An Apology for Women* (1609), a tract defending women which he was commissioned to write by an unidentified noble lady:

> I could never approue those too too holy women-gospellers, who weare their testament at their apron-strings, and wil weekely catechize their husbands, citing places, clearing difficulties, & preaching holy sermons too,

if the spirit of their devotion moue them. For sure I am, antiquity helde silence to be a womans chiefest eloquence, & thought it their part to heare more then to speake, to learne rather then to teach.[8]

The presence of these assertive Puritan women indicates that some women, having found alternative ways to understand the meanings of the Scriptures, were already putting these interpretations into practice in the early Jacobean period. However, it was Puritanism itself that contained a contradiction concerning women's independence of thought and freedom of expression. Coexisting with teachings on the necessity of women's silence and their obedience to male authority was the stress in Puritan thought on the dictates of individual conscience; and this emphasis fostered in women the habit of building a sense of self in relation to God. Even though they were not officially allowed to speak in church, large numbers of women flocked to sermons and lectures;[9] for not only men, but also women and 'even' servants, were taught to strive to understand the Bible for themselves. The seriousness of women who attended sermons was noted by their contemporaries; some preachers were annoyed by women taking notes or transcribing sermons in shorthand.[10] In religious meetings, even women were encouraged to express their views during discussions on the meanings of the Scriptures.[11]

In these circumstances the Puritan emphasis on the exposition of God's Word through preaching and lecturing must have greatly assisted the development of rational thinking and articulateness in women. Moreover, all Puritans agreed that women could and should instruct their families in religious matters. Wives' responsibilities for the spiritual life of their families must have made them, as well as the members of their families, very conscious of the deeper meaning of their language. Thus, while persuading women to conform to the ideal of female silence and obedience, Puritan doctrine paradoxically encouraged them to form habits of independent thought and self-expression.

Puritan women's awakening to their sense of self, then, started in the private sphere – that is, in their personal efforts to examine the self in relation to God. The division between private and public sphere easily disappeared, however, especially when women had ideological support for their activities. Considering it also their duty to enable others to understand God's Word, some Puritan women overstepped the boundary of the private into the public sphere, and started to preach openly. Furthermore, society's over-reaction to Puritan women's changing consciousness made that change even more publicly visible. In particular, contemporary plays drew public attention to Puritan women's changing attitudes through dramatising the various social implications of those attitudes.

Society's fears about the liberating aspects of Puritan thought are reflected in the stereotypical portrayals of Puritan women in early Jacobean plays. Stock features of the female Puritans in these plays are lechery and volubility. Simon Shepherd, in his exploration of the significance of lechery in Puritan women in drama, argues that such a portrayal represents a common reaction against the Puritan emphasis on love and affection, especially as found among the radical Puritan sects like the Family of Love. Such attitudes could lead to the celebration of love and sex and, more dangerously, to the concept of female equality, which might pose a serious threat to the patriarchy.[12] The stock features of volubility in female Puritans on stage in this period also seems to suggest a common reaction against the freedom of expression and independence of thought which Puritan women were developing at the time. In earlier plays, such as Middleton's *The Family of Love* (1602) or *The Puritan, or The Widow of Watling Street* (1606), the Puritan women are shown to hold independent points of view and engage in free speech, thus contradicting Jacobean assumptions about the female virtues of silence and modesty. Here, however, their self-assertive speech is presented only in terms of their hypocrisy; that is, as being merely a strategy designed to conceal their sexual drive or material greed.

III

Simon Shepherd maintains that sympathetic treatment of Puritans is rare in literature of the period.[13] However, in some later plays the speech of women who show Puritan inclinations is dealt with in a positive light. Even though they violate the ideal of female silence, they are presented as women of integrity. Here the self-assertive speech of Puritan women is designed to indicate a moral stance in the plays, one which represents the Puritan principle itself, the levelling attitudes of Puritan Parliamentarians, or the Puritan concept of marriage. This phenomenon is particularly clear among plays of the 1630s when Puritan opposition leaders were increasing in power, and some City magnates were trying to use the stage as a means of propaganda in their conflict with the crown.[14] In most cases, the overt function of these Puritan women's speech is not to construct their subjectivity. None the less, the fact that they show no hesitation in speaking out, frequently at length, in order to express their refusal of assumptions about social status or the position of women, deserves attention.

IV

Thomas Drue's *The Duchess of Suffolk* presents a heroine the function of whose speech is to put forward the Puritan principle. The play was performed at the Fortune in 1624, after being 'much reformed' by Sir Henry Herbert as 'full of dangerous matter'.[15] It therefore belongs to the Jacobean period in a chronological sense, but the levelling attitude and Puritan belief endorsed in the play also relate it to the later drama. Curiously, the play contains some parallels with the situation in Webster's *The Duchess of Malfi* (1613), although the difference in the authors' attitudes to the crucial issue underlines Drue's overtly democratic stance throughout his play, which was written a decade after Webster's tragedy. The two plays are both based on historical fact, and the emphasis of each is on the inequality of marriage. The Duchesses of the two plays are both widows who choose their stewards as second husbands. Both Duchesses make advances to the men they are in love with, by playing with the double meanings of the word 'husband'.[16] Yet the authors' attitudes towards the issue of unequal marriage differ greatly: while Webster maintains an ambiguous distance from his heroine's assertion of will, Drue unequivocally approves the Duchess's democratic behaviour.[17]

Drue establishes his heroine as a Puritan duchess right from the beginning. The play starts with her giving alms to beggars, while she expresses her concern for the purity of religion in a Puritan vein:

> There should we read, vpon the naked walls,
> The first creation of our wretchednesse;
> There no intruding obiects of gaie clothes,
> Imbrodered hangings, or rich tapistrie,
> Shall wound the seruice which we owe to heaven. (sig. C1v)

When the Duchess chooses her virtuous steward, Bertie, to be her husband in Act I, refusing royal and aristocratic suitors, her unconventional choice evokes criticism from her noble friends. One of them, Arundel, calls her 'madcap Dutches' (sig. B2r). But her levelling attitude, in contrast to that of Webster's Duchess, soon gains approval from both her friends and her servants. Addressing Bertie, one of her servants delivers a justification of the Duchess's unequal marriage:

> She lessens not her honours in your choyce,
> But makes you Lord of her affections,
> And them we serue not, but her royalties,
> Which, as they are not lessened, why should we
> Shrinke from their seruice. . . . (sig. B2v–B3r)

The Duchess is portrayed as an outspoken woman throughout the play. At the beginning, she relentlessly mocks the Papist bishops Bonner and Gardiner as they are being led to prison. Although this mockery precipitates their later revenge upon her, the act of speaking out is represented as a courageous Protestant challenge to popery. The rest of the play concerns the ordeal of the Duchess and her family, who are persecuted by the Papist bishops and forced to flee from England, wandering from one place to another on the Continent. At the accession of the Protestant Elizabeth, they finally return to England in triumph. In the end, the Duchess is again seen giving alms to poor beggars.

The historical Duchess of Suffolk – as described in Foxe's *Acts and Monuments*, on which Drue's play is based – was an important patron of London Puritan preachers.[18] More importantly, as Margot Heinemann and Jerzy Limon argue,[19] the Duchess's sufferings as a refugee in Europe seem to have been intended as a stage parallel with those of Queen Elizabeth of Bohemia, King James's daughter, who was an English national heroine on account of her commitment to Protestantism. At the time when Drue's play was performed at the Fortune, Queen Elizabeth and her husband were being forced to wander on the Continent in an attempt to escape the persecution of the Habsburgs.

Elizabeth was not a Puritan, but because of her marriage in 1613 to the Elector of Palatine, Frederick V, who was looked upon as the Protestant hope on the Continent, she was idealised as a Protestant champion by the English people. Because of the couple's projected role as the conquerors of the Catholic Antichrist on the Continent, Elizabeth was often associated with Queen Elizabeth I, who had defeated the Armada. When they were forced to live in exile after Frederick's defeat by the Habsburg forces in 1620, their sufferings were associated by the English people with those of the Protestant victims of Catholic persecution in the past. This feeling was especially strong among Puritans in the City, who tried to help the royal couple by offering financial aid and petitioning the King for their political rescue.[20] When Drue's play was performed, many people in the audience must have recognised the parallel between the Duchess of Suffolk, a sixteenth-century Puritan leader, and Queen Elizabeth of Bohemia, their own Protestant champion.

Queen Elizabeth of Bohemia was said to be a woman of great spirit and strong personality. Her assertiveness, in contrast to her husband's constant indetermination, is shown in various anecdotes. When Frederick decided to accept the Crown of Bohemia, Elizabeth seems to have exerted considerable influence upon her husband. When she and her husband had to flee from Prague, she showed no sign of fear. The English ambassador was said to have called her 'our blessed undaunted lady'.[21] She was also a woman of practical ability, well able to take resourceful action. Elizabeth wrote letters – albeit in vain – to her father, King James, and his favourites at court, asking them for help; she tactfully christened her daughter Louisa Hollandina and 'asked the Dutch States to be godfathers'; and she is also said to have 'dazzled ambassadors and substituted the currency of her favours for the money which her husband had not got'.[22] Her daring actions and speech, which might seem to violate the Jacobean ideal of womanhood, were looked upon by English people as representing integrity, since their purpose was to promote the Protestant cause.

Jerzy Limon has made a strong case for Drue's use of past history as a political allegory for the present, arguing that the underlying purpose of the play was to act as an open criticism of James's failure to attempt a rescue of the royal couple.[23] Further Protestant propaganda may be suggested by the fact that in Drue's play the Duchess gives birth to Peregrine Willoughby, since the historical Lord Willoughby, as Heinemann points out, was a noted commander against Spain in the Low Countries in 1587.[24] An explicit parallel between Queen Elizabeth I and Queen Elizabeth of Bohemia is also implied by the play: in her eulogy on Queen Elizabeth I in Act v, the Duchess mentions a phoenix arising from her ashes to 'enlighten Christendome' (sig. I1r), which the audience would have connected with Queen Elizabeth of Bohemia. Heinemann sees the play as 'the very model of a plebeian, lower-class way of seeing the contemporary crisis'.[25] The Duchess's assertive speech is thus justified because she is motivated throughout by religious ardour.

V

Similarly, Robert Davenport's comedy *A New Trick to Cheat the Devil*, published in 1639, illustrates the function of the female characters' speech as an embodiment of levelling attitudes. The play focuses on the familiar themes of the conflict between City and court, the values of the trading class and those of the nobility, but its most remarkable feature is that it powerfully contradicts most of the social assumptions underlying the contemporary plays which deal with the same issue, such as Massinger's *A New Way to Pay Old Debts* (1621) or *The City Madam* (1632).

Master Slightall, a young gentleman, is deeply in love with Anne, a citizen's daughter, and finally succeeds in becoming betrothed to her. Although Anne's father, Changeable, blesses her betrothal, his wife has higher social ambitions for her daughter and tries to marry her off to Lord Skales. At first Anne is charmed by the glamour attached to her social advancement, but when she is actually introduced to the young Lord she finds him personally disagreeable and regrets her wavering from Slightall. Changeable is on his daughter's side, and by devising an intrigue which involves disguising himself as the Devil he frees her from the prospective marriage and succeeds in facilitating the reunion of the young lovers.

Anne and her domineering mother, Mistress Changeable, are the characters who dictate most of the play's action, though the final resolution is made possible by Changeable's extraordinary intrigue. Mistress

Changeable, like Lady Frugal in *The City Madam*, is a stereotypically ambitious citizen wife who aims at obtaining social prestige through her daughter's marriage into the aristocracy; in pursuit of this end she shows no hesitation in destroying Anne's betrothal to Slightall.

By contrast, Anne's personal characterisation is very different from that in previous portrayals of City women. She is presented as an outspoken woman – which, it is true, is often the case with bourgeois women in contemporary plays. Yet the aim of her speech is not to indulge herself in emotion, the motivation typically ascribed to the speech of talkative women in other plays. It is rather to express her views and to question the social assumptions to which she is expected to conform. For her, language functions as a means to establish a point of view which is independent of the value system of society. Although at first she almost yields to her mother's standard of human values, when she realises her dislike of the young Lord she begins to question the value of nobility:

ANNE:	Mother, a word I pray.
WIFE:	What sayes my Child?
ANNE:	Which is his Lord-ship?
WIFE:	He that kiss'd you last.
ANNE:	Troth I felt no more honour from his lippes
	Than from another man, nay scarce so much;
	For *Slightall* kisses better. (II. i. p. 212)[26]

Anne, in high spirits, openly challenges the traditional concept of the superiority of the aristocracy:

> Till now I had thought your Lords, and Noble men
> Had bin possess'd of many worthier parts,
> Where meaner men are scanted; but I see
> All's one, or little difference. (II. i. p. 214)

Regarding the Lord's title as no more than 'a cold Bed-fellow' (II. i. p. 215), she points out its emptiness in real life: 'Can honour helpe in Child-birth? or Nobility/ Us privilege from throwes?' (II. i. p. 215). Anne's dismissal of the value of nobility strikes a sharp levelling note. At one time she even falls into scolding, greatly embarrassing the Lord, his men and even her parents:

ANNE:	You are a Noble Thiefe.
LORD:	Ha?
ANNE:	You are a gentle foole.
CHANGEABLE:	How?
ANNE:	I am as cold as Ice, and you a scold.
WIFE:	Minion, how?
ANNE:	You are a Trencher friend.

TREATWELL:	That meant by mee?
ANNE:	And thou a slave and Pander.
GEFFREY:	Speake it not,
	Ile not believe it Mistris.
ANNE:	This Ile prove.
CHANGEABLE:	Why Daughter, daughter?
WIFE:	Sure the Girle's growne franticke. . . .
LORD:	But, Mistris *Changeable*,
	Why did you call me thiefe?
ANNE:	Stand but in row,
	And as I am a woman Ile make all this good;
	You here, you there, and everyone in order:
	First, in particular, and next in generall,
	I will goe over you. (III. ii. pp. 246–7)

She then goes on to justify her rejection of Lord Skales and his aristocratic moral code by proposing the Puritan view of matrimony:

> A noble Thiefe, that was your Character . . .
> . . . but you more great,
> Under pretext of your Nobility,
> And countenance in Court, have from a Husband
> Stolne a contracted and a married Wife;
> For Contract upon Earth in Heaven is marriage,
> And celebrate by Angels (III. ii. p. 247)

Here Anne, unlike other scolds in the drama of the period and despite her public abuse of the people around her, is not treated as an object of ridicule.

The clash of values is thus resolved entirely in favour of levelling attitudes. Margot Heinemann considers the feeling throughout the play to be 'pre-revolutionary'.[27] Anne is certainly endowed with intriguing possibilities of growing into a woman of independent mind. In the face of her mother's aggressive interference, she continues to insist on autonomy in the choice of her own husband:

> Good mother,
> 'Tis me, not you, whom this affaire concernes;
> You gave your owne free answer to my Father,
> So give me leave to doe where I affect;
> The good or bad is mine; not touches you
> That are disposed already. (II. i. p. 214)

However, the author's purpose in characterising Anne as an outspoken woman is apparently only to advance a levelling attitude in the context of increasing tension between court and city. Anne's questioning of social values stops at a political level; her questioning does not develop into an exploration of her own consciousness.

VI

Another talkative female character with a Puritan inclination is Dorotea Constance in Walter Mountfort's *The Launching of Mary or The Seaman's Honest Wife*. Mountfort was not a professional playwright, but an official of the East India Company. He wrote the play on a voyage home from India in 1632.[28] The play consists of two plots: the main one functions as a defence of the activities of the East India Company, drawing upon Thomas Mun's tract *A Discourse of Trade from England unto the East Indies* (1621).[29] The secondary plot, however, relates the story of Dorotea Constance, the chaste and hard-working wife of a sailor who is away in the service of the East India Company. While she deeply misses her husband, she defends her virtue staunchly against the approaches of various men, including a courtier, a captain and even a parson. Her Puritan attitudes are revealed by her frequent recourse to prayer and her invocations to heaven to assist her in her virtuous life. Because of her rigorous morality, she is taunted as 'mistres puritan' (l. 933)[30] by the wanton wives of other seamen, Mall Sparke and Tibb Nutt. However, she is presented not as a narrow-minded Puritan but as a lively and intelligent woman who even goes to the theatre. She expresses strong resentment of the social attitude which regards a woman as morally loose on such trivial grounds as visiting the theatre:

> Am I suspected for incontinent
> because sometymes to recreate my selfe
> I see a playe. . . . (ll. 701–3)

Her only weapon against her suitors' approaches is language. She is one of the most talkative heroines in the plays of the period; at times her speeches exceed thirty lines. Dorotea herself is fully conscious of the power of her speech: 'Good wordes doe sooner blunt the edge of wrath then fierie language' (ll. 2122–3). The method she employs for defeating her male opponents is verbally to dissuade them, as if she were preaching to them. Moreover, the men are impressed by the power of her discourse. A land Captain admires her eloquence: 'You would become the Academie well since you are growne so good a disputant' (ll. 843–4). Another admirer, Captain Goodman, thinks that she does 'argue well' (l. 2182), while Tallow, a workman in the shipyard, is also overcome by the power of her speech: 'her very tongue hath done more then the strongest man in the yard Could haue done' (ll. 2550–51). However, Dorotea employs her language not only to fight against male sexual assaults but also to refute common assumptions about female frailty. She associates her would-be seducers with the contemporary detractors of women, such as the notorious Swetnam, declaring:

> I know there are a packe of Satyrists,
> malignant Swetmans [Swetnams], drunken poetasters
> w[hi]ch farce & bumbast out theyr spurious lines
> w[i]th raylinge language 'gaynst our feeble sex,
> Others there are w[hi]ch out . . . of Idiotisme,
> and shallow apprehension speake theyr pleasure,:
> thus palefacte enuy, and dull ignorance
> (twinns of disorder) are our enymies.
> such pestle heads, such silly sotts as you
> are of the number which I named last:
> who, cause you know but little, dare belch out
> that little, to no purpose, gaynst poore women.
> makinge no difference twixt the good & bad,
> T'were tyme yll spent to tell you, you are base
> because t'is too well knowne. . . . (ll. 2514–28)

When the men laugh at her outburst, regarding it as a typical example of the female offence of scolding, she defies them by asserting her sense of self – which is, she insists, related to God, and therefore independent of other people's views:

> Tis not your follie that canne make me mad
> nor is [i]t your laughinge that canne make me mourne.
> my maker hath not made me such a Creature
> to be impatient at scurrilitie
> yet I dare saye you are vnmannerlie. (ll. 2531–5)

Though the ideas expressed in Dorotea's speeches are little more than conventional concepts about female virtues, her self-assertion is represented as embodying the morality of a citizen and thus, indirectly, serves to support the City's propaganda for the East India Company. Heinemann thinks that the play was probably used by some City magnates as part of this publicity effort; its performance was a subsidised one intended for an invited audience.[31]

It is noteworthy that in the plays of Drue, Davenport and Mountfort the heroines, who must have been immediately identified as Puritans by the audience, are endowed with great articulateness. Moreover, it is their speech which represents the plays' Puritan moral stance and makes the greatest impact on the other characters. Thus, these plays bring to public attention Puritan women's changing attitudes to their private selves. The political implications of these heroines' eloquence are twofold. First, their speeches endorse the Puritan stance with respect to current political and social affairs, such as King James's foreign policy, the conflict between the values of the City and those of the nobility, and the City's publicity for the East India Company. Secondly, presented in a positive perspective, the heroines' articulateness posed a challenge to society's norm of women's silence and modesty, a challenge that threatened the dominant patriarchy.

VII

Not surprisingly, the change in the stage representation of female Puritans in the 1620s and 1630s is closely paralleled by various tendencies in contemporary society. First, there was society's changing attitude to Puritanism itself; in the late Jacobean and early Caroline periods, as public awareness of the dangers of absolutism and the moral degeneration of the court increased, more people began to turn to the Puritan outlook on life as a possible way of improving their state of living. Especially in the 1620s, after the Thirty Years War had started on the Continent, this sympathy with Puritanism increased in London; the Puritan opposition leaders of the City were among those who most daringly countered King James's policies, both domestic and foreign.[32] The playwrights could now expect a more favourable audience response to articulate women on stage if their speeches supported Puritan attitudes. Secondly, there had been a change in the relationship between Puritans and the theatre. It has been commonly believed that the Puritans' antagonism towards the theatre was the main cause of the satirical portrayals of Puritans in earlier plays. However, as Margot Heinemann has made clear, in the 1620s and 1630s close ties seem to have developed between Puritans and the theatres in London. Some Puritans began to see the theatre as a possible medium for propaganda, and actually used the stage for this purpose.[33] It is hardly surprising, then, that some plays of this period present Puritan women as women of integrity eloquently asserting Puritan thought.

Furthermore, this transformation of stage representation seems to indicate society's increasing recognition of the significance of the role played by both contemporary and historical Puritan women. Keith Thomas, in 'Women and the Civil War Sects', maintains that preaching by women began in some Baptist churches in Holland, and that by the 1640s the phenomenon had reached London.[34] However, as is clear from William Heale's reference in *An Apology for Women*, preaching by women seems to have started much earlier in England.[35] Unfortunately, in contrast to the considerable quantity of extant documents concerning women preachers in the 1640s and 1650s, evidence of women preaching in pre-Revolutionary England is too slight for us to know the true nature of the impact of their activities upon society.

That some Puritan women had come to believe by this time in the necessity of expressing their views can also be seen in Rachel Speght's prompt response to the publication of Joseph Swetnam's famous anti-woman pamphlet *The Araignment of Lewde, idle, froward and unconstant women* in 1615.[36] Swetnam's pamphlet was no more than a collection of misogynist commonplaces of the time; however, probably because of its very commonness, as Ann Rosalind Jones suggests,[37] it proved extremely popular, going through ten editions by 1634. The pamphlet provoked five answers, including three pamphlets by authors using women's names.[38] The author who launched the counterattack upon Swetnam was Rachel Speght. The daughter of James Speght, the rector of more than one London church, she was twenty when, in 1617, she published her pamphlet, *A Movzell for Melastomvs, The Cynical Bayter of, and foule mouthed Barker against Evahs sex.*

Speght's Puritan stance is clear from her argument against Swetnam; she counters his attack on women through the Puritan defence of marriage and discredits his references to biblical examples of women's inferiority by pointing out his misreadings of the Scriptures and offering what she thinks are their real meanings. The method she uses to conduct her counterattack recalls that employed in the exposition of the Scriptures by Puritans in their preachings and lectures. Speght's Puritan position is confirmed by the fact that throughout her poem published four years later, *Mortalities Memorandum, with a Dreame Prefixed imaginarie in manner; reall in matter*, she appears to have used the Geneva Bible as her scriptural source.[39] Ester Sowernam (pseudonym), the writer who next attacked Swetnam, refers to Speght as 'a Ministers daughter' (sig. A2v).[40] At the beginning of her pamphlet, Ester writes that she had heard about Swetnam's outrageous pamphlet while having supper with some friends, and that later she was told about Speght's forthcoming response (sig. A2r–A2v). Therefore it seems to have been fairly well known at the time that the first criticism of Swetnam came from a Puritan woman.

Speght uses the tactic of presenting herself as a woman who embodies the Puritan ideal of modesty. Adopting a meek, modest, mild pose, she apologises for venturing on the immodest, unfeminine act of publishing her writing, especially because of her 'insufficiency in literature and tenderness in years' (sig. A4v); she is 'vnworthiest of thousands' (sig. A3r), for she has *'not as yet seene twenty years,/ Though in her carriage older she appeares'* (sig. B4v). Speght's self-deprecating pose seems to have irritated Ester Sowernam so much that she decided to launch her own attack on Swetnam. Yet Speght's tone is in fact quite misleading; from the beginning her criticism of Swetnam is conducted with great self-confidence. She starts by accusing him of blasphemy, for condemning women – the 'excellent worke of Gods hands' (sig. B2v) – as a curse upon men. Throughout the pamphlet her argument is eloquently delivered and well structured, lucidly pinpointing the logical flaws in Swetnam's pamphlet.

Moreover, as Ann Jones has pointed out,[41] Speght extends the Puritan concepts of marriage and womanhood to present her own views on sexual equality. Using a tactic often employed in contemporary tracts on matrimony, she returns to the creation story in Genesis, but her purpose is to assert the equality of man and woman by making use of ambiguities in the text:

> . . . man was created of the dust of the earth, but woman was made of a part of man, after that he was a liuing soule: yet was shee not produced from *Adams* foote, to be his too low inferiour; nor from his head to be his superiour, but from his side, neare his heart, to be his equall; that where he is Lord, she may be Lady . . . (sig. D1v)

Because Eve is created as a respectable helpmate to Adam, men and women were promised equal authority: 'he makes their authority equall, and all creatures to be in subjection vnto them both' (sig. D1v). Speght's view of marriage is typically Puritan in that she acknowledges husbands' authority over wives and the importance of their mutual assistance, and accepts the common analogy of the role of husband in the family with Christ's role as head of the Church. However, her emphasis is actually upon the husband's responsibility, as the head, to create a harmonious relationship between spouses:

> the *Man is the Woman's Head*; by which title yet of Supremacie, no authoritie hath hee given him to domineere, or basely command and imploy his wife, as a seruant; but hereby is he taught the duties which hee oweth vnto her. . . . For he is her *Head, as Christ is the Head of his Church*, which hee entirely loveth, and for which hee gave his very life . . . (sig. D4v)

She even goes on to challenge marital absolutism, the view which insisted on the necessity of wives' submission even to evil husbands, advocated by many Puritan divines such as William Gouge. Speght asserts:

> women are enjoyned to submit themselves unto their husbands no otherwais then as to the *Lord* . . . as the Lord commandeth nothing to be done, but that which is right and good, no more must the husband . . . (sig. E1r)

In spite of her apologetic tone, Speght's pamphlet consistently demonstrates her firm belief in the necessity for women to speak out against injustice and to use their capacities for rational thinking. Her argument stands in sharp contrast to contemporary stereotypical views of women as silent and lacking rationality. Speght's belief is demonstrated again in her next published work, *Mortalities Memorandum*. As in her pamphlet, while assuming a modest, meek pose she forcefully advocates the equality of the sexes and women's right to make the most of the intellectual capacities endowed upon them by God:

> Both man and woman of three parts consist,
> Which *Paul* doth bodie, soule, and spirit call:
> And from the soule three faculties arise,
> The mind, the will, the power; when wherefore shall
> A woman have her intellect in vaine,
> Or not endeavor *Knowledge* to attaine.

The talent, God doth give, must be imploy'd,
His owne with vantage he must have againe:
All parts and faculties were made for use;
The God of *Knowledge* nothing gave in vaine.
'Twas *Maries* choyce our Savior did approve,
Because that she the better part did love (p. 71, lines 127–38)

In the dedication of her poem Speght reveals her irritation at the hostility directed against her unwomanly act of writing and publishing her pamphlet, and especially at the accusation that her father wrote it. In spite of these reactions against her work, however, in publishing her pamphlet and poem she at least publicly exhibited women's right to use their ability of speech to protest. Her tract and poem thus reveal a new attitude of Puritan women to their sense of self and speech, an attitude which was later to be embodied in the articulate heroines of the plays by Drue, Davenport and Mountfort.

VIII

While the female virtues of silence and obedience were constantly emphasised in Puritan preachings and writings, there were clearly quite a few English women in the early seventeenth century who openly defied this sense of 'virtue'. From the late 1610s onwards, women's self-assertive acts seem to have caused particular concern in society. Moreover, several of these rebellious women show a distinct connection with Puritanism.

Among women of the upper and middle classes, female insubordination was not unusual in this period. William Gouge complained that when he preached on 'Domesticall Duties' in St Anne's Church at Blackfriars, some of his audience exhibited their dissatisfaction by murmuring and shifting in their seats.[42] Another male response to the increasingly self-assertive London women was King James's exasperation with their 'insolence', especially in donning mannish clothes. As Chamberlain's much-quoted letter to Carleton on 25 January 1620 relates, the King's fury culminated in his order to all the preachers in London to inveigh against the insolence of women.[43] Another letter by Chamberlain less than three weeks later (12 February 1620) shows that not only priests but also playwrights and ballad-writers responded immediately.[44]

The King's order also prompted the publication of a pair of pamphlets, *Hic-Mulier: Or, the Man-Woman* and *Haec-Vir: Or the Womanish Man* (1620). *Hic-Mulier: Or, the Man-Woman* is hardly more than a repetition of conventional diatribes against women, but has special significance in having been accompanied by the interesting pamphlet *Haec-Vir: Or, the Womanish Man*. Hic-Mulier in this pamphlet attempts to justify women's defiance of conventional assumptions about womanhood, and in reply to Haec-Vir's attack on her transgression of gender boundaries she gloriously asserts freedom of choice for women:

> we are as free-borne as Men, haue as free election, and as free spirits, we are compounded of like parts, and may with like liberty make benefit of our Creations. . . . (sig. B3r)[45]

Judging from the levelling attitudes asserted in it, Simon Shepherd thinks that the pamphlet indicates some sort of Puritan position.[46] Indeed, the declaration of female equality here recalls that of Rachel Speght in her poem and the Duchess of Suffolk, Anne, and Dorotea in the plays discussed here. Among the numerous treatises upon women written in this period, *Haec-Vir* is the only pamphlet which draws attention to contemporary women's awakening sense of independence. The declaration of independence by Hic-Mulier in this pamphlet poses a challenge to the dominant social ideology. Yet the writer's unease in adopting this attitude is betrayed at the end, where both Hic-Mulier and Haec-Vir agree to return to the traditional sexual norms.

IX

In Puritan thought women were not granted such complete spiritual equality as they were in the later radical religious sects. The spiritual equality allowed to women by Puritan doctrine was circumscribed by one fundamental condition: supremacy still rested in men; their wives were simply their helpmates. However, the ambiguities and contradictions contained in the Puritan ethic allowed women more opportunity than before to develop their sense of self, and to justify their independence of thought and freedom of expression. The positive attitudes to the speech of the Puritan women displayed in the plays examined in this essay seem to reflect the growing confidence in their speech among contemporary Puritan women – one which we may already observe in Rachel Speght's tract and poem written many years earlier – and to be a sign of society's recognition of the possible virtues of women's eloquence. Although these plays may be of little literary worth judged by traditional canonical standards, such attitudes merit note, in view of the fact that in most English Renaissance plays female eloquence is identified as a transgression.[47]

That many women in seventeenth-century England were dissatisfied with the passive, subordinate rolesassigned them by Church and society can be seen in the examples of female insubordination glanced at in this essay. This tendency is also understood by the fact that a great number of sectarians were women, attracted to these radical religious groups which offered complete spiritual equality and the opportunity to preach or even hold priestly office. Despite constant attack from men of orthodox views, women preached and prophesied in England in the 1640s and 1650s. During these decades some even turned to activism, presenting petitions to Parliament and organising demonstrations.[48] Puritan women's changed attitudes to their sense of self had now moved beyond the private world and were fully manifested in the public sphere.

Puritanism could serve to provide ideological support for women's growing sense of self and desire for self-expression in pre-Revolutionary England. While producing well-educated, independent-minded Puritan women of orthodox views, such as Lucy Hutchinson and Mary Countess of Warwick, Puritanism also laid the foundation for the activities of the women of the radical sects. These Puritan women thought that their own speech was justified, since the purpose of such expression was to worship God and to enhance others' faith. Yet since the bounds of such justification could be easily extended to non-religious spheres, women, even non-Puritans, would invest their language with meaning and integrity. Puritan women sowed the seeds of another, albeit minor, English revolution – the transformation in women's attitudes to self-expression.

NOTES

1. For instance, Rachel Speght, *A Movzell for Melastomvs, The Cynicall Bayter of, and foule mouthed Barker against Evahs sex* (London, 1617), sig. D1v; see pp. 198–200.
2. Thomas Adams, 'Mystical Bedlam; or, The World of Madmen', with a memoir by Joseph Angus, in *The Works of Thomas Adams* (Edinburgh: James Nichol, 1861), vol. I, p. 278.
3. Speght, sig. D1v; see pp. 198–200.
4. Thomas Becon, *The Golden Boke of Holy Matrimony* (London, 1560), quoted in William and Malleville Haller, 'The Puritan art of love', *Huntington Library Quarterly*, 5 (1942), pp. 244–5. For the Puritan concept of love and marriage, I am indebted to this article.
5. William Gouge, *Of domesticall duties eight treatises* (London, 1622), p. 272.
6. R. Valerie Lucas, 'Puritan preaching and the politics of the family', in Anne M. Haselkorn and Betty S. Travitsky, eds, *The Renaissance English Woman in Print: Counterbalancing the canon* (Amherst: University of Massachusetts Press, 1990), pp. 228–31.
7. John Dod and Robert Cleaver, *A Godlie Forme of Householde Government* (London, 1612), p. 104.
8. William Heale, *An Apology for Women* (Oxford, 1609), pp. 35–6. Heale's pamphlet is dedicated to the Ladie M.H., whose 'commaunde', he says, 'is effected' (sig. A2r).
9. Christopher Hill, *Society and Puritanism in Pre-Revolutionary England* (Harmondsworth: Penguin, 1986), pp. 65–7; Patrick Collinson, *The Elizabethan Puritan Movement* (London: Methuen, 1967), p. 85; R. Valerie Lucas, 'Puritan preaching', pp. 226–7.

10. R. Valerie Lucas, ibid.

11. Collinson, *The Elizabethan Puritan Movement*, pp. 378–82.

12. Simon Shepherd, *Amazons and Warrior Women: Varieties of Feminism in seventeenth-century drama* (Sussex: Harvester Press, 1981), pp. 55–62.

13. Ibid., p. 65.

14. Margot Heinemann, *Puritanism and Theatre: Thomas Middleton and opposition drama under the early Stuarts* (Cambridge: Cambridge University Press, 1980), pp. 200–36.

15. Joseph Quincy Adams, ed., *The Dramatic Records of Sir Henry Herbert, Master of the Revels, 1623–1673* (New York: Benjamin Blom, 1917), p. 27.

16. Thomas Drue, *The Life of the Dvtches of Svffolke* (London, 1631), sig. A4r; F.L. Lucas, ed., *The Complete Works of John Webster* (New York: Gordian Press, 1966), vol. II, I. i. 413, 434. All subsequent references to the edition of Drue are made in the text of the essay.

17. M.C. Bradbrook, *John Webster: Citizen and dramatist* (London: Weidenfeld & Nicolson, 1980), pp. 181–2. Bradbrook discusses the influence of Webster's tragedy upon Puritans, particularly upon Thomas Adams in his sermons.

18. Collinson, *The Elizabethan Puritan Movement*, p. 87. For life of the Duchess of Suffolk, see Cecilie Goff, *A Woman of the Tudor Age* (London: John Murray, 1930); Pearl Hogrefe, *Women of Action in Tudor England: Nine biographical sketches* (Ames, Iowa: Iowa State University Press, 1977), pp. 82–103; Evelyn Read, *Catherine, Duchess of Suffolk: A portrait* (London: Jonathan Cape, 1962).

19. Heinemann, *Puritanism and Theatre*, p. 205; Jerzy Limon, *Dangerous Matter: English drama and politics 1623/24* (Cambridge: Cambridge University Press, 1986), pp. 40–61.

20. Limon, ibid. (pp. 51–7).

21. C.V. Wedgwood, *The Thirty Years War* (London: Methuen, 1984), p. 127.

22. Ibid., p. 149. For life of Queen Elizabeth of Bohemia, see C. Oman, *Elizabeth of Bohemia* (London: Hodder & Stoughton, 1938).

23. Limon, *Dangerous Matter*, pp. 40–61.

24. Heinemann, *Puritanism and Theatre*, p. 208.

25. Ibid., p. 206.

26. A.H. Bullen, ed., *The Works of Robert Davenport*, Old English Plays, new series, vol. III (London and Redhill: The Hansard Publishing Union, 1890). All subsequent references are made in the text of the essay.

27. Heinemann, *Puritanism and Theatre*, p. 229.

28. G.E. Bentley, *The Jacobean and Caroline Stage* (Oxford: Clarendon Press, 1967), vol. IV, p. 922–4.

29. Ibid., p. 924.

30. John Henry Walter, ed., *The Launching of the Mary or The Seaman's Honest Wife* (Oxford: Malone Society, 1933). All subsequent references are made in the text of the essay.

31. Heinemann, *Puritanism and Theatre*, p. 210.

32. Ibid., especially pp. 151–71, 200–36.

33. Ibid.

34. Keith Thomas, 'Women and the Civil War sects', *Past & Present,* **13** (1958), p. 47.

35. Heale, *An Apology*, pp. 35–6; see pp. 187–8. Keith Thomas himself notes ('Women and the Civil War Sects', p. 58, Note 23) isolated references to women preaching in England before 1640.

36. Joseph Swetnam, *The Araignment of Lewde, idle, froward and unconstant women* (London, 1615).

37. 'Counterattacks on "the Bayter of Women": The pamphleteers of the early seventeenth century', in *The Renaissance English Woman in Print*, pp. 45–6.

38. These responses were: Daniel Tuvil's *Asylum Veneris, Or A Sanctuary for Ladies* (London, 1616); Rachel Speght's *A Movzell for Melastomvs, The Cynicall Bayter of, and foule mouthed Barker against Evahs sex* (London, 1617); Ester Sowernam's *Ester hath hang'd Haman: Or An Answere To a lewd pamphlet, entituled, The Arraignment of Women* (London, 1617); Constantia Munda's *The Worming of a mad Dogge: Or, a Soppe For Cerbervs the Iaylor of Hell* (London, 1617); an anonymous play, *Swetnam, The Woman-hater, Arraigned by Women*, licensed on 17 October 1619 (London, 1620).

39. Germaine Greer *et al.*, eds, *Kissing the Rod: An anthology of seventeenth-century women's verse* (London: Virago, 1988), p. 76. All subsequent references are made in the text of the essay.

40. Ester Sowernam, *Ester hath hang'd Haman: Or An Answere To a lewd pamphlet, entituled, The Arraignment of Women* (London, 1617). All subsequent references are made in the text of the essay.

41. Jones, 'Counterattacks', p. 52.

42. R. Valerie Lucas, 'Puritan preaching', pp. 233–4.

43. Norman Egbert McClure, ed., *The Letters of John Chamberlain* (Philadelphia: The American Philosophical Society, 1939), vol. II, pp. 286–7.

44. Ibid., vol. II, p. 289.

45. *Haec-Vir: Or the Womanish Man* (London, 1620).

46. Shepherd, *Amazons and Warrior Women*, p. 87.

47. Catherine Belsey, *The Subject of Tragedy* (London and New York: Methuen, 1985), pp. 149–91; Belsey brilliantly discusses this identification in English Renaissance drama and society.

48. For these women's activities, see Christine Berg and Philippa Berry, ' "Spiritual whoredom": An essay on female prophets in the seventeenth century', in Francis Barker *et al.*, eds, *1642: Literature and power in the seventeenth century* (Colchester: University of Essex, 1981), pp. 37–54; Patricia Higgins, 'The reactions of women, with special reference to women petitioners', in Brian Manning, ed., *Politics, Religion and the English Civil War* (London: Edward Arnold, 1973), pp. 177–222; Phyllis Mack, 'The prophet and her audience: Gender and knowledge in the world turned upside down', in Geoff Eley and William Hunt, eds, *Reviving The English Revolution: Reflections & elaborations on the work of Christopher Hill* (London and New York: Verso, 1988), pp. 139–52; Christopher Hill, *The World Upside Down: Radical ideas during the English Revolution* (Harmondsworth: Penguin, 1978), especially pp. 306–23; Thomas, 'Women and the Civil War Sects'.

10

'Who May Binde Where God Hath Loosed?': Responses to Sectarian Women's Writing in the Second Half of the Seventeenth Century

HILARY HINDS

'Who may binde where God hath loosed?':[1] if this question is considered in relation to women's writings from the radical sects in the second half of the seventeenth century, it is one that prompts two rather different interpretations. It can be seen as a rhetorical question, celebratory of the outpouring of God's Word through the medium of women in the sects. It can also, however, be seen as indicative of a certain anxiety on the part of the authors about critics' attempts to 'binde' or stifle these utterances. Both readings have a central relevance to the position of sectarian women's writing at this time; the greatly increased production of texts by women must be seen in the context of the hostile responses they encountered.

Noting the increase in women's published writing during the period, many critics have argued that there was indeed cause for celebration. Patricia Crawford has called the Civil War and Commonwealth 'the high points of women's publication',[2] both in the sense that women published a greater quantity than previously, and in that women's writing diversified, ranging from political controversy to prose fiction. The radical sects were of particular importance in this expansion: amongst the Quakers, for example, there are records of 650 writers between 1650 and 1700, at least 82 of whom were women.[3] Despite setbacks at the Restoration, this increase was never reversed thereafter. Important though it is to give due weight – and due celebration – to these increased figures, it is equally important to see them in perspective. Although they do represent an increase in absolute terms in women's writing, they do not in any significant way shift the balance between men's and women's publications. For example, Quaker women represent no more than 12½ per cent of the output by Friends in this period – this in a sect which, until the

Restoration at least, incorporated a belief in the active equality of the sexes amongst its tenets. Similarly, no more than about 10 per cent of the spiritual autobiographies written in the second half of the century were by women; and Elaine Hobby estimates that, overall, women's works comprise less than 1 per cent of the total number of texts published between 1649 and 1688.[4]

'Who may binde where God hath loosed?': these words, then, can be said to indicate a confidence, emanating from the assurance that God is present in the production of this ever-increasing number of texts; for who could oppose a project motivated by the power of God and hope to succeed in this opposition? This indeed is a justification often used by women writers in these texts – that it is not with them that their works originate, but with God, so that they can be neither praised nor blamed for their writings. However, as well as this confidence, the question also suggests anxiety. Despite the emphasis placed by women writers on the spiritual origin of their work, they were aware that it was being received in an environment intolerant of – even hostile to – any activity that was seen to break the bounds of modesty and silence; and this becomes particularly apparent when the question is seen in its textual context. In the preface to Anna Trapnel's *The Cry of a Stone* (1654) the author, just before asking 'Who may binde?', begs people not to reject her message, not to 'bind up the goings forth of the most free and Eternal Spirit' in any 'Law, custom order, or qualification of man, how antient or accustomed soever'. Here, the possibility that God's Word can be successfully 'bound up' or silenced by any number of man-made impediments – impediments supposedly powerless in the face of God's omnipotence – is quite clearly countenanced and feared.

Not surprisingly, perhaps, experience justified this fear. Reactions to women writing were largely hostile, and often hysterically so. Dorothy Ludlow suggests that this hostility was reserved especially for women who wrote, preached or prophesied any kind of political message. The divine calling in itself, she asserts, was not generally feared by men. It was only when women overstepped the boundary between the private and the public sphere that men felt that they had to register their opposition, for this showed a concern for current affairs, in which women supposedly had no part to play.[5] Whilst fear certainly surrounded public activities such as preaching or prophesying, I want to suggest that there is no such easy distinction to be made in terms of writing. Although it is possible to classify some writing as overtly 'political' (public) and some as 'spiritual' (private), this ultimately made no difference to the male audience who reacted with almost uniform hostility to all kinds of publications, whether they were spiritual autobiographies, tracts, pamphlets or political prophecies.

It was not, then, the nature of the writing, whether 'political' or 'spiritual', 'public' or 'private', that determined this response. It was the very existence of writing by women that offended men – not only because it broke the bounds of modesty and silence, but also because even the most 'private' of texts had overtly 'public' and didactic ends. This combination – the rejection of the bounds of modesty and an engagement with the public sphere – was enough to incur the wrath or dismay of men both outside and inside the radical sects.

Daniel Rogers, in his marriage manual *Matrimoniall Honour* (1642), gives a clear indication that it was the context of woman's religious activity to which he objected, not the subjects of their writing or preaching. He wrote that such women have 'shaken off the bridle of all subjection to their husbands, . . . not blushing one whit'. Even if what they say is sound, they are still of the Devil's ranks, because they are usurping authority:

> Such immodesties and insolencies of women, not able to containe them-
> selves within the boundes of silence and subjection, I am so farre from
> warranting, that I here openly defie them as ungrounded, and ungodly.[6]

To Rogers, then, the question 'Who may binde where God hath loosed?' would have seemed irrelevant, for it stood in contradiction to the position of 'silence and subjection' that God had ordained for women in relation to their husbands. Any spirit provoking women to preach or write, thereby breaking these 'boundes', was therefore thought to be the work of the Devil. Women, Rogers's words imply, are unruly; they need a 'bridle' in order to keep them subject to their husbands. Immodesties and insolencies are never far below the surface and so have to be 'contained' within certain bounds. The images he uses suggest constraint, restriction and containment of forces that threaten to disrupt. I shall return to the more specific significance of these images later, but at this point I want to consider the various forms of sectarian writing, the reactions this writing actually received, and the reactions predicted by the writers. An exploration of these makes clear the limitations of the political/spiritual and public/private division; moreover, it clarifies the common ground behind diverse forms of writing, as well as behind men's reactions to these texts.

The tracts and pamphlets that appeared in such numbers in the 1640s and 1650s are, on first appearances, the most overtly 'political' of the literature produced in the sects. Generally very short – often only two or three pages – and usually with an overwhelming sense of urgency and imminence, titles such as Grace Barwick's *To all present Rulers, whether Parliament, or whom soever of England* (1659), Hester Biddle's *Wo to thee City of Oxford* (1655) and Dorothy White's *Upon the 22 day of the 8th Month, 1659* (1659) give some indication of the highly topical and heterogeneous nature of the material.

Nevertheless, the authors were unified in their modes of inspiration. Usually, they claimed, the command to write came directly from God. Dorothy White begins *Upon the 22 day*:

> The Word of the Lord came unto me, saying, Write, and again I say, Write with speed, to the Heads and Rulers of this Nation; Oh! earth, earth, earth, hear the Word of the Lord . . .[7]

Grace Barwick's message from God instructed her to travel a hundred and fifty miles to deliver the Word of God to 'all present rulers'. In addition to their common motivation, these two tracts are also typical in that they are addressed to a specific audience – generally consisting of the rulers of the nation, as here – or to a local audience. Jeane Bettris, for instance, addressed the inhabitants of Aylesbury in these words: 'saith the Lord, For I have measured thee as I measured Sodome in the day of her highnesse, and the same sin that I found in her is found in thee.' Bettris's tone of warning and admonition is common to many radical tracts of the period: Anne Audland warned a Justice of the Peace who tried and sentenced her for disrupting a service at a 'steeple-house' in Banbury that God 'will visite you for these things, and plead with you for all your hard speeches, and all your ungodly deeds: and give you your portion with hypocrites, except you speedily repent.' Similarly, Sarah Blackborow urged people to leave 'Adultery and Transgression' and to 'hearken diligently to hear the voice of God'.[8]

The concern with the present and the immediate future, the imminence of God's judgement and thus the necessity of speedy repentance, is characteristic of all these Quaker writers, and precludes the apologies or justifications for writing and publishing that customarily accompany the work of other women writers in the radical sects. No mention is made of their unfitness to write: they have a message to convey, and there is no room for false modesty. Anne Audland writes: 'when the book of Conscience is opened, thou mayst remember that thou wast forewarned in thy life-time. . . . And so your false blasphemy I do deny, and the living God will judge between me and you.' Her sense of her own role and her own importance in God's scheme is very clear, and should be recognised by others, not only by herself. Mary Howgill's opinions are just as clearly and straightforwardly expressed. She condemns Cromwell, telling him: 'thou hast chosen the glory of the world, and art as a stinking dunghill in the sight of God . . . and when the day comes upon thee, thou shalt me remember, that thou wast warned of all thy evil'.[9] Typically, the imminence of Christ's second coming is intimately connected with the current political situation, the 'present rulers' and the attitudes and activities of individuals and communities known to the writers.

The strength of this concern is all the more apparent in comparison with the writings of Quakers after the Restoration, when the attitude towards political affairs was quite different and they seemed determined to distance themselves from any such controversial matters. Mary Mollineux, for example, suggests that the status quo, however inequitable, is there to be transcended rather than challenged. The title of her collection of poems, *Fruits of Retirement* (1702), itself suggests this more quietist spirit, and one poem in particular, 'Of a happy Life', confirms this stress on the inner life to the exclusion of the outer. Its subject is 'The honest man, that lives in Health/ Enjoying still sufficient Wealth':

> That hath an equal loyal Spouse,
> An Handsome, habitable House;
> Inherited, or purchas'd, that
> He need not fear the sullen Threat
> Of griping Landlord; but if not,
> Finds true Content in any Lot;
> Since in the Closet of his Mind
> Dwells Solace not to be defin'd.[10]

Compared with the earlier Quaker tracts of the mid seventeenth century, which were resonant with warnings and exhortations, attacks on tithes and 'hireling priests', this tone of acceptance, a turning inward to find 'solace' in the mind despite all external conditions, is markedly different. It illustrates the change of political climate after the Restoration, when the passing of the Conventicle Acts in 1664 and 1670 forbade all religious meetings except those where the liturgy of the Church of England was used; the penalties for such disobedience were fines, imprisonment or deportation. The contrast also emphasises how, during the Commonwealth period, spiritual hopes and expectations were closely integrated with political and material ones.

This integration is perhaps most apparent in the prophecies of Fifth Monarchist writers such as Anna Trapnel and Mary Cary, in which the second coming and the establishment of the New Jerusalem were perceived in very material terms. King Jesus's arrival was thought to be imminent, and would entail the downfall of all earthly monarchies. This, though inevitable, had none the less to be worked and fought for; and consequently Trapnel's prophecies include both spiritual and political visions that together fulfil God's promise to His people. She writes: 'the Army . . . was then drawing up towards the City, in which I had a little discovery of the presence of the Lord with them, in which day I had a glorious vision of the New Jerusalem.' Later she continues: 'I conversed with God by prayer, and reading of the Scriptures, which were excellently opened to me touching the proceedings of the Army'.[11] Yet God did not communicate with Trapnel solely on the subject of the army. In her *Report and Plea* (1654) she claims that He 'filled me that day with prayer, and singing, and discovering the tottering, shaking condition of Clergie-Function'.[12]

Through her prophecies, then, Trapnel criticises any institution or person that she feels stands in the way of the preparations for the Second Coming, and this includes a detailed criticism of Cromwell's career. Previously, she suggests, he had been 'Gideon, going before Israel, blowing the Trumpet of courage and valour'. Later, after she felt that he had betrayed the Fifth Monarchist cause, she had a different vision, one 'of the deadnesse of Gideons spirit to the work of the Lord, shewing me that he was laid aside, as to any great matters, the Lord having finished the greatest businesse that he would employ him in'. She also described another, even less equivocal, vision in which Cromwell appeared at the head of a herd of cattle, and ran at 'many precious Saints that stood in the way of him'.[13] Since the Saints were to take power until the arrival of King Jesus, here was a clear case where God's plan needed assistance in its fulfilment from the Saints themselves.

The interpretations of biblical prophecies by Mary Cary, another Fifth Monarchist, were equally 'political'. Indeed, the politics and the prophecies are not only linked in her vision but wholly integral, each gaining significance and meaning in the light of the other, for prophesying was not so much foretelling the future as an apprehension and interpretation of God's will through a 'reading' of signs, including scriptural texts. Cary makes clear just how wide a definition 'prophecy' could have: 'all might prophesie, that is, (in the lowest sense) be able to speak to edification, exhortation and comfort'. Elsewhere, she writes:

> the things that are here spoken of, being now in a great measure accomplished: for all prophesies are best understood in the fulfilling of them.[14]

This commentary gives us a sense both of the timelessness of biblical prophecies for Cary, and also of their topicality and immediate relevance to her. Their interpretation and realisation are not an ideal for some distant future, but a crucial feature of present circumstances.

The manner in which Fifth Monarchists anticipated preparing the way for the arrival of King Jesus, and the portions of the Bible they concentrated on to justify these actions, indicate just how threatening such an integration of the spiritual and the political could be. Christopher Hill has made clear the importance, for the sectaries of the period, of the idea of 'the world turned upside down' as an image from the Bible that had a particular significance for the shaping of contemporary ideas.[15] The phrase indicated not only that those currently in power would be toppled, but also that they would be replaced by those hitherto powerless in society, 'the Saints':

> [those that] doe covet to treasure up most riches for themselves, and to poll, and rob, and cheat the people, to inhance their own estates, and make themselves great in the world, and their children gay and splendid amongst

men; as doe Kings, Princes, and evill Governours, (not to mention some sorts of Committee-men)[16]

shall become the 'basest and vilest' amongst men. Instead, 'Kings, and Nobles, and mighty men, are to be subjected to his Saints', who will seek 'the public weale, and safety, and happinesse, and salvation of all'.[17] Trapnel makes it clear from which sections of society the Saints are primarily to be drawn, predicting that Christ is coming 'for to inrich them that/ Before were poore and mean'. She distinguishes between true and false religion, as between the socially advantaged and the disadvantaged, finally identifying those most likely to be closest to God:

> there are many fleshly, nationall, Religious ones, but the poore, fatherlesse and widow are the companions of the pure Religious ones.[18]

The people Trapnel cites are those without a voice, or at least a public voice: the poor, and the 'fatherlesse and widow', women without men and therefore not 'owned' by anyone, and so without a mouthpiece or spokesman. But with the coming of Christ, she implies, they will find their voices.

The concept of an egalitarian future is echoed by many sectarian writers. Mary Cary wrote:

> the time is coming . . . when not onely men but women shall prophesie; not only aged men, but young men; not only superiours but inferiours; not only those that have University-learning, but those that have it not; even servants and handmaids.[19]

Again, she implies that the world was to be turned upside down, the usual hierarchies upended: women, the young, 'inferiours', the uneducated, servants and handmaids shall be equal to (or, the implication is, above) their so-called superiors. Her reference to servants and handmaids prophesying is an allusion to Acts 2: 17–18, part of which Anne Audland uses as an epigraph to her pamphlet *A true Declaration of the suffering of the innocent* (1655):

> And on my Servants, and on my handmaidens, I will poure out in those dayes of my Spirit, and they shall prophesie.

This passage from Acts (together with 1 Corinthians 1: 27–8) was often referred to, and used as a justification of activities that were readily condemned by those opposed to the sects. In a sense, these verses epitomise the political and spiritual aspirations of the sectaries.

Whilst the political implications of this kind of women's writing are explicit, and the threat they were felt to pose is similarly apparent, there is none the less no clear demarcation between these 'political' texts and other 'spiritual' ones. Although spiritual autobiographies, for example, seem at first to be much more limited in scope, more introspective, and interested in a personal past rather than a national future, their political implications are just as far-reaching.

It is true that the apparent structures of the more overtly political texts and of the spiritual autobiographies contrast quite sharply. The all-inclusiveness of the tract literature, the integration of the personal and spiritual with the political and prophetic, is different in emphasis from spiritual autobiography's emphasis on the work of God in its narrowest manifestation: His role in the individual's journey through sin, conversion, doubt and faith. Because of this, it is possible to characterise it as having a more limited perspective, focusing solely on the doubts and hopes of an individual Christian, instead of on the whole Christian community. Undoubtedly, there are ways in which this generalisation holds true. The mood of Jane Turner's *Choice Experiences* (1653), for example, is very different from Trapnel's prophecies. Trapnel's *The Cry of a Stone* is dedicated to 'all the wise Virgins of Sion', but it also has a much wider application: 'it is not for you only, but for all'. Turner, on the other hand, addresses her work to 'the Churches of Christ who worship God in Spirit and truth . . . especially those my dear Brethren at Newcastle, Barwick and Scotland'. Turner's husband, too, reinforces this sense of restriction in a prefatory letter to the work:

> I know it would seem very strange to you, if this following Treatise should come to your hands without my publick owning of it, as indeed well it might, considering my near relation with the Author.[20]

From the outset the gender boundaries are established. The rules of propriety, in the sense both of ownership and of correctness, are observed. Not only does Turner's husband circumscribe her activities by owning them, but Turner herself excuses the act of writing by saying it was done 'at several times in my Husband's absence, which may be some satisfaction as to my spending that time. I did intend them only for my own private self.'[21] To write when her husband was at home would have broken one of the rules of propriety; to intend the writing for anyone other than herself would have broken another. Whilst Trapnel and Cary were 'pressed in spirit' to publish their writings, to communicate them to as many people as possible, here it is Turner's husband who is 'pressed in spirit' to publish, 'judging it might be profitable to some precious souls . . . though it be written but in a broken scittering way'. Trapnel and Cary aimed to communicate their message of the imminence of the realisation of God's kingdom on earth. Turner wrote 'as a remembrancer of the old loving kindness of the Lord towards me, and twas not in the least in my thoughts that ever it should have been presented to a publike view'.[22]

Turner's writings, then, do not have the urgency of Trapnel's, Cary's, or some of the Quaker tract-writers', nor an intimate and immediate concern with the directly political issues of Parliament or the leadership of the country. They are calm, reflective and personal, interspersing 'experiences' with 'observations', drawing religious precepts from personal events. So far, distinguishing the 'political' from the 'mystical' does, to some extent, describe the differences between the writings of Turner and other spiritual autobiographers, and those of women such as Trapnel and Cary.

However, this is a very partial description of women's spiritual autobiography, one that ignores the context in which it was written or received. Nor does it give voice to the stated or implied intentions of the authors, which at times seem to contradict the apologies or justifications at the beginning of their texts. These contradictions, as much as anything else, broaden the implications of autobiography as a political genre, and help to explain the hostile reactions they so often elicited from men.

The increase in the numbers of spiritual autobiographies written after 1640 is generally taken to be associated with the rise in influence and numbers of the Protestant sects, a change that allowed an individual to play a much more active part in determining his or her own spiritual well-being. In fact, all individuals were thought of as equal in grace in the sight of God, a concept that was especially significant for women. While social and sexual inequality was generally accepted, this new spiritual equality allowed women a sphere of activity in which to articulate their faith, instead of having to be receptacles of received religious ideas and dogma. Such liberty manifested itself with increasing force in many areas, in preaching and parish protest as well as in prophesying, tract-writing, and spiritual autobiography.

It was especially in the area of spiritual autobiography that women could, and did, claim equality with men. Because the individual of any class and either sex – 'illiterate men and silly women . . . (so called)'[23] – was important, the very fact of writing autobiography made this plain, provoking complaints about immodest or even ungodly behaviour. From some of the texts, it would seem that men were threatened by the idea that any form of spiritual activity would deflect women from their ordained position of subordination. Jane Turner's stress on the fact that she wrote in her husband's absence is one indication of this; other women's reluctance to publish is another. As was written of Elizabeth Stirredge, 'altho' the Lord had given her a large Gift in verbal Testimony, yet she was backward to appear therein'. And Stirredge herself feared the reaction she would receive: 'Lord, look upon my affliction, and lay no more upon me than I am able to bear. They will not hear me that am a contemptible Instrument. And seeing they despise the Service of Women so much, O Lord make use of them that are more Worthy.'[24] Women, despite being equal to men in the sight of God – equal to the extent that He calls upon them to undertake His work and convey His message to His people – were by no means received in the same way in the fulfilment of this work as the men with whom they were supposedly equal.

There are passages in several autobiographies that indicate how writing could be perceived as disruptive or subversive. Joan Vokins writes: 'I could take no comfort in Husband or Children, House, or land, or any visibles, for want of the Marriage Union with the lamb of God'.[25] This, although addressing the spiritual, implies a comparison with the material: the earthly marriage and spiritual union with Christ. There is no doubt which liaison is more important to her. Cynthia Pomerleau suggests that this illustrates part of the function of religion in Vokins's life:

> it allowed her to find by turning inward the meaning, mystery, exaltation and ceremony that were lacking outwardly. In effect, she could admit that she was not satisfied with her domestic lot without actually rebelling against it.[26]

The inadequacy of Vokins's material lot, perhaps more than her dissatisfaction with it, is suggested by other passages in the text. Writing of her husband and children, for whom she had a 'true and tender love', she comments:

> if I had disobeyed the Lord, to please them, I might have provoked him to have withholden his Mercies from us all, and to bring his Judgments upon us. . . . Then Husbands, and Wives, and Parents, and Children, and Servants, shall receive according to their doings; and none that disobeys the Lord can be excused.[27]

Vokins implies that the best way of serving her husband and children is by serving God, in order that He does not withhold his mercies from them all. What is also clear, however, is how much her own peace of mind depends upon following her divinely initiated course:

> The feeling of his sweet refreshing Life that he communicates to my soul, is a hundred-fold better than Husband or Children, or any other outward Mercies that he hath made me a partaker of, though very near and dear to me.[28]

Vokins's husband and children take a definite second place to her relationship with God. Interestingly, it is almost only in the comparisons between God's demands and her family's that her family is mentioned at all.

It was perhaps this emphasis on the spiritual, to the virtual exclusion of the material, that disturbed many male readers of women's early spiritual autobiographies. It is, in fact, one of the characteristics most often noted by critics in relation to spiritual autobiographies of this time in general, although men handle spirituality differently in the autobiographical mode. Thus Owen Watkins writes of George Whitehead's journal:

> His life story, like those of all the Quaker preachers, is a record of his public service and contains hardly any reference to family and personal relation-

ships. And the national life as a whole is referred to only when it impinges on the activities of Friends, mainly in times of persecution.[29]

This spiritual experience, as opposed to any other, is seen as part of the general Quaker reliance on the 'inner light' as a source of authority and truth: 'all guidance came from the power within and final authority was to be found not in the teaching of the Church, nor in the Bible, but only through personal experience'.[30] Yet this was not limited to the Quakers alone. Dean Ebner writes of Bunyan's autobiography: 'The world of Bunyan was a severely interior world from which important human experiences of a more external nature, chiefly historic and domestic, were all but eliminated.' Of Trapnel's *A Legacy for Saints* (1654) he writes: 'No persons, places, or times mentioned during this narrative are unrelated to the history of spiritual illumination.'[31] The importance of this is seen as entirely spiritual: the world under examination was internal, so that all things material were of no importance.

This assumes, however, that this 'impersonal' tendency has the same meaning for all the sectaries, irrespective of gender. But there is another perspective, again offered by Watkins, which comes closest to what I would suggest is the significance of this tendency for women writers, although Watkins is actually writing about autobiography in general. Commenting on the didactic nature of spiritual autobiography and the implications this has for the sense of self created in the work, he writes:

> in publishing his [*sic*] record he would repudiate the idea that it should be read because he was an exceptionally interesting person, a unique personality; no one in the seventeenth century could have done this without having to admit to the most monstrous egotism. . . . But, of course, whether the writer's concern was pastoral or evangelical or prophetic, he found himself involved in presenting a 'self' to the reader, if only because he was the main subject of the story. . . . The charge of vainglory would more readily stick to the writer who implied that his life and character were of intrinsic interest because of his career, travels, or other adventures, and distinct from the particular ways he fulfilled his function as God's instrument or exemplified God's workmanship.[32]

For women writers, the private/public dichotomy presented a 'double-bind'. To include details of their homes, families and selves in any material sense would have laid them open to charges of vainglory and immodesty (charges whose meaning was very different for women and for men[33]); yet to ignore these aspects was to imply that their 'proper' areas of concern were of secondary or even peripheral importance. Given the choice, in almost all cases women chose finally to omit all references to their outward circumstances. As became apparent, however, even this was not enough for them to escape recrimination, for men felt that the female 'self' was too much present – not only *in* the text, but because of the very *existence* of the text. Daniel Rogers strongly suggests this: the 'bridle of subjection' and the 'boundes of silence' within which women should 'containe themselves' implies that the yardstick by which their utterances are measured is silence, not the quality of their words. The very act of writing – and particularly of publishing – or preaching was itself an indication of immodesty or profligacy, an inability to contain oneself within one's proper bounds.

This reference to the 'boundes' of silence presents a particular view of the nature of women, one that Natalie Zemon Davis characterises as the 'disorderly woman'.[34] Such disorderliness, far from being an aberrant state, was based in nature, in the particular combination of cold and wet humours found in women, which left the woman in the sway of her womb and her baser passions, so that the lower elements ruled the higher. This tendency, if left unchecked, was thought to lead to chaos. Moreover, women would try to reproduce this disorderly pattern in society by dominating those above them in the social and sexual hierarchy. In Roger's words, women had to be 'contained' within the 'boundes' of silence and subjection to ensure that this intrinsic disorderliness was kept on a tight rein. The resulting humility and modesty was not, then, natural, but had to be achieved or enforced. Rogers's train of thought goes some way towards explaining the nature of the responses women writers received, and also men's fear and vehement hostility, as disorderliness threatened to break out. The 'bridle' of which Rogers wrote was more than a metaphor for this desired subjection. Rather, it was a concrete response to women's 'disorderliness'. In 1655, Dorothy Waugh spoke in a marketplace in Carlisle, for which she was seized and put in prison, where an iron bridle was brought:

> that which they called so was like a steele cap and my hatt being violently pluckt off which was pinned to my head whereby they tare my Clothes to put on their bridle as they called it, which was a stone weight of Iron by the relation of their own Generation, & three barrs of Iron to come over my face, and a peece of it was put in my mouth, which was so unreasonable big a thing for that place that cannot be well related, which was locked to my head, and so I stood their time with my hands bound behind me with the stone weight of Iron upon my head and the bitt in my mouth to keep me from speaking.[35]

In reality, the constraints upon women's activities were much more than verbal or written disapproval and discouragement. Women faced not only iron bridles but also imprisonment in Bridewell, and violent assaults from those they preached to:

> And as Mary Prince and I was coming Arm in Arm from a Meeting, that was at George Bishop's House, there was a Rude Man came and abused us, and struck off Mary Prince her hat, and ran some sharp Knife or Instrument through all my Clothes, into the side of my Belly, which if it had gone but a little farther, it might have killed me.[36]

The same writer records that during the course of her travels she was imprisoned wherever she went, whipped at Exeter 'till the Blood ran down my Back', and threatened by a butcher who 'swore he would cleave my Head in twain; and had his Cleaver up ready to do it' when he was restrained by a woman in the crowd.[37]

The number and diversity of the reactions to women's religious activities were striking. As well as the physical violence encountered by women preachers, women writers also faced violent condemnations of their work. Edward Burrough, later a leading Quaker, wrote a pamphlet response to Turner's *Choice Experiences*, castigating it as 'nothing but aiery imagination and confusion'. Her language, he said, 'is the language of Babylon wholly; and she is yet a servant in bondage in Babylon unto the Mistresse of Witchcraft'. Most tellingly, he suggests that she has broken the bounds of both silence and modesty by writing in this way: 'let her mouth be stopped, and let shame strike her in the Face, who professes her selfe to know the Lord'.[38]

This catalogue of accusations was by no means unusual. Elizabeth Poole, who recorded her visions and their connections with contemporary events, was condemned in a Royalist pamphlet as a 'monstrous witch full of deceiptful craft'.[39] Anna Trapnel was habitually the subject of such abuse:

> England's Rulers and Clergie do judge the Lords hand-maid to be mad, and under the administration of evil angels, and a witch, and many other evil terms they raise up to make me odious, and abhorr'd in the hearts of good and bad, that do not know me.[40]

She recorded the surprise of those who came to hear her preach: 'as some have said, they thought I had been a Monster, or some ill-shaped Creature, before they came and saw, who then said, they must change their thoughts, for I was a woman like others, that were modest and civill'.[41] A woman preaching was evidently felt to be so much 'out of order' that her body must reflect this state and be 'ill-shaped'. To see that this was not so, to find her 'modest and civill', within accepted social boundaries, necessitated a re-evaluation of established ideas, for this challenged all social preconceptions. Later, Trapnel answered more specific charges laid against her: those of witch, imposter, vagabond, whore, and 'dangerous seditious Person'.[42]

Accusations and recriminations came from within as well as outside the radical sects. The Quakers and Muggletonians accused each other of witchcraft. Anne Wentworth was accused by her detractors (fellow Baptists) of being 'a Proud, Passionate, Revengful, Discontented and Mad woman . . . that has unduly published things to the prejudice and scandal of my Husband, and that hath wickedly left him'. Once again, the sins of pride, passion, revenge, discontent and madness are linked with the activities of publishing her writing and rebelling against the natural order by usurping the authority of her husband. Wentworth defends her actions as necessary to save herself from her husband's 'cruel usage', and also as crucial if she was to continue the work to which God had called her, specifically her writing, which her 'earthly husband in a most cruel manner hindered me from performing, seizing and running away with my Writings'.[43] Wentworth plainly sets limits on the authority ascribed to her husband, just as Katherine Chidley did when she asked:

> what authority this unbeleeving husband hath over the conscience of his beleeving wife; It is true he hath authority over her in bodily and civill respects, but not to be a Lord over her conscience; and the like may be said of fathers and masters.[44]

In the light of statements like these, it is clear why religious activities could be interpreted as threatening or provocative.

The common element, I have suggested, behind these diverse accusations of witchcraft, immodesty, madness, pride, whoredom, sedition, deception and revenge was the prevalent image, outlined by Davis, of women as essentially disorderly. If, then, a woman demonstrated her disorderliness by writing, publishing or preaching, this could be expected to be matched by other characteristics of the disorderly woman, such as those just listed. Yet Davis also suggests that this image was ambiguous: on one level it was restrictive and repressive, clearly condemning all activities outside its boundaries; whilst on the other it was liberating, in that it could be used by women to excuse socially unacceptable behaviour. Women could not in the end be accountable for what they did. In the grip of their baser passions, they were beyond the dictates of reason and logic, and so had to be in the constant guardianship of a man, either a father or a husband, who bore the final responsibility for them.

Men, it seems, felt that women exploited this lack of responsibility. In 1605, the Court of Star Chamber complained that women rioters tearing down enclosure fences were 'hiding behind their sex'.[45] Certainly, images of women as subverting the social and sexual hierarchies by dominating or outwitting their husbands or masters, and disguising themselves and living as men, would have been available through comic literature, theatre, broadsheets and ballads, and 'the world of play' – festivals, songs, folk stories and customs. At the same time as mocking or condemning these women, they also showed them to have real power and influence in their own lives and in their family or community. Davis does not, therefore, entirely disagree with those who argue that these inversions of gender roles are ultimately sources of order and stability, in that they clarify the structures of the society and provide a safety valve for conflicts within the system. But she also argues that they go further in that they undermine as well as reinforce the assent given to this hierarchical order. The complexity and ambiguity of the images of the disorderly woman allow for multiple interpretations: 'Play with the concept of the unruly woman is partly a chance for temporary release from traditional and stable hierarchy; but it is also part of the conflict over efforts to change the basic distribution of power within society.'[46]

Expanding the sectarian perspective is Bakhtin's theory of the 'carnivalesque'.[47] Bakhtin suggests that there is continuity between the carnivalesque in its medieval manifestations – feasts, festivals, and so on – and the prose fiction of early post-Renaissance Europe: 'these, written in the vernacular, harness the energies and orientations of the culture of folk humour or carnivalesque, in celebrating difference, otherness, human potential both mimetic and fantastical, through the medium of an essentially comic structure'.[48] These texts were internally heterogeneous, open-ended, in contrast with closed, 'pure' literary genres such as the epic or lyric. Instead of a 'single, unitary language' such as that pertaining to either of these literary forms, these fictions bring different languages or viewpoints into contact with each other, granting none the status of the 'sole verbal and semantic centre of the ideological world'.[49]

Although this perspective refers specifically to prose fiction and its 'dialogised' structure, it shares a number of striking parallels with that outlined in relation to radical sectarian writers of the seventeenth century. These women writers, like most writers in the sects, were outside the 'centralising and unifying' influences of both religion and religious writing, so that they were not concerned to reinforce the status quo of the established church or civil government. The Quakers, in particular, wrote in a style that was often criticised at the time[50] for being insubstantial, overly metaphorical and thereby incomprehensible, as well as for being subversive in its reliance on the 'inner light' as opposed to any external, even scriptural, authority. Although in other sects the Scriptures played a more centrally definitive part, the personal relationship between the writer and God and the experience of the command to write or preach was at the centre of the activity. Without the belief that they had no choice but to write or preach, the Quakers could not reconcile such an activity with their belief in the prevailing social hierarchies.

Despite the common assertion that 'there is no selfe in this thing',[51] the central reference point remains the self. As Jane Turner puts it, 'True Christian experience . . . is truth brought home to the heart with life and power, by the Spirit of God'.[52] The decisive factor is internal, an individual apprehension of the 'spirit of God', an individual consciousness. While this did not necessarily challenge the dominant social ideology, it did not baulk at doing so if that was what this apprehension demanded. The precedent, the authority, for spirituality therefore was not fixed, formalised or institutionalised, but as fluid as the consciousness of the

219

individual concerned. Consequently it was difficult, if not impossible, to define boundaries beyond which writers should not go; for if God called, a writer could not refuse to follow. The texts of a writer such as Anna Trapnel, for example, are open-ended in the sense that no area of her life, her thoughts or her experiences was out of bounds. The possibilities were limitless, provided that they were prefaced with a call from God to enact them. This fluidity or receptivity to the hitherto unacceptable is one important element in the threat that women writers of spiritual treatises posed to male commentators of the time.

Once again, critics must return to the lack of boundaries, in several senses, as a crucial feature of these writings. In writing at all, women such as Anna Trapnel were believed to be overstepping the limit; in the writings themselves, the only boundary is the one imposed by God through the consciousness of the writer. In this context, the charge of 'looseness' or immodesty against these women is particularly apposite, as well as ironic.

Apposite, too, is another of the dominant images that occur throughout these texts, an image that broadens still further the implications of the charge of 'looseness': the image of 'opening'. George Fox wrote: '& soe ye Lords power op[e]ned to him as hee began to have great understandings of ye Lords truth and mercyes . . . & ye Scriptures were very much opned to him.' Thomas Dockrey wrote of Margaret Fell: 'she soon came to enjoy the Glorious Opening of Power of God, by which she was opened to answer both Priests, Professors, and Prophane, and stop'd their Mouths and Writings from replying again.'[53] In these examples, opening is associated with a sense of liberation: for Fox's subject, a liberation through understanding; for Fell, a liberation not only of understanding but also of confidence and power, since she is able not only to answer her critics but also to turn the tables on them by silencing them.

Precedents for this use of 'open' exist in the Bible, although the implications of these usages are much more limited. In Psalm 49, for example, it is written: 'I will open my mouth in a parable: I will utter dark sayings of old'. Luke 24:32 states: 'And they [the disciples] said to one another, Did not our heart burn within us, while he talked with us by the way, and while he opened to us the Scriptures?' Here the implications concern an increase in understanding – in the first passage through parables and 'dark sayings'; in the second through explanation or commentary (perhaps closer to the spirit of Fox's usage than Dockrey's). For most women writers, the implications of this 'opening' seem to go further, however, suggesting if not a liberation, at least a breaking down of boundaries, an impulse outward from the restrictions imposed by social hierarchies and religious prescriptions.

The practical sense of 'opening' as 'explaining' also pervades the texts. Hugh Peter writes that in Mary Cary's work we will find the 'scriptures clearly opened, and properly applied'. Anna Trapnel writes: 'I conversed with God by prayer, and reading of the Scriptures, which were excellently opened to me touching the Proceedings of the Army'.[54] Here the movement begins with prayer and Scripture-reading, and moves outward to encompass the elements of immediate political relevance. Most telling, though, is Alice Curwen's account of how the call to write came to her:

> The 10th day of the 11th moneth, when I was retired in my Mind waiting upon the Lord, it was opened in my Heart by the invisible Power of the living God, the vertue of which I felt, and the Spring of Life being witnessed, I was moved to write of the Dealings of the Lord with me, and of my Travels and of my Testimony in writing, since I went from my outward being.[55]

In this passage, a sense of stillness contrasts with a sense of movement. When she was 'retired in my Mind', her heart was 'opened', which 'moved' her to write of a movement she had made in the past, when she had left her 'outward being'. Curwen's sense of movement has been both outward, in that she travelled to America, and inward, in that she followed the dictates of the 'inner light', leaving her 'outward being' for her inward or spiritual self. The impulse to write, too, is expressed in terms of movement. These types of images, contrasting with Rogers's metaphors of bridles and bounds, suggest a rejection of limits or restrictions, an unwillingness to keep within these 'outwardly' imposed boundaries. Indeed, at one point in Alice Curwen's husband's prefatory testimony, Thomas Curwen uses the word 'contain' in a way directly reminiscent of Rogers: 'the Lord's Presence was with her, wherein she could not contain her self, but she breathed forth Praises to the Lord'.[56] In contrast to containment there is, then, a breathing *forth*: again the impulse is outward. Similarly, Trapnel writes that she was 'carried forth in a spirit of Prayer and Singing', and Mary Cary, in a phrase similar to the one quoted in the title of this essay, predicts that those who try to hinder God's work will inevitably fall, for 'they cannot hinder his work, *for who can let it?*'.[57]

Images of constraint and movement are found in all types of writing, whether prophetic or autobiographical, and indicate a common concern with the 'movement' of that individual and, further, the consequent movement of the reader. The private necessarily becomes public, despite any claims that may initially be made that a piece of writing was intended as no more than 'a remembrancer of the old loving kindness of the Lord towards me', and thus only for 'my own private self'. These words by Jane Turner, stressing the private nature of the experience of writing for her, are contradicted by something she writes later on, when she recommends:

> a close walking with God in all spiritual duties, meditations, self-examination, self-watching, self-judging, self-humbling and prayer . . . not

> that these private duties are above publick but that they prepare for publick, and by these we are acquainted with our own hearts.[58]

Examination of the self and the resulting self-knowledge are not, therefore, ends in themselves but preparations for 'publick' duties, and the words Turner has written are intended to facilitate this self-knowledge. As John Gardner wrote in his preface to Turner's work: 'These inward Experiences are not intended to limit others, but to provoke self-examination and spiritual quickning'.[59] Once again, the contrast is between limiting and 'quickning', constraint and movement. Turner's husband, however, is concerned to define the limits of this movement. He seeks to maintain this 'public' (because published) act of his wife within private boundaries by stressing his own role in it: his surprise when he first learnt of its existence, to the point that it actually silenced him ('I knew not what to say of it'), followed by his regaining control of it by writing that he was 'very much pressed in spirit to publish it'.[60] The private part of the activity, the writing of it, he ascribes to his wife, and the public part, its publication, to himself. This, to some extent, protected her from accusations of immodesty and vainglory. It also allowed him to maintain his position of control over both her and her writings. By trying to deny her any 'public' intention in writing – which is of course belied by her own statements about the private being a preparation for the public – he established limits that were of as much benefit to him as they were to her.

The public implications of writing on such apparently private subjects as outlined above are even clearer in Anne Wentworth's *Vindication*. She defends all that she has written, including that which was 'to the prejudice and scandal' of her husband, on the grounds that she was commanded by God to write and publish. Her writings, she says, are both public and private: they concern 'the peace of my own Soul, and of the whole Nation'. When Baptists, her fellow 'professors', came and rebuked her for what she was doing, she was confident that God would make the significance of this clear. He:

> will search out this matter, and make a true and manifest judgement of it, for there is nothing *hid* from him, and this matter is now become a *publick figure*.[61]

That her personal and private experiences have importance and relevance in a wider and more public sense is something that God has already made clear to her:

> He afterwards revealed to me, (what I did not then know) that my *oppressions* and *Deliverance* had a Publick Ministry and *meaning* wrapt up in them . . . and he also revealed to me what wrath shall fall upon the *same spirit* throughout the Nation, which every where oppresses the true seed, as I have been oppressed by it.[62]

The private and public implications of her experiences and her writings are inseparable and interdependent. Events happening to an individual do not occur in isolation but are connected with 'the same spirit throughout the Nation', so that the meaning is both personal, spiritual and private, and also political and public. This interdependence is central to an understanding of why 'personal', spiritual texts like spiritual autobiographies were perceived as so subversive and threatening. As Owen Watkins wrote, all these works had a 'palpable design' on the reader: 'They were written to persuade, to cause reading to issue forth in action.'[63] Action, as opposed to mere reflection, was the desired end: 'it is not the hearers but the doers that shall be justified'.[64] Neither reading nor writing was a passive activity, and it was in the 'active' area of choice regarding both these that the threat was felt to lie. This involved choosing to write, choosing to place God's command before social strictures and before the family, choosing to read of and learn from another's experiences, choosing to act accordingly, and to take heed of prophecies. To make a choice is to assume power and control, something actively discouraged from all quarters.

On a more sobering note are the longer-term effects that the image of the disorderly woman, which underlay these disparate reactions, had for the status of women. Although the ambiguity of this image allowed women to exploit their own putative lack of rationality and responsibility for their actions (thereby allowing them to get away with proscribed activities), the fact that this reinforced the prevalent view of women opened the way for later repression. Phyllis Mack suggests that women's right to exercise 'public authority' by preaching, prophesying and publishing was based not on any recognition that they possessed previously unnoticed qualities of leadership but, on the contrary, on traditional beliefs in their greater receptivity to the prophetic or spiritual message because of their irrationality and passions. The beliefs that allowed women to speak and write within the sects were the same as those that later restrained them. Thus the way to repression and silencing was never closed off; a simple, temporary diversion was taken. This, she suggests, is why after the Restoration women were so easily and successfully restricted to their 'silent' status once more.[65] During the revolution, when 'the world turned upside down', ideas about women's passivity allowed them to receive the Word of God more readily than their male counterparts, and to broadcast it to others without restraint. After 1660 these same beliefs turned into a reason to keep silent.

The arguments of the 1640s and 1650s that justified women's writing and preaching were later used to silence them, and changing social and political conditions encouraged retrenchment and a more 'quietist' spirit. However, the Restoration was not a disaster for women's published writing. In terms of writing from the sects, it is certainly true that the 1660s saw a marked decline in women's publications, especially prophecy, apart from those produced by the Quaker movement. But women did not retreat into silence on matters of public and social concern – or at least, not for long:

> A hostile environment may have silenced some women, but others were undeterred. By 1700 it was no longer a wonder that a woman should write for publication.[66]

Indeed, by 1700 Aphra Behn had written some incisive exposés of the double standard resulting from the unequal opportunities, educational and otherwise, afforded men and women; Anne Finch had observed that a woman writer would be ridiculed, ignored or dismissed as 'an intruder on the rights of men'; and Mary Astell had denied that the differences between men and women were divinely ordained or 'natural' and argued that, rather, they were a result of socialisation:

> Women are from their very infancy debarred those advantages, with the want of which they are afterwards reproached, and nursed up in those vices which will hereafter be upbraided in them.[67]

The site and terms of resistance to the status quo have changed, but resistance none the less remains. If dominant arguments altered in order to silence women in the sects in the 1660s and 1670s, then other women asserted their presence in different areas of the debate. The emphasis had shifted from the radical challenge presented by the women in the sects, which was, after all, a challenge of background and class as well as of the controversies in which they engaged. It was principally upper-class women who made their mark in these later debates, often arguing for the education of women of their own class alone. There were, then, substantial losses, as well as some gains, in the years following the Restoration. It can none the less be stated quite unequivocally that the silence of women for which men strove, either before or after the Restoration, was never achieved.[68]

NOTES

1. Anna Trapnel, 'To all the wise Virgins of Sion', in *The Cry of a Stone* (London, 1654).
2. Patricia Crawford, 'Women's published writings 1600–1700', in Mary Prior, ed., *Women in English Society 1500–1800* (London: Methuen, 1985), pp. 211–82.
3. Hugh Barbour and Arthur O. Roberts, eds, *Early Quaker Writings* (Grand Rapids, MI: William B. Eerdmans Publishing Co., 1973), p. 14.
4. Elaine Hobby, *Virtue of Necessity: English women's writing 1649–1688* (London: Virago, 1988), p. 6. For estimates of the numbers of women writers, see Cynthia S. Pomerleau, 'The emergence of women's autobiography', in Estelle

C. Jelinek, ed., *Women's Autobiography* (Bloomington: Indiana University Press, 1980), pp. 21–38; Phyllis Mack, 'Women as prophets during the English Civil War', *Feminist Studies*, 8: 1 (Spring 1982), pp. 19–45.

5. Dorothy Paula Ludlow, ' "Arise and be doing": English "preaching" women, 1640–1660' (unpublished PhD thesis, Indiana University, 1978).

6. Daniel Rogers, *Matrimoniall Honour* (London, 1642), quoted in Barbara Gerd Samuelsen Yoshioka, 'Imaginal worlds: Woman as witch and preacher in seventeenth century England' (unpublished PhD thesis, Syracuse University, New York, 1977), pp. 425, 427.

7. Dorothy White, *Upon the 22 day of the 8th Month, 1659* (London, 1659), p. 1.

8. Grace Barwick, *To all present Rulers, whether Parliament, or whom soever of England* (London: 1659), p. 1; Jeane Bettris, *A Lamentation for the Deceived People of the World* (London, 1657), p. 1; Anne Audland, *A true Declaration of the suffering of the innocent* (London, 1655), p. 3; Sarah Blackborow, *Herein in held forth the Gift and Good-will of God to the World* (London, 1659), p. 3.

9. Audland, *A true Declaration*, pp. 2, 3; Mary Howgill, *A remarkable Letter of Mary Howgill to Oliver Cromwell called Protector* (London, 1657), pp. 1, 4.

10. Mary Mollineux, *Fruits of Retirement* (London, 1702; this edn 1772), p. 141.

11. Trapnel, *The Cry of a Stone*, p. 4.

12. Anna Trapnel, *Anna Trapnel's Report and Plea* (London, 1654), p. 9.

13. Trapnel, *The Cry of a Stone*, pp. 6, 10, 13.

14. Mary Cary, *A new and more Exact Mappe or Description of New Ierusalems Glory* (London, 1651), p. 237; Mary Cary, *The Little Horn's Doom and Downfall* (London, 1651), p. 36.

15. Christopher Hill, *The World Turned Upside Down* (London: Maurice Temple Smith, 1972; republished Harmondsworth: Penguin, 1975). Hill prefaces his book with three biblical references to 'the world turned upside down': Psalms 146: 9; Isaiah 24: 1–2, 20–21; Acts 17: 1–6.

16. Cary, *New Ierusalem*, pp. 56–7.

17. Ibid., pp. 62, 56.

18. Trapnel, *The Cry of a Stone*, pp. 33, 30.

19. Cary, *New Ierusalem*, p. 238.

20. Jane Turner, 'Epistle Dedicatory', in *Choice Experiences* (London, 1653); Captain John Turner, 'Epistle Dedicatory', in ibid.

21. 'A Word from the Author to the Reader', in Turner *Choice Experiences*.

22. Ibid.

23. Christopher Feake, 'Epistle to the Reader', in Cary, *The Little Horn's Doom*.

24. John Thornton, 'Testimony', in Elizabeth Stirredge, *Strength in Weakness Manifest* (London, 1711), p. 70.

25. Joan Vokins, *God's Mighty Power Magnified* (London, 1691), p. 35.

26. Pomerleau, 'The emergence', pp. 28–9.

27. Vokins, *God's Mighty Power*, pp. 23–4.

28. Ibid., p. 70.

29. Owen C. Watkins, *The Puritan Experience* (London: Routledge & Kegan Paul, 1972), p. 186.

30. Ibid., p. 161.

31. Dean Ebner, *Autobiography in Seventeenth Century England* (The Hague: Mouton, 1971), p. 29.

32. Watkins, *The Puritan Experience*, pp. 226–7, 236.

33. On the importance of modesty and chastity for women, see Hobby, *Virtue of Necessity*, pp. 2–3.

34. Natalie Zemon Davis, 'Women on top', in her *Society and Culture in Early Modern France* (London: Duckworth, 1975), pp. 124–51.
35. 'A relation concerning Dorothy Waughs cruel usage by the Mayor of Carlile', in *The Lambs Defence Against Lyes* (London, 1656), pp. 29–30 (p. 30).
36. Barbara Blaugdone, *An Account of the Travels, Sufferings and Persecutions of Barbara Blaugdone* (London, 1691), p. 10.
37. Ibid., pp. 15, 27.
38. Edward Burrough, *Something in Answer to a Book called Choice Experiences* (London, 1654), pp. 3, 7, 12.
39. Quoted in Yoshioka, *Imaginal Worlds*, p. 384.
40. Trapnel, 'To the Reader', in *Report and Plea*.
41. Ibid., p. 49.
42. Ibid., p. 52.
43. Anne Wentworth, *A Vindication of Anne Wentworth* (London, 1677), pp. 2, 4–5.
44. Katherine Chidley, *The Justification of the Independent Churches of Christ* (London, 1641), p. 26.
45. Davis, 'Women on top', p. 146.
46. Ibid., p. 131.
47. Mikhail Bakhtin, *Rabelais and His World*, transl. Helene Iswolsky (Bloomington: Indiana University Press, 1984).
48. Kate Holden, 'Women's writing and the carnivalesque', in *Literature Teaching Politics*, 4 (1985), pp. 5–15 (p. 6).
49. Ibid., p. 7.
50. See, for example, Joseph Glanvil, *An Essay Concerning Preaching* (London, 1677). The denigration of the Quaker style has continued this century; see Ebner, *Autobiography*, p. 123.
51. Trapnel, *The Cry of a Stone*, p. 42.
52. Turner, *Choice Experiences*, p. 202.
53. George Fox, *Journal*, ed. Norman Penney (Cambridge: Cambridge University Press, 1911), p. 13; Thomas Dockrey, 'Testimony', in Margaret Fell, *A Brief Collection of Remarkable Passages and Occurrences* (London, 1710).
54. Hugh Peter, 'Epistle Dedicatory', in Cary, *The Little Horn's Doom*; Trapnel, *The Cry of a Stone*, p. 4.
55. Alice Curwen, *A Relation of the Labour, Travail and Suffering of that faithful Servant of the Lord Alice Curwen* (London, 1680), p. 1.
56. Thomas Curwen, 'Thomas Curwen's Testimony concerning his Wife', in ibid.
57. Trapnel, *The Cry of a Stone*, pp. 15, 1; Cary, 'To the Reader', in *The Little Horn's Doom*. Cary's words actually show more confidence than the biblical passage which she is misquoting: 'Yea, before the day was, I am he; and there is none that can deliver out of my hand; I will work, and who shall let it?' Isaiah 43: 13.
58. Turner, 'the Author to the Reader', in *Choice Experiences*.
59. John Gardner, 'To the Reader', in ibid.
60. Captain John Turner, 'Epistle Dedicatory', in Turner, *Choice Experiences*.
61. Wentworth, *A Vindication*, p. 11.
62. Ibid., pp. 12, 13.
63. Watkins, *The Puritan Experience*, p. 233.
64. Elizabeth Hooton et al., *False Prophets and false Teachers described* (London, 1652), p. 4.
65. Mack, 'Women as prophets', p. 35.
66. Crawford, 'Women's published writings', p. 231.

67. See Joan Goulianos, ed., *by a Woman Writt: Literature from six centuries by and about women* (London: New English Library, 1974) for selections from the work of Aphra Behn and Anne Finch. Astell quoted in Dale Spender, *Women of Ideas (and what men have done to them)* (London: Ark, 1983), p. 56.

68. Complete modern editions of the texts discussed in this essay are not currently available. However, substantial extracts from Anna Trapnel, *Anna Trapnel's Report and Plea*, Anne Wentworth, *A Vindication of Anne Wentworth*, and Joan Vokins, *God's Mighty Power Magnified*, together with other autobiographical writings from the seventeenth century, are available in Elspeth Graham, Hilary Hinds, Elaine Hobby Helen Wilcox, eds, *Her Own Life: Autobiographical writings by seventeenth-century Englishwomen* (London: Routledge, 1989).

Index